FREE MARKET MORALITY

FREE MARKET MORALITY

The political economy of the Austrian school

ALEXANDER H. SHAND

ROUTLEDGE

London and New York

First published 1990 by Routledge
11 New Fetter Lane, London EC4P 4EE
29 West 35th Street, New York, NY 10001

Printed and bound in Great Britain by
Biddles Ltd, Guildford and King's Lynn

British Library Cataloguing in Publication Data

Shand, Alexander H.
Free market morality: the political economy of the
Austrian school
1. free markets

I. Title
338.5,22

Library of Congress Cataloging-in-Publication Data

Shand, Alexander H.
Free market morality : the political economy of the Austrian
school / Alexander H. Shand.
p.   cm.
Bibliography: p.
Includes index.

1. Austrian school of economists—Moral and ethical aspects.
2. Capitalism—Moral and ethical aspects.   I. Title.
HB98.S483   1989
330.15'7—dc19

ISBN 0-415-04045-0. — ISBN 0-415-04189-9 (pbk.)

To George Shackle

CONTENTS

vii

CONTENTS

I wish to express my thanks to the Trustees of the Leverhulme Fund for their financial help towards the costs of writing this book, during my tenure of an Emeritus Fellowship, 1986–87.

INTRODUCTION

This book aims to give the general reader or student some understanding of one of the most important sources of the political and
economic philosophy of the so-called New Right. It is now clear that
during the last decade many confident and widely agreed beliefs as to
the ability of the state or its agencies to shape human affairs wisely
have been severely shaken, not only in the western democracies but
even in China, the Soviet Union, and its East European satellites,
where the ruling party élites continue to move uncertainly towards
the introduction of what they seem only vaguely to understand: the
free market.

There are many different reasons for this: some connected with
political changes and power struggles; and some with disillusion-
ment, as the record of collectivism has unfolded to reveal its
deficiencies. The term 'radical' is no longer automatically associated
only with socialism. There is now a radical Right whose ideas come
from several different sources: 'anarcho-capitalists' such as Murray
Rothbard and David Friedman (Milton Friedman's son); the
Chicago school represented by Milton Friedman – 'the monetarists'
(a term widely used but little understood); the public-choice school
who have applied economic analysis to politics (represented by
Tullock and Buchanan); and the Austrian school of economics
(represented chiefly by Friedrich A. Hayek and Ludwig von Mises).

The main emphasis in published work on the Austrian school has
tended to be on its economic aspects but free market economics has
consequences also for individual freedom and equality. It is the aim
of this book to consider some of these consequences and to compare
them with some competing ideas.

Part I explains the philosophical roots and associated methodology of the Austrian school. Part II has a brief account of the nature

ogy of the Austrian school. Part II has a brief account of the nature and functions of free markets but concentrates chiefly on the rather less discussed question, at least within an Austrian context, of the morality of markets. Part III, on freedom and equality, is the core of the book. In Part IV, four topics have been selected, which are the subject of much topical controversy: the welfare state, unemployment, inflation, and economic growth – in which various views are compared with the Austrian position. Lastly, the concluding chapter includes a brief assessment of the record of the British governments of the 1980s under 'Thatcherism'.

The most important difference between the Austrians and other elements of the New Right lies in the way in which Austrian policy prescriptions may be traced to their underlying philosophy. The Austrian view of problems such as unemployment, inflation, freedom, and equality can be seen to follow quite clearly from their methodological individualism and subjectivism. It is a central aim of this book to bring out these connections.

A word on political labels; I use the terms Left and Right. But the possibilities of confusion and lack of clarity associated with the unthinking use of these well-worn terms are many and varied. An especially bizarre example is the way they are now used in describing the present political scene in the Soviet Union. The Right are those who find a great deal to admire in Stalin; the Left are the reformers who wish to 'roll back the state'. 'Conservative' and 'Liberal' are almost equally capable of such elasticity of definition. My preferred contrast in political economy would be something like collectivist/holist as opposed to individualist/libertarian, but such mouthfuls were rejected for the sake of brevity and to follow customary usage. Collectivist/holists see no need for further analysis when the word 'community' is qualified by almost any noun defining an individual: as in Christian; immigrant; business; gay; single-parent. Individualist/libertarians tend, by contrast, to be typically suspicious of such verbal constructions because they may obscure individuality and suggest a spurious solidarity.

The term 'political economy' is the old name for economics, before it became fashionable to treat economics as a science like physics, which it clearly is not, since the economist's material, in the words of G. L. S. Shackle (1973: 122), 'is flooded by the human powers of discovery and origination'. The Austrian emphasis on the market as a discovery process is not widely appreciated even by conservatives.

There is a persistent belief that we must have a 'national' policy for anything that happens to get into the news. The public's perception of the true nature of things is clouded by the continual publicity given to matters it is assumed only the government is capable of dealing with – what Mises referred to as 'non-problems'. This may be because of the neglect by the educators of the virtues, as opposed to the vices, of free market capitalism – especially through their teaching of history.

A central dilemma for libertarians is the conflict between having a general sympathy for freedom and the humane desire to help the more vulnerable members of society: the young, the old, and the sick. Hayek's views on such questions are by no means so dogmatically libertarian as some other elements of the New Right, nor indeed as some of his opponents suggest. Hayek's traditionalist leanings render such views simplistic. But he constantly directs our attention to the underlying reality; that ultimately, whatever system of government we live under, it is the behaviour of individual men and women that determines whether the society we live in is caring or callous, enterprising or slothful, civilized or barbarous. Governments can only assist or hinder; over-reliance on the state as the main agent of progress is doomed to be disappointed.

Only since completing this book has Hayek's latest volume been published – too late, unfortunately, for full consideration. I have, therefore, briefly noted some of its contents in an Appendix.

Part I

PHILOSOPHY

Chapter One

PHILOSOPHICAL ROOTS AND METHODS

The general system of ideas known as the Austrian school of economics was first clearly formulated in Carl Menger's *Principles of Economics* in 1871, (see Menger, 1950). It was, however, Ludwig von Mises at the University of Vienna, together with other followers of Menger – Wieser and Bohm-Bawerk – who formed the first generation or 'older' Austrian school. It was this group that began to spread abroad the Austrian ideas. Austrian economics today is chiefly represented by Ludwig Lachmann, Israel Kirzner, Murray Rothbard, and pre-eminently by Friedrich von Hayek.

Hayek himself has distinguished four 'generations' of Austrians – the fourth generation including Gottfried Haberler, Fritz Machlup, Oskar Morgenstern, and himself. For further discussions of the origins of the Austrian school see Schumpeter, (1954: 844–9).

DIVERSITY IN THE AUSTRIAN SCHOOL

Although there has, in the recent past, been much publication on something known as 'Austrian economics' it should first be noticed that this body of ideas is not monolithic; quite profound differences of view are to be found under the same 'Austrian' label. There is no doubt that Austrian economics refers to the theories of the founder, Carl Menger, but since then there have been a number of divergent and conflicting followers and interpreters of this Austrian tradition. For example, although Hayek was a student of Mises, there are some quite important differences in their respective methodologies. Hayek extended the subjectivism of Menger and Mises from economics to political philosophy and law. On the other hand, in one fundamental respect he differed from his mentors; he never accepted Mises' axiomatic approach in its entirety. He was not anti-empiricist though his empiricism was of a special kind. For present purposes, which are to consider the relevance and impact of Austrian ideas on recent political and economic trends, we wish to have some general outline of the main strands in Austrian methodology. These concepts have implications for attitudes to some important politico-economic matters such as: free markets, macroeconomics, inflation, individualism, collectivism, freedom, and equality. Accordingly it seems reasonable to present Austrian methodology with a fairly broad brush, considering several key ideas and, for the most part, ignoring finer divergencies.[1] There is, inevitably, a certain degree of artificiality in dividing methodology into selected separate topics as I do in this chapter since strong interconnections exist between them and they overlap and support one another to form a whole complex system of ideas. However, it is hoped by this approach, to achieve greater clarity and concentration on each topic. It has to be admitted that doing this means considering, to a great extent, the ideas of Hayek, who is without doubt the most influential of the Austrians, and because his interests have spread so widely from the confines of economics. There is one subject, however, in which Mises is the chief figure and Rothbard is today's outstanding exponent and we begin with this.

PRAXEOLOGY

Praxeology is the general science of human action, and economics in Mises' theory becomes simply a branch of praxeology. He starts by proposing that all the statements of economic theory follow deductively from a few axioms that he holds to be true a priori. The fundamental axiom is that human beings act purposefully to achieve certain ends; from this starting point Mises weaves the whole of his economic theory in his *magnum opus, Human Action*, and apart from economics the entire social structure is examined on this basis (Mises, 1966). Those members of the Austrian school who believe that their enquiry can be conducted *a priori* derive their position from the essentialism of Aristotle; they believe that there is an essence of man – elements about him that are part of his definition. Thus when Austrians say 'man acts purposefully' it is of the essence of man to act purposefully and can therefore be known a priori. Now this in itself may not seem to be a possible cause for the fierce criticism amounting to derision that has been directed at Mises by 'mainstream' economists. By mainstream I mean what is described as neoclassical economics, the dominant methodology that proceeds on the principle that it is possible to formulate propositions about the real world that may be tested empirically and ideally, by falsification.[2] This orthodox positivism includes the famous precept suggested by Milton Friedman: that the initial assumptions need not be verified so long as the deductions that follow from them can be satisfactorily tested.

What has horrified most mainstream economists about Mises' prescription is twofold: first, that such a priori statements are either useless or confused, and second, his apparently perversely dogmatic attitude to the testing of the deductions that follow from his initial axiom. In particular Mises appears to rule out the verification of theorems by appeal to experience but argues that their correctness or incorrectness may be decided by reason alone. Such a position led Samuelson to 'tremble' for 'the reputation of my subject'. On the face of it, then, Mises' methodology is extremist and in conflict with what many people would see as acceptable and reasonable – and 'alien to the very spirit of science' (Blaug, 1980: 93). However, before dismissing Mises' ideas too hastily there is something more to be said. For one thing Mises' a priorism does not stand alone and unsupported; certain other economists do support his methods.[3] But Hayek's position, as we shall see, is different, with special features of its own. Now the question of the standing of a priori statements in economics – or in any other context – is a complex and controversial one that is a continuing subject for philosophical debate. Nevertheless, some brief account is needed in order to judge the validity of Mises' method.

Another way of describing a priori propositions is to say that they are 'necessary truths'. Such propositions are knowable a priori because they hold true for all cases at all times and in all places. Such statements (known as 'analytic') need no verification – for example – '2 plus 2 equals 4'; 'if A precedes B and B precedes C, then A precedes C'; 'one can't be in two places at the same time'. These statements appear to require no previous experience of the world in order to determine their truth. Economic positivists[4] take the view that a statement that cannot be tested empirically can tell us nothing about the world and is of no use to any scientific study. The implications of this for Mises are that his a priori statement: 'human beings act

9

purposefully' can make no contribution to our knowledge of the economic world. The question for Mises is: are there conceivably any statements that are analytic – self-evidently true – that can tell us anything about the world? A statement that does give genuine information about the world is known as a 'synthetic' statement. Those who believe that there can be no synthetic a priori truths are empiricists; those who believe that there are synthetic a priori truths are known as rationalists. The most obvious field in which synthetic a priori statements exist is mathematics. Consider the statement, 2 plus 2 equals 4. One way of looking at it is to point out that it is logically possible that we might find an exception to its truth; but no-one ever has and we are so sure of its correctness and that it is self-evident that it must surely be synthetic a priori. In spite of this it can still be argued that such mathematical propositions are analytic. What does '4' mean but '2 plus 2', and what does '2' mean but '1 plus 1'? But do we not get useful information from such statements? The room for argument concerning the possibility that such statements as 'human beings act purposefully' are synthetic a priori becomes somewhat less obvious than might at first sight have been imagined. Clearly there is a great deal more to be said on the subject.[5]

Philosophers have not finally settled the question one way or the other; the orthodox view that there is a precise distinction between 'analytic' and 'synthetic' is still being questioned.[6] Bertrand Russell observed that empiricism as a theory of knowledge is self-refuting:

> For however it may be formulated, it must involve *some* general proposition about the dependence of knowledge upon experience; and any such proposition, if true, must have as a consequence that itself cannot be known. While, therefore, empiricism may be true, it cannot, if true, be known to be so.[7]
>
> (Russell, 1965: 156–7)

A rather surprising implication of Mises' a priorism is that econometric studies contain nothing more than recent economic history:

> in the field of human action statistics is always history and .... the alleged 'correlations' and 'functions' do not describe anything else than what happened at a definite instant of time in a definite geographical area .... As a method of economic analysis econometrics is a childish play with figures that does not contribute anything to the economic reality.
>
> (Mises, 1978: 63)

According to Mises the fallacy that pervades such research lies in the belief that the methods of the natural sciences are also appropriate for the study of human behaviour. But economics is not history; it is a branch of praxeology, the aprioristic theory of human action. This raises the question: can there be one scientific method appropriate to all fields of study – natural science as well as social science? Should the social sciences use a different methodology from, say, physics? Apart from Mises' 'extreme' position there are some quite respectable arguments for not using entirely the same methodology in all the sciences. Popper, for instance, although proposing a 'unity of method', that is, the view that all the sciences – social and natural – should use the same method, concedes that there are some important differences (Popper, 1960: 130–43). One objection to the proposal for a unity of method between the natural and the social sciences starts from the concept of *Verstehen* or 'understanding', which will be explained later in this chapter.

The derision with which Mises' apriorism has been greeted by orthodox economists is, one suspects, itself the product, partly at least, of some element of apriorism. One reason for this, apart from the sincerely held belief in Friedmanite positivism may be that Mises' major works remain comparatively unread. A close attention to the first few chapters of *Human Action* 1966 and *The Ultimate Foundation of Economic Science* 1978 reveals some very careful reasoning, the subtleties of which tend to be neglected by the repetition of sentences wrenched out of context. Mises' apriorism derives from the view that the axioms of praxeology because 'they involve necessary categories of the mind' are synthetic as well as a priori – they say something about the real world. To his positivist critics Mises points out that all geometrical theorems are already implied in the axioms – yet nobody would deny that geometrical axioms add to our knowledge; Euclidean geometry may be relied on in building bridges. As one writer on methodology points out, to invoke positivist concepts against Mises is to miss the point and is itself unscientific: 'the fact remains that ... a critique of one system (no matter how perverted that system's tenets may seem) based wholly on the precepts of its rival (no matter how familiar those precepts might be) establishes nothing' (Caldwell, 1982: 124). One line of questioning of Mises' apriorism is to look closely at the concept of purposive human action. Some behaviour – Pavlovian conditioned reflexes – presumably would not be regarded as pur-

11

poseful. But what about action that is conditioned by rewards and punishments – so-called operant behaviour? This is a form of conditioning in which behaviour is controlled through systematic manipulation of the consequences of previous behaviour. Can we know a priori that such conditioning does not apply to human behaviour? (Nozick, 1977: 364).

Rothbard, although a staunch supporter of Mises' methodology, offers a somewhat different argument in support of the action axiom. Whereas Mises, following Kant, considers the axiom a law of thought and therefore a categorical truth a priori to all experience, Rothbard prefers to regard it as a law of reality rather than of thought: empirical rather than a priori.

> For (1) it is a law of reality that is not conceivably falsifiable, and yet is empirically meaningful and true; (2) it rests on universal *inner* experience, and not simply on external experience, i.e. its evidence is *reflective* rather than physical; and (3) it is clearly *a priori* to complex historical events.
>
> (Rothbard, 1957: 318)

Disposing of, or rather leaving unclear, the whole analytic/synthetic distinction in this way does not in itself of course in any way undermine the neoclassical programme of gathering evidence about the economic world. But it may be used as Mises does as the starting point from which some of what he sees as the pretensions of economic research can be criticized. 'Economics is not history.... The economist does not base his theories upon historical research, but upon theoretical thinking like that of the logician or the mathematician' (Mises, 1978: 73). When he says 'does not' Mises means 'should not'. All that activity involving 'alleged economic research': collecting various facts, forecasting the future, advising the government on what to do about the economy, the setting up of economic 'workshops' analogous to science laboratories is not, according to Mises, economics. Although it 'may be highly appreciated from some points of view ... it is not economics. It is economic history of the recent past' (Mises, 1978: 74). This attitude might cause us to declare that the study of distant galaxies in astronomy or last year's weather are also fruitless as aids to forecasting future developments. What makes economics different? Mises' answer would presumably be that since human beings are free to act and to change their minds, prediction is inherently more difficult than in the physical sciences.

Mises' apriorism places him is some strange company. The politico-economic conclusions of his whole economic philosophy point, as we know, to an uncompromising advocacy of the liberal free-market order. But there are other apriorists whose political preferences and goals are quite the reverse. Some Marxian economists have also been busy attacking positivism and neoclassicism in economics on the basis that they rely on the analytic-synthetic distinction. Whether or not all modern Marxist economists now wish to entirely welcome apriorism, there is certainly an enthusiasm evident among some of them.[8]

Professor Hutchison asks, with considerable logic, how total contradictions regarding apodictic certainties could ever be settled between Marxian and Austrian apriorists with empiricist testing eliminated?

> Perhaps each side holds that conflicts cannot arise with regard to *their a priori* 'critical judgements', or 'apodictic certainties', because of the infallibility of those who pronounce them .... A priorist Austrians might be warned that Marxian 'scientific communities' have their own effective methods of establishing a consensus – as in Cuba, Kampuchea and Afghanistan – which certainly have no regard to 'positivist' and 'empiricist' criteria.
>
> (Hutchison, 1981: 297)

The dangers of apriorism in economic methodology are clear: without some empiricist criteria the field is open to anyone who wishes to set up their particular prejudice as an unarguable dogma. But it may well be that dogmas, although all of course deplorable on scientific grounds, have differing influences on political goals and policies. A firmly held belief that you are on the side of history and that history says that a particular race or class will inevitably be victorious must surely have greater potential for misery than some other cherished a priori beliefs. Holding the view that man acts purposefully while being indifferent to the consequences of such action might tend to foster lack of sympathy for those afflicted by poverty and other misfortunes, but it is unlikely to support mass extermination of a class or race; the individualistic element in Mises' a priorism for example, whatever its methodological faults, ensures his unyielding opposition to forms of oppressive collectivism. Of

13

course, some might believe there to be worse possibilities than oppressive collectivism – 'rampant' individualism?

Hayek and apriorism

Although Hayek is now regarded as the personification of the Austrian school, in some aspects of basic methodology his position with regard to Mises' praxeology is not clear cut. In fact, one might justifiably assert that there is such disagreement between authorities that it would be simplistic to try to state the essence of Hayek's position in a short statement. For example, Barry claims that Hayek tries to combine two incompatible methods: praxeology with its rejection of testability and Popperian falsificationism (Barry, 1979: 40). Gray, on the other hand, can see no evidence that Hayek ever endorsed Mises' a priorism (Gray, 1984: 19), but points out that Barry has since abandoned his view that Hayek's position contains the contradiction referred to. Hutchison discerns two stages in the development of Hayek's methodology. He shows, by a 1933 quotation, Hayek's belief in the importance of prediction in economics, a fundamental difference from Mises (Hutchison, 1981: 216). But not until 1937 is there a fundamental shift in his ideas when he first refers to Popper's influence. In 1975, although he is maintaining the essential differences between the natural and the social sciences, he nevertheless is stressing that it is possible – in economics – to make 'predictions which can be falsified and which therefore are of empirical significance' (Hayek, 1978: 33). Clearly this is poles apart from Mises' extreme apriorism. Yet Hayek's empiricism is of a particular kind and is perhaps best exemplified by a passage from *The Sensory Order* (Hayek, 1976: 166–72). In this he emphasizes that although he may be thought to be anti-empiricist, this is not the case. His rejection of some aspects of empiricism stems from 'a more consistent and radical application of its basic idea'. Experience itself builds up in our minds 'linkages' that then enable us to assess future experiences. The mind is not a *tabula rasa* but itself brings to experience an apparatus of classification that has been built up by 'pre-sensory linkages'. What this means is that because all our knowledge is due to experience it must contain elements that cannot be contradicted by experience. Experience presupposes 'an order of experienced objects which precedes that experience and which cannot be contradicted by it, though it is itself due to other, earlier

14

experience'. This certainly sounds like an attempt to synthesize apriorism and empiricism in a quite subtle way. The mind absorbs facts about the world through the medium of the senses; these facts are clarified or labelled by the mind into different 'boxes'. Hayek's point is that this ordering function of the mind is *prior* to the images perceived. This is because all the data we have ever received has been subjected to this classificatory process in the mind itself. With further experience of the way the world is, the mind's capacity to sort out and classify becomes more and more developed.

For the purpose of drawing out the politico-economic implications of Austrian methodology the subjects that remain to be discussed are the most relevant. These make a formidable list: scientism, subjectivism, methodological individualism, historicism, knowledge and its limitations, and the unintended consequences of human action. A particular view of these matters is now associated with the modern Austrian school although they have no exclusive monopoly of this view nor is there unanimity among its adherents. These subjects are very much interrelated and overlapping; there is a sense in which one cannot be discussed without reference to the others. It is difficult to be certain which of the ideas is the dominant one – the key to the others. If a choice had to be made as to the dominant theme, then it would most likely be scientism or subjectivism. But a reading of the relevant texts shows the extent to which these ideas are interdependent. This is especially the case with Hayek's *The Counter-Revolution of Science* which has a convincing claim to be the 'bible' of modern Austrian methodology (Hayek, 1979). Whilst bearing in mind this interdependence we shall, for the sake of clarity, try to treat the various ideas separately, so far as possible; the connections between them should become obvious.

SCIENTISM

Although Hayek first used this term in 1941,[9] it has not found its way into the two-volume edition (1973) of the *Shorter Oxford Dictionary*, even though it was in use in France in the 1930s. 'Scientism' means the slavish and 'inappropriate' imitation of the method and language of science. The application of scientism is to be described as 'scientistic', and it is important to note the difference between the terms scientistic and scientific. To be scientific is to be free of prejudice in deciding the most appropriate method of study of

15

particular problems; to be scientistic is to apply the methods of science mechanically and uncritically in an unthinking habitual way to fields of thought for which they are unsuited. Scientism assumes that the methods of the natural sciences – especially physics – are the only true source of factual knowledge of any kind including that of human society. This contrasts with the view that the social sciences are different in nature and are not amenable to study through the methods of physics. Hayek emphasizes that he is certainly not against the methods of science 'in their proper sphere', which he regards very highly. The progress of science has involved struggling to get away from conclusions about the world around us based merely on the way in which human senses interpreted events. In the prescientific periods of history 'common sense' or ordinary folklore produced all manner of nonsensical explanations of natural phenomena such as the attribution of thunderstorms to gods or spirits. The work of science has been to demolish myths and constantly to revise our understanding of the true nature of the physical world through experiment and testing. The systematic testing of phenomena and substances established new classifications and explanations quite different from our own innate view of the world. Measurement and numerical statements gave great precision to the natural sciences. The clear and dramatic success of the application of such methods to the study of nature inevitably led to the idea that human behaviour generally, including the fields of politics, economics, and sociology would yield to the same sort of approach. The origins of such enthusiasm – 'the source of the scientistic hubris' – are to be found in eighteenth-century France:

> Both the two great intellectual forces which in the course of the nineteenth century transformed social thought – modern socialism and that species of modern positivism, which we prefer to call scientism sprang directly from this body [École Polytechnique founded by the Revolutionary convention in 1794] of professional scientists and engineers which grew up in Paris.
>
> (Hayek, 1979: 185)

This scientistic hubris eventually spawned all manner of absurdities and dangerous enthusiasms, culminating in the literary field in Wellsian visions and utopias in which all problems have been solved by science and all bishops, politicians, military men, and the like have been banished from power to be replaced by the cool rational scientific sanity of the men in white coats moving endlessly and trouble-free amongst the gleaming white towers and transport systems of 'science cities'. A legacy of the scientistic utopianism which found such powerful support in the 1960s, is the hellish groups of tower blocks that, in the 1980s, are the focus of such intractable problems in areas where the slums were, now euphemistically described as 'inner cities'.

The mistake of scientism is to leap from explaining how the world really is as opposed to how we 'unscientifically' may, as human beings think it is, to the assumption that our (subjective) knowledge of the world is not only often wrong but should, therefore, be ignored. The point is not how far the world fits the facts, but to what extent what people believe determines their actions. The picture that men have of the world is just as important in explaining their behaviour – is no less a reality – than is the objective scientific view. The social sciences, therefore, are not concerned with the relationships between material things – the field of true science – but with what men think about things themselves and other men.

Scientism, as applied to the study of society, found its clearest and most influential formulation in the work of the early nineteenth-century sociologist and mathematician, Auguste Comte. He is regarded as the founder of positivism. He predicted rightly that the human race would universally come to shed the attempt to explain events anthropomorphically or by invoking abstract entities like 'nature'; positivism would be the adopted method in mathematics, physics, and astronomy. Once this transition had come about, Comte saw the obvious next step as the introduction of positivism into sociology, economics, ethics, and politics. But in these fields, the question remains open.[10]

Finally, we must note the change that has occurred in Hayek's view of scientific method since the 1940s. In 1966 he wrote that through the influence of Karl Popper he now understood the scientific method to be different from the account he had used in *The Counter-revolution of Science* (1952 edn). In his later work he accepted the Popperian conception of science as deductive and that theories are tested by trying to falsify their predictions through observation of the world. But Hayek, although he acknowledges that, from Popper, he has learnt that the differences between the natural and social sciences have been greatly narrowed, keeps up the argument 'only because so many social scientists are still trying to

17

imitate what they wrongly believe to be the methods of the natural sciences' (Hayek, 1967: viii).

In his *Objective Knowledge* Popper notes Hayek's 'very generous acknowledgement that the methods actually practised by natural scientists are different from "what most of them told us ... and urged the representatives of other disciplines to imitate"' and describes the fashionable occupation of 'labouring the difference between science and the humanities' as having become a bore (Popper, 1979: 185). Professor Hutchison sees Hayek's movement away from Mises and towards Popper as putting them 'literally poles apart' (Hutchison, 1978: 33).[11]

There remain other aspects of 'the slavish invitation' of the scientific method when applied to society that mislead and may be disastrous for human wellbeing. Hayek's change of view by no means disposes, as some writers seem to think, of his arguments against scientism. Other elements of scientism are very much with us and continue to be deeply influential.

The dominant theory influencing the monetary and fiscal policy of many governments from the end of the Second World War until the later 1970s is seen by Austrians as a good example of the scientistic approach. This theory – roughly synonymous with Keynesianism – asserts that there is a simple correlation between total employment and aggregate demand and led to the widely held belief that full employment may be permanently maintained by government management of macroeconomic variables. The main reason for the failure of such policies lies in a preoccupation with measurable data. In economics and other social sciences the amount of quantitative data is necessarily limited. In the natural sciences it is rightly assumed that most of the important aspects of phenomena will be measurable but it is mistaken to carry this procedure over in its entirety to the social sciences. To concentrate only upon the measurable excludes the consideration of those facts that may be important though unquantifiable. Hayek has illustrated the dangers of this in his contention that the obsession of governments in the 1960s and 1970s with correlation between aggregate demand and total employment led to policies that made matters worse (Hayek, 1978: 23–6). Aggregate demand and total employment were, so he argues, apparently the only variables for which there existed quantitative data. Simply because these aggregates were measurable did not mean the theory was sound, since it ignored the unmeasurable causal factors. Hayek saw the problem of inflation as brought about by the actions of governments under the influence of this faulty theory.[12] The influence of scientism was seen in the mistaken belief of governments and their advisers that in trying to manipulate the measurable variables they were being truly scientific; this was the opposite of the truth. Hayek saw the problems of unemployment and inflation as caused by 'discrepancies between the distribution of demand among the different goods and services and the allocation of labour and other resources among the production of those outputs' (Hayek, 1978: 25). These distortions in the operation of market forces had been brought about by 'monopolistic or government price fixing.'

Whether or not Hayek's theory is to be preferred to Keynesianism depends on their respective results – not an easy matter to be definite about. But the relevant point about which it is possible to state a fairly confident conclusion is that government policies of the 1970s failed to maintain full employment in a period of high inflation: that this is, at least partly, ascribable to scientistic hubris seems quite plausible. These criticisms should not lead us to the rather despairing view that trying to measure economic variables and allowing these data to guide policy is entirely harmful and a complete waste of time; the proper lesson to be learned is that economists are not 'men in white coats'; the complexity of events in human societies should counsel the need for caution in macroeconomic 'management' and a realistic recognition that much that is important cannot be known to a government.

SUBJECTIVISM

In a very general way subjectivism is the theory that holds that the private experience of the individual is the only foundation of knowledge of the world. In the history of economic thought, subjectivism refers to the theory of value adopted by Jevons, Menger and Walras in the 1870s. They abandoned that search for a means of calculating objectively the value of goods and services, which had long preoccupied most of their predecessors. Subjectivism became one of the chief characteristics of the Austrian school, as well as entering into mainstream economics in demand theory. However, in the 1930s the review by Piero Sraffa of Hayek's *Prices and Production* marked the start of the neo-Ricardian counterattack, an interesting account of which is given by Lachmann in Grassl and

Smith (1986). Sraffa's review marked the first shot in the battle, which attained new vigour in the 1960s, and still continues, the best known aspect of which is the labour theory of value. In Marx's version of the productive resources theory – which holds that the value of a good or service equals the sum total of productive resources (factors of production) embodied in the good or service – labour is the only productive resource. Any higher price than the cost of the labour used in the production of a good is an unearned surplus and is 'exploitation'.[13]

The Austrian view is entirely opposite to that of the neo-Ricardians or Marxists. As Mises puts it with regard to the still prevalent notion, which has its roots in the medieval 'just price' – that there is some correct level that prices 'ought' to be:

> one deludes oneself or practises deception if one calls such wishes and arbitrary value judgements the voice of objective truth. Value judgements are necessarily always subjective, whether they are passed by one man only or by many men, by a blockhead, a professor, or a statesman.
>
> (Mises, 1966: 395–6)

The idea of subjective value in economics is now known considerably to predate the Austrians and Jevons. Rothbard's 'New light on the prehistory of the Austrian school' (Dolan, 1976: 52–81) shows many examples of men who grasped quite well the idea of subjective value among the Scholastic philosophers of the Middle Ages and particularly in sixteenth-century Spain. Schumpeter saw 'Smith and Ricardo not as founding the science of economics, but as shunting economics onto a tragically wrong track, which it took the Austrians and other marginalists to put right' (Dolan, 1976: 53). The 'right' track had evidently been followed also in the middle of the seventeenth century (1651) by Thomas Hobbes when he wrote: 'And in other things, so in men, not the seller, but the buyer determines the Price' (Hobbes, 1984: 152).

The best account of Austrian subjectivism is probably Chapter 3 of Hayek's (1979) *Counter-revolution* and subjectivism remains a strong influence in his subsequent writings, even though the original emphasis on the difference between the natural and the social sciences referred to on p. 18 has been considerably weakened. Popper believes in the unity of the sciences, natural and social, hence in his view there must be objective knowledge in the social sciences and

holds that any subjective knowledge, obtained perhaps by introspection, must be tested by his falsification principle – the normal
method of science. He does, however, concede that most of the
objects of social science are theoretical constructions – such as 'the
war' or 'the army'. These are 'abstract concepts'. What is concrete is
the many who are killed (Popper, 1960: 135). (These ideas raise the
question of methodological individualism – our next section.) The
most important aspect of subjectivism, as described by Hayek, which
still has relevance for economic and political affairs is this: that in
those matters that influence how society works it is what people
think is the (objective) truth that determines the course of events.
Thus although money can be defined objectively as 'little round discs
of metal' this would not help our understanding of the role of money
in the economy, which depends on human subjective evaluations.
The same considerations apply to all goods and services:

> In fact most of the objects of social or human action are not
> 'objective facts' in the special narrow sense in which this term is
> used in the Sciences. . . . So far as human actions are concerned the
> things *are* what the acting people think they are.

> (Hayek, 1979: 44)

This disposes of the apparent mystery of why some old paint on a
piece of canvas put there by some long-dead artist can be sold for
millions of pounds. This might be seen as labouring a fairly obvious
point that the majority of people are well aware of without tedious
explanation, were it not for the uncomfortable feeling that in the case
of a substantial segment of the population – at least of Britain – the
belief is held that the government is responsible for prices.[14] Understanding of the subjective nature of prices and costs cannot be taken
for granted; this is why subjectivism is relevant for politics and
economics.

Dissatisfaction with subjectivism caused economic theorists to
strive to banish it from their discipline, in such theories of consumer
demand as 'revealed preference'. The basic idea is that an individual's
preferences are revealed by his choices. Thus if he buys A rather than
collections of goods B, C, or D we say he has revealed a preference
for A. Assuming transitivity, that is, if he prefers A to B and B to C,
he must prefer A to C, and a 'preference map' may be drawn. Rather
surprisingly Hayek appears to accept that revealed preference purges
consumer theory of that form of subjectivism based on the idea that

valid observation in the social sciences necessarily involves understanding (*Verstehen*) of the meaning of the actions of human beings because the observer is also human (Hayek, 1978: 277).[15]

The important point is that subjectivism entails the belief that the data of the social sciences are simply the attitudes, values and opinions of acting humans; Hayek has maintained that there can be no true statements about social matters independent of these (subjective) beliefs. There are no social 'facts' as such. However, there is evidence in his later work that he wishes to stress as a distinguishing feature of social science not so much its subjectivist nature as its essential complexity (Hayek, 1967, Chapter 2).

The implications of Austrian subjectivism find their most complete expression in the writings of Ludwig M. Lachmann who was once a student of Hayek's. Lachmann regards subjectivism as the really important heritage of the Austrian school. In his view, subjectivism inevitably pervades every aspect of economic life whether it be in defining 'cost' in terms of foregone opportunities or expressing the market rate of interest as an expression of the individual time preferences of individuals (Lachmann, 1977: 4). To take one example: it is customary for government statisticians to produce data comparing the total capital stock of, say, Britain with that of West Germany; such figures, which appear quite objective, contain an important subjective element. It is not a question of the accuracy of the figures but of the method by which they are arrived at. To compute a total of capital stock, firms must be asked to value their own plant and equipment. These values are in turn derived from an assessment of the future earning power of machines and plant. They are necessarily subjective estimates, since no-one can forecast future prices, which will affect the value of the consumer goods that the capital goods being valued are helping to produce.

The general drift of science has been towards escaping from subjectivism, as in the teaching of Comte, who denied the very possibility of introspection to many of his followers who adopted behaviourism, that school of psychology that studies only unambiguously observable, and preferably measurable behaviour; it leaves out of account introspection. Hayek regards behaviourism as naive in the respect that it does not in practice follow its own logic. For example, a behaviourist may be satisfied that he is being entirely objective in studying people's reactions to various external stimuli such as *asking them* to describe what they experience when presented with phenomena such as a colour or a sound. To be consistent, behaviourists would want more than this: they would want to *measure* changes subject to different frequency sound or light waves in the retina or auditory nerve (Hayek, 1979: 79). However, Ernest Nagel has criticized this Mises/Hayek version of behaviourism as a caricature of the behaviourist approach. 'The attack is levelled against a straw man' (Nagel, 1961).[16] Nagel further argues that the fact that the social scientist is able to 'understand' human motivation because he is human, does not itself affect the validity of the phenomena he is studying; the social scientist's empathy does not, by itself, constitute knowledge and his identification with his subject does not do away with the need for objective evidence. Clearly, subjectivists, although they have illuminated some dark corners and banished a few myths should not be too set in their ways. The truth, as so often, may lie in between. Extreme subjectivism is difficult to defend but so are some forms of behaviourism. The philosopher C. D. Broad has described behaviourism as 'one of those philosophical theories which must be described as "silly"' if it is interpreted as meaning that people are simply ingenious machines produced by other machines when considering human reactions to colour or sound; as well as the sensation brought about by molecular phenomena in the brain there is also my 'awareness' of the sensations. It is, says Broad, obvious that 'awareness' (of a colour or sound) is not the same thing as a molecular movement in the brain.[17] But this does not dispose of the issue. 'Awareness' may of course itself be simply the result of some other molecular movement in the brain. It may be that in time new discoveries in the fields of neurobiology or artificial intelligence will render accessible the nature of the working of the human mind to the same scientific method by which we have so successfully obtained knowledge of atoms and stars. The theory that contends that the mind is inherently inaccessible to one's own mind[18] may eventually go the way of the phlogiston theory, when oxygen was discovered; it may be a provisional hypothesis that will be modified or banished altogether by the discoveries of future knowledge. Possibly future developments will replace this particular form of scientism with true science. Subjective states of mind are, as Professor John Searle has said, objective facts, therefore science cannot ignore them.[19] It is, however, interesting to note the modern tendency evident in the field of subatomic physics to have lost confidence in the possibility of objective reality. One observer of the progress of physics writes: 'The "exact sciences" no longer study an objective reality ... the distinction between objective and subjective has vanished .... If the new physics has led us anywhere, it is back to ourselves....'[20]

A similar view was expressed by Russell Stannard, Professor of Physics at the Open University, who pointed out that the Danish physicist, Niels Bohr claimed that science tells us nothing about the world as it is in itself – 'it tells us the way we *interact* with the world'. Bohr went on to say that there is a frontier of the *knowable* – a barrier that would never be breached, *The Times*, 3 December, 1983; this is rather similar to Hayek's (1976) view as expressed in *The Sensory Order*.

Subjectivism, public policy, and cost theory

Returning finally to economics, consider two further examples of the implication of subjectivism that are of everyday relevance. These will only be stated briefly here as we shall return to them. The first example is that of 'public goods'. A public good is defined as one whose consumption by one person does not reduce the amount available to any other person and that which is difficult (too costly) to exclude any individual from consuming; the classic case is that of a lighthouse. Since consumption is non-rival – the marginal cost of an extra person's consumption is zero – it has often been argued that the market reaches an inefficient solution. In the case of a bridge, for example, which is not crowded, an extra person crossing will not generate any extra cost but a private owner of the bridge would find it feasible to levy a toll on this additional costless user. Reducing the use of it in this way is an inefficient use of the bridge. Therefore, it is often argued, bridges should be owned by the government and so should any similar properties for which exclusion can be applied but consumption is non-rival. The subjectivist criticism of this classic argument for certain forms of public ownership is that its concept of marginal costs is wrong – it fails to recognize that costs are subjective. The fact that the cost incurred by the extra user of the bridge is zero, is irrelevant to a decision to build the bridge in the first place. The original decision to build the bridge is subjective in the sense that other opportunities of investing the money would have presented themselves at the time and these were rejected in favour of building the bridge. Although some objective data would have been available to the bridge owner, the ultimate course of action is subjectively chosen (Brownstein, 1980).

The second example of how subjectivism should be taken into account is the general area of public-sector economics, the first example being essentially one aspect of this wider field. The main subjectivist thesis in this context is that economists, politicians, and civil servants have deluded themselves and many other people into the belief that 'the economy' is analogous to a ship or a complex machine that can be 'managed' from the centre. The assumption underlying this attitude is that the data that directs the economic activity of millions of individuals within the bounds of a society can be known and measured objectively (Mishan, 1984). Subjectivists contend that these phenomena are not objective facts. One of the delusions of the objectivist approach is that economic efficiency may be accurately quantified and promoted. It is in the field of welfare that objectivism may be potentially the most harmful. When policy is prescribed using costs that it is assumed may be quantified by an outside observer, ignoring the way in which costs are subjectively assessed by acting individuals – in partial ignorance and uncertainty – then the policymakers' prescriptions may well fail to reflect the wishes of the individuals whose welfare the planners are trying to augment. The question of subjectivism and public policy underpins much of the Austrian school's doubts as to the potential beneficence of 'planning'.

From the London School of Economics in the 1940s and 1950s emerged a wholly subjectivist approach to the theory of cost that added to the accepted concept of opportunity cost the idea that the true cost of choosing one action rather than some other is the loss, prospective or realized, of the foregone possibility of using those things alternatively.[21] Also this cost cannot be discovered by a third person who observes these channels because cost exists only in the mind of the decision-makers. There can never be an objective way of measuring cost because the relevant alternative – the real measure of cost – can never be realized and therefore there can be no money flow to measure (Buchanan and Thirlby, 1973).

Shackle's subjectivism

The contributions of G. L. S. Shackle to subjectivist thought are unique and original but some economists have found his philosophy 'extreme', 'despairing' or even 'nihilistic'. Such comments would appear to overlook the fact that Shackle's subjectivism is not so much extreme as 'different'. He sees human affairs – all we experience – as originating in the thoughts of individuals who each imagine for themselves alternative feasible uses of the means to hand and – the critical point – imagine for each use many possible outcomes. All possible alternative actions present themselves first to individual minds – this is the only possible source. An important corollary of this view is the belief that human events are inherently unpredictable. It is impossible to encapsulate the full significance of Shackle's subjectivism in a few sentences – his work must be read; but the following quotation will indicate the general nature of his philosophy:

> My theme thus avers that choice, if its nature is that of a *beginning*, is necessarily made amongst skeins of rival conceptions of the sequel of action.... Choice is an exploitation of unknowledge. It allows the chooser to ask himself: What can be the sequel of such-and-such a course? .... Epistemic standing, for the chooser's purpose of gaining access for practical imagination, is *possibility*, freedom from discernible obstruction.
>
> (Shackle, 1979: ix)

What should economists do?

Austrian subjectivism, especially in its more extreme forms is repellent to mainstream economists who take much pleasure (and profit) in the exposition and elaboration of the satisfying models of positive economics. Do the Austrians deserve to be scorned or ignored? The question has been more than once asked: if Austrians are totally sceptical concerning the possibility of predicting economic events – as some of them seem to be – why do they continue to call themselves economists at all? This question contains the unsupported assumption that economists *ought* to be engaged in forecasting. Exactly what economics is *for* is not all that simply stated. Certainly, economists have had some success in this direction: predictions of the inflation rate in the UK have been fairly accurate and useful. But the general record is not such as to cause one to place much faith in the statistical cataracts that pour forth from the various institutes. E. J. Mishan, who although notable for ruffling orthodox feathers, could not possibly be regarded as a dogmatic subjectivist writes: ... regarded as a science, as an empirical science at least, it [economics] has proved to be something of a fiasco. Certainly any physical sciences which formulated so few dependable generalisations would be regarded by natural scientists with amused contempt' (Mishan, 1986: 78). Nevertheless we must concede that there is something worrying, not about the belief that human beings act subjectively – this is surely a reasonable and arguable point of view – but concerning some of the policy implications that some of its adherents have claimed for it.

One economist has complained that subjective logic leaves nothing for the economist to 'do' and 'then the only problem that remains is that of subjugating one's conscience long enough to draw one's salary' (Coddington, 1983: 61). If the 'messianic' element in the Austrian subjectivists became dominant 'we would then be faced with a situation akin to one in which there was an outbreak of Christian Science among the medical profession or a passion for telekinesis among airline pilots' (Coddington, 1983: 61–2). On this view the whole profession should 'shut up shop'. The implication seems to be that unless economists can produce 'results' in the manner of doctors or accountants then they are not worth their keep. This objection would apply to many university academics other than economists and contains too much of an initial assumption that economists are for managing and advising others on the 'running of economic systems' (see also the essay by James Buchanan (1979) *What Should Economists Do?*).

Leland Yeager has, in a well-balanced essay entitled 'Why Subjectivism?' deplored what he sees as Austrians reciting 'slogans that reinforce cosy feelings of camaraderie among members of an elite' (Yeager, 1987: 28). Yeager reviews favourably the case for the largely subjective nature of costs and prices but finds some Austrian scepticism concerning the possibility of objective factors, exaggerated. What is to be done, he asks, when real world decisions must be taken, such as building an airport or enacting laws regulating the pollution of the environment? 'Does one simply ramble on about how imponderable everything is, or does one try to quantify benefits and costs' even though these figures may not be entirely accurate? (Yeager, 1987: 26). Of course, the answer must be that the attempt must be made to measure relevant data and to reach some decision. The beneficial effect of Austrian subjectivism (perhaps its real claim to be 'useful' to policy-makers) is to curb exaggerated claims of accuracy and to temper expectations of ability to 'manage' economic phenomena, with some degree of scepticism. The tendency to treat economic variables too reverently (such as the inflation rate) as having the same truthfulness as temperatures when measured by an accurate thermometer, only serves to foster delusion and possibly too much self-importance among politicians.

Another example is the prevalence of 'league tables' comparing, say, Britain and Japan as to their wealth or income per head. Such comparisons, though they have their uses, tend to ignore the unquantifiable factors in economic welfare such as congestion, or the quality and amount per head of housing. The Austrian critique, which points out the subjective elements in many apparently entirely objective phenomena, is at least a usefully corrective influence especially in assessing the significance of the size of economic aggregates. National income statistics, for example, are notoriously unsatisfactory and unawareness of this can lead to mistaken policy goals. Changes in the quality of goods over time are not shown in comparing gross national product (GNP) whether over time in one country or between countries. This is only an obvious example of the many ways in which GNP may be over- or understated, through ignoring unmeasurable factors affecting well-being, which are to various degrees subjective.

METHODOLOGICAL INDIVIDUALISM

One of the most pervasive disputes among students of the social sciences is between what we might broadly designate as individualism versus collectivism. This problem is on two separate levels: the question of *how* to study economics, sociology, and politics on the one hand and the Platonic question of what is the 'good' society on the other. There is a wealth of literature on the subject, which indicates its importance and casts doubt on the belief of one writer that the whole controversy rests upon a 'sterile polarity' (Burman, 1979).[22]

If, as Austrians believe, the subjectivist nature of human action should be uppermost in the minds of students of the social sciences, then it follows from this that the starting point for all statements as to the nature of economics and sociology ought to be from the perspective of the individual.

Methodological individualism (MI) is in contrast to methodological holism:[23] they are two opposite approaches to the social sciences. They differ in their answers to such questions as: is it necessary always to refer to the individuals constituting 'social wholes' in order to describe phenomena such as 'the economy', 'the government', or 'the crowd'? Do such combinations of individuals have functions of their own or are such functions properly seen as merely the resultant of their individual members? Can we speak, for instance, without self-delusion, of a committee as if it possessed some sort of collective mind distinct from its individual members? In answering such questions MI tends to regard social wholes as of less importance than the individuals of which they are composed; even to see social wholes as entirely abstract formations having no separate reality. The Austrian's rejection of holism explains much of their criticism of the theory of macroeconomic aggregates and their inter-actions – featuring such concepts as the general price level or aggregate demand. Expressions in common usage such as 'the economy' or 'the needs of society', which are beloved of politicians and are examples of holism, are anathema to Austrians. Not only is such terminology loose and even unscientific, but it may lead to fallacious beliefs (as Austrians see it) such as the idea that there exists a national economic 'cake' – the GNP – and that it is some agency's responsibility to distribute it among the individuals in society.

Origins

The influence of religion on the origins of this question can be seen in the Protestant insistence that the only thing that mattered was the individual's relationship with God. Opposition to individualism from the nineteenth century onwards came from collectivist (holist) thinkers such as Saint-Simon and Comte. The latter regarded a society as no more decomposable into individuals than a geometric surface is into lines or a line into points. The denial of MI influenced all social studies in nineteenth-century Germany in history, economics, law, and psychology, especially among the Hegelians and Marxists (Lukes, 1973: 111). In psychology it was known as Gestalt: a pattern or organized whole with qualities different from those of its component parts. Gestalt psychologists conceived this argument as applying to fields of study such as philosophy and science; enquiry should proceed from above, downwards. One must not start with the supposed components and try to envisage them as wholes, but rather look at the wholes to discover what their parts are.

29

Austrian objections to holism

Mises does not contest the idea that social wholes are real – they do exist. Far from denying this he sees it as one of the main tests of MI 'to describe and to analyse their becoming and their operation' (Mises, 1966: 42). Against the argument that man is a product of social evolution, that real man is necessarily always a member of a social whole, and that there is no thinking that does not depend on language – a social phenomenon – Mises replies that 'thinking and acting man emerges from his prehuman existence already as a social being ... the evolution of reason, language and co-operation is the outcome of the same process' (Mises, 1966: 43). All these processes by which man developed consisted of changes in the behaviour of individuals – there is nowhere else they could have occurred. All collectives or wholes, according to Mises, are the product of our mental processes, which lead us to recognize social entities. To start the study of human action from the examination of wholes also faces an insurmountable obstacle: individuals often belong to various collective entities simultaneously. This problem 'can be solved only by methodological individualism'.

From the position of advocating MI simply as the correct scientific principle on which to base a study of society – which might conceivably proceed in a politically neutral spirit – Mises later elaborates his 'scientific' objections to holism into a political value judgement. He sees holism as inevitably opposed to the individualist social philosophy that he so much admires and that has much of its origins in the eighteenth century. Holism or collectivism leads inevitably to the belief that the selfishness of the individual must be sacrificed for the benefit of society, since the latter is an entity living its own life. This has led historically to various forms of theological or metaphysical faiths. The secular methods of science give way to the idea that men must be forced to sacrifice themselves for a greater concept than themselves. 'It is of minor importance whether one calls this God, Weltgeist, Destiny, History, Wotan or Material Productive Forces' (Mises, 1966: 147), or, one might add, 'the economy', or 'society'. This philosophy is characteristic of the primitive tribal stage of human history whose metaphysical doctrines were demolished by the eighteenth-century rationalists and which influenced economics through Smith and his followers. Hayek fully developed the implications of tribalism and his critique of the idea of 'social justice' starts from the assertion that the 'demand for "social justice" is indeed an expression of revolt of the tribal spirit against the abstract requirements of the coherence of the Great Society with no such visible common purpose' (Hayek, 1982: 144).

Mises concludes that collectivism is necessarily 'theocratic'. All varieties of collectivism: religious, rationalistic, or socialist, postulate the existence of a superhuman entity that the individuals must obey:

> It does not matter whether the autocrat bases his claims on divine rights of anointed Kings or on the historical mission of the vanguard of the proletariat. . . . The terms society and state as they are used by the contemporary advocates of socialism . . . signify a deity.
>
> (Mises, 1966: 151)

Thus does Mises switch from methodological individualism as a way of looking at society to using it for his uncompromising attack on socialism in all its forms.[24]

Hayek closely follows Mises on this question. He refers to collectives such as capitalism, the economic system, or imperialism as no more than 'provisional theories, popular abstractions' which must not be mistaken for facts (Hayek, 1979: 64). They are 'pseudo-entities'. The social scientist must begin with the ideas that motivate individuals. This is 'the characteristic feature of methodological individualism which is closely connected with the subjectivism of the social sciences' (Hayek, 1979: 64). Hayek rightly asserts that social 'wholes' would be meaningless ideas without the actions of the individuals who constitute them. The phenomenon that we call society – or rather the multitude of phenomena that constitute society – would remain in existence even if the abstraction 'society' vanished from our vocabulary.

The Austrian position receives strong support from Karl Popper; '. . . the "behaviour" and the "actions" of collectives, such as states or social groups, must be reduced to the behaviour and to the actions of human individuals' (Popper, 1966, vol 22: 91). Rousseau's answer to Plato's question: Who should rule? is seen by Popper as an example of the disastrous political effects of holism. Rousseau's answer was that the 'people' should rule – not the will of an autocrat, a king – but the will of all. The people were to be regarded as a single person embodying the 'general will'. Unarguably the subsequent uses made of this holistic concept in human history have been, on balance, bad.

31

Popper links holism with utopianism; holists not only study society 'by an impossible method' they plan to 'control and reconstruct our society as a whole!'. He describes this in the famous phrase: 'the totalitarian intuition' (Popper, 1960: 79). However, Popper has apparently also given his blessing to what the Austrians most oppose in human affairs: 'social engineering'. But he qualifies this by referring to *'piecemeal'* social engineering. This involves the re-modelling and servicing of social institutions by analogy with the methods of the physical engineer. 'Social institution' is used here in a very wide sense – it may be a business, a small shop, a school, a Church, or a law court. Hayek's objection to the use of the term 'social engineering' – in the piecemeal sense – is however conceded by Popper. Hayek's criticism is, of course, that social engineering implies the centralization of all knowledge in a single head or group of heads, whereas unlike the problems of physical engineering, social problems are made up of knowledge that is dispersed among millions of individuals and cannot possibly ever be centralized. Popper defends his use of 'social engineering' by proposing that Hayek's objection is now included as part of the 'technical knowledge' of the social engineer – by becoming the hypothesis that social knowledge cannot be centralized (Popper, 1960: 64–5, 90). This leaves Popper's position somewhat ill-defined but the most important implication of his use of the term 'piecemeal' is his stress on his opposition to wholesale change on a large scale; change should be carried out cautiously. The holist approaches problems by what is essentially an unscientific method. He rules out in advance any limits to the possibility of the wholesale reconstruction of human institutions; also he fosters the impulse to 'mould' human beings to fit into the preconceived design and ignores the possibility of unavoidable surprises arising from the unpredictability of individuals.

It has been pointed out by Kenneth Minogue how the mortality of the individual compared with the continuity of social wholes like the state leads to the mistaken belief that the wholes are more important, more real than individuals and he writes of the way in which 'large and cloudy entities like society' are brandished in argument (Minogue, 1985: 111).

Defending holism

J. R. Lucas opposes MI on the grounds that its contentions are false. Man, he argues, is a social animal – just as Aristotle had spoken of man as a political animal. 'What other people mean to a man, constitutes a large and essential part of what it is to be that individual man' (Lucas, 1985: 273). And 'individualists have a wrong view of human nature. They fail to recognise how sociable and how fallible we are'. What bothers Lucas about individualism is not only that he sees it as simply incorrect to see a society as only a collection of individuals, but that he deplores the way in which individualism has led to the abandonment of certain traditional values that give coherence to a society. It has led to the secular state, 'on the grounds that communities ought not to espouse values, but only individuals should' (Lucas, 1985: 275). The American liberals in their pursuit of individual freedom 'installed Mammon in the place of the departed gods'. All that is left when individualism is carried to its logical extremes is to elevate the making of money to be the one value, whereas it should be regarded merely as a means to an end. This criticism reminds us of what has been seen as a fundamental conflict in the Hayek version of individualism in that he wants, on the one hand, to promote the freedom of the individual whilst at the same time stressing that the individual must be bound by traditionally evolved rules. 'The freedom of the British was a product of the fact that the law that governed the decisions of the courts was the common law, a law existing *independently of anyone's will* ... (Hayek, 1982, vol. 1: 85; my emphasis). Lucas (1985: 275) sees that individualism contains sound arguments for freedom but that it sweeps aside worthwhile 'social values and moralities'. This position is of course the one currently favoured by the opponents of Thatcherism, who condemn it more on the grounds of immorality and heartlessness, the thrust of the anticapitalist critique having shifted more to this than to the alleged waste and inefficiency of the free market (not that this has by any means disappeared altogether).

Ernest Gellner, in imaginative mood, offers some novel and witty explanations of the Popper/Hayek enthusiasm for individualism. He depicts it as a 'curious sub-species of Manicheanism in which the Evil Principle has a very short run in the world, a mere three or four millenia ....' (Gellner, 1985: 49). To Hayek and Popper, collectivism is a bad habit that mankind picked up during the tribal stage of history; in the interest of its own best nature and prosperity, it should get rid of it. Gellner sees the common Viennese origins of Hayek and Popper as the key to their passionate opposition to collectivism, as they noted 'with distaste the obstacles presented to liberalism ... by the surge of ethnic communalisms from the more backward parts of the Hapsburg empire'. Holism and collectivism were, in this Austrian view, the evidence of a *temporary* emergence of a Manichean dualistic world with a powerful Principle of Evil' (Gellner, 1985: 50). Gellner regards this as similar to other forms of theodicy: occupied with questions such as, why is there evil at all in a basically good world? There is quite possibly some point in Gellner's 'sociology of knowledge' explanation but the fact that living in Vienna at a certain point in history influenced someone's ideas is no more a valid criticism of the actual substance of those ideas than would be a similar reaction to Kepler's health as having some bearing on his laws of planetary motion. It would be equally irrelevant if we were to pass judgement on the soundness of Professor Gellner's opinion of the Popper/Hayek position by reference to some other formative experiences of *his* life. We are all moulded by our own particular experience but our ideas should be considered as they are in themselves, as well as by how they have been determined.

One critic of MI, Ernest Nagel (1961: 537–46), refers particularly to Chapter 4 of Hayek's (1979) *Counter-revolution of Science*. Before his comments on this, however, he condemns the way in which historical 'forces' have been used as 'instruments for justifying social iniquities', such as Rousseau's 'general will'. Such interpretations 'have been useless as guides in inquiry and sterile as premises in explanations'. Even so, Nagel does not accept that all collective terms are explicitly definable exclusively by way of individual terms. He offers as examples terms such as 'parades' and 'crowd hostility'. To deny that such entities cannot be observed is like saying that we cannot observe a forest but only the individual trees.[25] In economics, Hayek and Mises, Nagel contends, try to use microeconomic theory based on MI to 'explain the operation of the total economy of a society by deducing propositions characterising those operations from premises dealing with dispositions, beliefs and resources of individual economic agents' (Nagel, 1961: 543). Is this really what Hayek tries to do? He is constantly stressing what he views as the *folly* of deducing macroeconomic aggregates from individual decisions; to take one example, in Hayek's (1983) *A Tiger by the Tail*, there is the section 'No causal connection between macro totals and micro decisions'. Nagel comes to the conclusion that there is, in the absence of careful comparative studies of the merits of the two types of explanation, no definite answer to the question of whether one type of explanation is superior to the other. This must be agreed.

Even supposing the thesis of MI is true, it does not immediately follow that the consequences for the social sciences are as the Austrians claim them to be. Also it is not obvious, in all cases, how the reduction of a whole to its constituent individuals is to be carried out. The situation may be compared with a similar one in the natural sciences: a physicist may believe that all the theories of biology are reducible to the behaviour of atoms and their constituent particles. This, so it has been argued, does not cause the physicist to condemn the biologist simply because he believes that ultimately all biological statements will be reduced to physics. 'Social scientists should be the last to claim that there cannot be a similar division of labour in *their* intellectual world' (Nozick, 1977: 361).

Although methodological individualists argue that all collectives are reducible by an observer to the actions of individuals, it does not follow that the members of the group do not *believe* in its autonomous existence and that that influences *their* behaviour. They may, of course, if the thesis of MI is true, all be mistaken, but Austrians have a problem since they also stress the subjectivism of individual behaviour: it is what individuals believe that governs their actions. Furthermore, who can say with certainty that the 'observer' can himself clear his own mind of holism? How does he set about it? (See Gellner, 1968: 259).

Another argument against MI is that it does not really eliminate holistic entities. For example: 'to describe an individual as a "working-class deferential Conservative" is question-begging because the social context in which the individual is located is incorporated into the description of the individual' (Lukes, 1973: 122). This is to sweep 'social phenomena under the carpet'. The term 'deferential' seems to present no difficulty to MI – it is an individual characteristic – and 'working class' depends on the holistic assumption that there is some group (a 'class') to which the individual belongs and whose general characteristics as discerned by sociology he cannot, as a mere individual, resist the influence of.

Conclusion

In spite of the reservations, refuting examples, and the dangers of dogmatism in methodological individualism, it seems to me that it has, on balance, the best of the argument, not only from a logical viewpoint, but perhaps much more importantly in saving us from the pernicious influence of historicism and related theories, which see the individual as being always at the mercy of powerful 'forces' that he can do little to influence. The central assumption of the individualist position 'is that no social tendency exists which could not be altered *if* the individuals concerned both wanted to alter it and possessed the appropriate information' (Watkins, 1968: 269–80). Of course human beings are influenced and develop by outside holistic phenomena, such as the rate of inflation, but this fact does not justify the conclusion that such phenomena are somehow impersonal and beyond control. Such attitudes can very well serve the purpose of some *individuals* in the desire to hide their own responsibilities: politicians of all parties love to talk about how they are 'fighting inflation' as if inflation is a dangerous dragon whereas it is reasonably certain that politicians – aided and abetted by others – actually create and feed the dragon.

'Vandalism' as used to describe the prevalence of destructive attacks on property is in danger of assuming a purely holistic meaning in the sense that it is an impersonal force rather than the true position, which is that 'vandals' are individuals (usually children) who have parents who might well be able to stop their offsprings' depredations.

Some opposition to the individualist position arises from the undoubted truth that individuals are often confronted by social facts that constrain their behaviour. The methodological individualist would not deny this; he only insists that the social environment (or social facts) consist of other individuals and not 'irreducible sociological or historical *laws*' (Watkins, 1968: 278).

In the next chapter further consequences and implications of the belief in the relevance of methodological individualism and subjectivism will be explored.

Chapter Two

UNINTENDED CONSEQUENCES, KNOWLEDGE, AND HISTORICISM

UNINTENDED CONSEQUENCES OF HUMAN ACTION

The common theme of this chapter is the inherent unpredictability of human affairs, if it is the case that methodological individualism and subjectivism contain a significant degree of truth as theories of social reality. Of course everyone knows that the unexpected can confidently be expected, and that knowledge of the future, though much desired, is virtually impossible to acquire. Yet, in spite of this, a great deal of human action, especially in the political field, goes on as if the truth about these matters is *not* known, or, if known, ignored. There is also much talk of the kind typified by such statements as 'We must do x or y in order to be prepared for the twenty-first century', or 'late capitalism' or 'the post-industrial age' – cloudy entities that rapidly become clichés.

Hayek asks us to consider the way in which footpaths are formed in open country. 'At first everyone will seek for himself what seems to him the best path. But the fact that such a path has been used once is likely to make it easier to traverse and therefore more likely to be used again' (Hayek, 1979: 70). The eventual result is the creation of a road that is the 'result of human action but not of human design', the title of Hayek's famous essay (Hayek, 1967, Chapter 6). More important examples that both the Austrians and Popper have mentioned are language, law, and the spontaneous order of the free market.

Of course, some unintended consequences may also be *unwanted*; there is no guarantee that beneficial results will always emerge. But neither is it the case that human institutions have been and are better for having been designed *ab initio*. Such a view leads to what Hayek describes as the 'constructivist' error. This is the idea that since man has created the institutions of society, he must also be able to alter them at will so as to satisfy his desires (Hayek, 1978, Chapter 1). Hayek built on the work of Menger, the founder of the Austrian school, who held that law, language, markets, and the state are the unintended results of historical development;[1] Mises added money to the list. Earlier examples are found in the work of Mandeville and of Adam Ferguson who, in 1767, wrote of 'the results of human action but not of design' (Hayek, 1967: 96) and David Hume, who had pointed out the way in which law and money had *evolved* rather than being the product of deliberate invention.

The route by which the idea of spontaneous order – the result of unintended consequences – reached the Austrians starts from Ancient Greece in which there prevailed a view of the world that everything was either natural or man-made. This thesis, which dominated European thought for centuries, left no place for any third category. Dr Bernard Mandeville in his *Fable of the Bees* (1728) appears to have been the first writer formally to show the possibility of a third way in which human institutions could have appeared, and he influenced David Hume, Adam Smith, and Edmund Burke. Popper suggested that Marx was the first to conceive social theory as the 'unwanted social repercussions of all our actions', based on a suggestion of Karl Polayni (Popper, 1966, vol. II: 323), but Hayek suggests that Marx was not the originator of the concept as he 'was unquestionably indebted' to Adam Smith and Adam Ferguson. Whatever is the truth of the matter, the more interesting point is that Marx appreciated the importance of the idea of unintended consequences. He used it to present an almost opposite picture of society from the rosy view of Adam Smith. Whereas Smith had seen self-interest as the engine of progress and increased wealth – working through no individual's intention to the mutual benefit of all, Marx interpreted all human intentions as 'merely part of the cunning by which individuals are manipulated in the interests of social evolution' (Minogue, 1985: 29). He was a methodological *collectivist*: it was the holist concept of the underlying productive process that gave rise to the unintentioned and *unwanted* evils of society, but that he explained in terms of individuals and their interactions. Charles Darwin's theories of evolution in biology are seen by Hayek as the 'culmination of a development which Mandeville had started' (Hayek, 1978: 265) though it is not suggested that Mandeville had any direct influence on Darwin. The ideas of Hume and especially of Burke reached Menger through the work of the German jurist, Friedrich Karl von Savigny. The latter described the 'constructivist' proposal to codify German law in the late-eighteenth century as like tearing off a body's skin in order to replace it by a synthetic product.

Hayek's and to some extent also Popper's versions of the doctrine of unintended consequences have a Darwinian type of evolutionary ingredient in that developed existing institutions are depicted not only as having been created by the unintentional actions of thousands of individuals, but also as being the optimum possible arrangements – being the outcome of a repeated competitive process. The institutions developed in a particular way because they achieved superior qualities and proved through their survival more suited to human purposes than the alternatives they displaced; in this way the institutions we have inherited are endowed with a kind of scientific and traditional legitimacy that it would be unwise to discard lightly.

Almost entirely opposed to the mainly British (specifically, Scottish) tradition in eighteenth-century social theory was the dominant school of continental constructivists such as Rousseau, Condorcet, Comte, and Saint-Simon who, strongly influenced by Descartes, advocated that only human institutions created deliberately can be beneficial; this induced a contempt for tradition and custom in general. This 'Cartesian rationalism' as further developed by Hegel and Marx is what Hayek has termed 'constructivism' or 'the engineering type of mind'. It is regarded by Austrians as naive, arrogant, and dangerous, resulting in its worst case in totalitarianism. Of all the human institutions that are the result of unintended action, such as the market and money, the rule of law is seen as vital in preserving that unintended spontaneous order that is an essential condition for the existence of liberty. Hayek, for example, sees the common law as the product of countless decisions made over centuries by kings or other rulers who were only able to 'declare or find existing law . . . and not create law' (Hayek, 1960: 163). The idea that has now become almost universally accepted, that it is the government's function to lay down detailed rules is seen as a threat to liberty; no group such as a government can possibly ever *know* all they would need to know for 'social' planning. This brings us to consider the Austrian and related theories of the limits of knowledge in the social sciences.

KINDS OF KNOWLEDGE AND THEIR LIMITATIONS

'What can we know, and how do we know it?' are questions central to philosophical enquiry. It is clear that there is no agreed definitive answer to these questions. Popper's answer, for example, is that there is no certain way of guaranteeing that any particular empirical knowledge is irrefutable; all knowledge and theories are provisional, and should be tested by attempts to falsify their predictions. Some philosophers have concluded that 'no one will be justified or at all reasonable in believing anything'.[2] This is mentioned only to give an idea of where epistemology may lead us. For a non-philosopher to venture into these thickets would seem like the height of unwisdom, therefore it must be stated that what is proposed in the following brief section, is necessarily limited in scope.

The generally accepted method of doing mainstream economics is based on positivism and this means that economic 'facts' and events should be studied by using similar methods to those of the natural sciences: the setting up of testable propositions whose predictions are capable of being falsified. There is some doubt as to whether economists actually follow this method in practice, although most of them would say that they ought to be doing something along these lines. How 'successful' economists have been in practice is hard to say both because there is no settled opinion about what criteria should be used and because what economics is *for* is by no means clear. It might seem in some ways sad to notice the extent of the self-criticism indulged in by eminent economists during the last fifteen years or so – almost in some cases as if they have lost confidence in the very foundations of their own past endeavours.[3] Such signs of weakened self-confidence in previously unquestioned assumptions concerning the nature of economics are, on balance, to be greeted with approval after the boastfulness and alarming growth in numbers of economists, especially in Whitehall, propelled by the ever-expanding output of economics graduates of the new universities and polytechnics.[4] Partly, the self-criticism is traceable to doubts over the limits to what can be known about society (although this is not the only source of the criticisms). The particular aspect of the theory of knowledge that is now to be considered is a very limited one: the implications of subjectivism for the status and limits of the knowledge of societal and economic facts and events. Some of these implications have been touched on in previous pages. Although subjectivism is not the preserve only of the Austrians – in Keynesianism there are sub-jectivist elements – it is their writings that provide the fullest exploration of the question of subjectivist knowledge; furthermore, the Austrians may be said to be committed to the view that subjectivism has been greatly overlooked as an important factor in the explanation of human society.

In Hayek's *The Sensory Order* (1976) we find a theoretical psycho-logical justification to support the contention that there are inherent limits to the mind's capacity to comprehend complex systems – to the degree when it would be possible to predict particular events – as in meteorology or biology and, in the human world, the market order. We may, however, develop complete theoretical knowledge of the mechanism by which, say, pressure systems develop in the atmos-phere without being able to predict the exact pressure gradient and consequent precise wind strength and direction for all points on the earth's surface at all future times (though the brilliant French mathe-matician Laplace – a man comparable in greatness to Newton – envisaged the possibility that by collecting enough data and knowing the 'forces by which nature is animated' the movements of all the atoms in the universe both past and future could be known with accuracy. It was simply a question of finding the right formulas.) Similarly, it is perfectly feasible to understand the principles of the free market without knowing or predicting the equilibrium of prices of all goods and services.

In addition to these limits to knowledge, which it is perfectly possible to envisage being extended as time passes – such as, for example, new theories of modifications of existing theories in meteorology – there also exists another, more restrictive limit to explanation, which is inherent in the mind itself. Hayek's thesis in *The Sensory Order* is that 'the human brain can never fully explain its own operations' (Hayek, 1976). His argument amounts to saying that for x to be capable of giving an explanation for y, x has to be more complex than y. Thus if x and y are the same thing – in this case the mind/brain – then x cannot understand y because it is incapable of comprehending itself. This argument has much in common with Gödel's theorem that Hayek was to use in later work.[5] In 1931 Gödel showed that a system's consistency cannot be proved within the system itself (his second Incompleteness Theorem). Gödel's theorem relates to axiom systems in which certain expressions are derived in accordance with a given set of rules from initial axioms. It has been accepted as carrying important inferences for mathematics and its relationship to logic, but whether it also falsifies theories that take the human mind to be nothing more essentially than a mechanical device – a living computer – remains a subject of controversy; this is especially so in the question of whether it is inherently impossible to build a computer that 'thinks' like a human brain – artificial intelligence. Hayek's answer to this is:

> To achieve this would require a brain of a higher order of complexity, though it might be built on the same general principles. Such a brain might be able to explain what happens in our own brain, but it would still be unable fully to explain its own operations, and so on.
>
> (Hayek, 1976: 189)

Another aspect of the question of what can we know, which has strong appeal for Austrians, is the thesis that in much of our behaviour 'we do not know what we are doing'[6] we often carry out actions according to rules of which we are not conscious. Michael Polanyi and Gilbert Ryle have both drawn the attention of philosophers to the importance and function of 'inarticulable' knowledge. It would be a false picture of the growth of knowledge to present it as only conscious, explicit knowledge – nor is all knowledge reducible to scientific statements. Much of the knowledge that society uses exists only dispersed among countless individuals and much of it is known unconsciously only to those individuals.

Akin to this view is the classification of knowledge as 'technical knowledge', which may be deliberately learned and practised such as driving a car or the technique of discovery in natural sciences; the second sort is 'practical knowledge'. The difference between the two kinds is that technical knowledge can be written down – formulated – whereas practical knowledge cannot. Unlike technical knowledge, practical knowledge gives the appearance of being imprecise and can neither be 'taught nor learned but only imparted and acquired' (Oakeshott, 1962: 11) in the way that a pianist acquires artistry as well as technique. The knowledge involved in political activity is of this dual character. Oakeshott saw a certain type of rationalism, which has become dominant in many fields of human activity, as despising his 'practical knowledge' as being no knowledge at all; and that only technical knowledge counts as knowledge. The source of this type of rationalism he finds, rather similarly to Hayek, in scientism: 'what commonplace minds made out of the inspiration of men of genius' (i.e. Bacon and Descartes) and this has led in the modern world to the worship of ideology which, unlike traditional rules and values, has the appearance of being self-contained:

> It can be taught to those whose minds are empty; and if it is to be taught to one who already believes something, the first step of the teacher must be to administer a purge, to make sure that all prejudices and preconceptions are removed, to lay his foundation upon the unshakeable rock of absolute ignorance.

(Oakeshott, 1962: 12)

A question related to any theory of knowledge so far as human affairs is concerned is to what extent future societal events can be predicted. Determinists contend that a human being's behaviour can be explained scientifically by such things as his genetic endowment, his state of health, his childhood experiences, etc.; in its extreme form determinism denies the reality of free will and it may follow from this that we cannot be held responsible for our actions. The next step in determinism is reminiscent of Laplace's ambitions and beliefs in the question of prediction: as the sciences that study human behaviour gain more insight so it will eventually become possible to predict exactly all the actions of any human being at any time and in any situation using genetics, physiology, neurology, and psychology. This reasoning has been attacked as faulty because it makes the mistake of treating the whole human being as a complex machine simply because separate parts may be so regarded. It is, however, a difficult theory to refute absolutely. Gilbert Ryle's view contained the assertion that 'men are not machines, not even ghost-ridden machines. They are men – a tautology which is sometimes worth remembering'.[7] However, for our present limited purposes, any further discussion of this mind/body problem must be curtailed in view of the fact that it occupies a very prominent place in philosophical controversy and the literature on it is dauntingly extensive. This might well be kept in mind by economists and sociologists who venture into this field. However, it should also be noted that theories in modern physics have undermined determinism. The legacy of modern nuclear physics in the form of Niels Bohr's quantum theory and Heisenberg's Uncertainty Principle[8] has completely undermined strict determinism. The dream of Laplace has been answered – nature will not permit such godlike prediction. The fact that the foundations of our concepts of matter have been shaken in the world of nuclear physics should not readily lead us to claim this as some supporting evidence for the version of subjectivism espoused by Austrian economics. It is quite unsound reasoning to suppose that because accurate prediction seems to be difficult in the subatomic world that we can bring this in to support the Austrian scepticism as to the possibility of prediction in the social sciences. For many purposes, outside the subatomic domain, traditional views still work: the path of an emergent light ray, for example, can still be predicted with certainty, providing we know the refractive index of the medium through which it has passed.[9] More useful argument as a support for Austrian subjectivism and the possibility of prediction is to be found in the work of Karl Popper. His thesis depends on the fact that 'tomorrow or a year hence, we may propose and test important theories of which nobody has seriously thought so far.' If knowledge grows in this way then it cannot possibly be predictable; ' ... we cannot anticipate today what we shall know only tomorrow'. Although Popper's proof of this thesis requires more than these bald statements[10] what they amount to is the purely logical contention 'that no scientific predictor, whether a human scientist or a calculating machine, can possibly predict, by scientific methods, its own future results' (Popper, 1960: vi).

The reliance placed on statistical frequency-ratio probability as a way of predicting economic behaviour is characteristically criticized by Austrians; but reservations concerning the validity of statistical methods are not confined to Austrians. It is sometimes thought that because statistics is designed to deal with large numbers, the problems of what Hayek calls 'complex structures' can be overcome using statistical frequency-ratio calculations. Although complex structures and patterns are relatively easy to recognize in the physical world and it is comparatively easy to find 'laws' governing these patterns, this, so it is argued, is not so in the structures of society – these are more complex. This view has been challenged by, for example, Ernest Nagel, but Hayek maintains that 'the increasing complexity as we proceed from the inanimate to the (more highly organised) animate and social phenomena becomes fairly obvious' (Hayek, 1967: 26). The weakness of the use of frequency ratios to analyse and predict the behaviour of complex structures lies in the fact that it ignores the relations between the individual elements and the differences between them. The beliefs and opinions that lead people to produce or sell certain quantities of goods are quite different from their ideas on the whole of the 'economic system' to which they belong. The individual responses to data within a system are the condition of the existence of the 'wholes' that would not exist without them. The application of frequency-ratio probability to economic prediction is somewhat unreal. 'A relative frequency is simply the ratio of the number of the members of a sub-class to the members of the class to which this sub-class belongs' (Shackle, 1972: 393) but the difficulty is to know how these classes should best be defined. The limitations of economic forecasting have frequently been pointed out by other economists of the Austrian tendency such as Lachmann and Loasby and others who are quite certainly not of their general persuasion.[11] The general theme of some Austrians and especially of Shackle is that prediction in economics looks to be impossible. This thesis has been taken up and used by liberal economists as yet another objection to government 'social engineering' and forecasting. Mises spoke contemptuously of economic advisers who, to comfort their customers, have developed the 'trend doctrine', which extrapolates the future from past trends. Certainly, the crashing sound of refuted forecasts is familiar: from the nineteenth-century prediction that coal would all be used up in a few years, to the forebodings about the coming 'crisis' in oil supplies which marked the 1970s and such monster reports as *The Limits to Growth* from the Club of Rome.[12] The scepticism of the Austrians has received ample empirical support as it will no doubt continue to do. The young J. M. Keynes wrote:

> Our power of prediction is so slight, it is seldom wise to sacrifice a present evil for a doubtful advantage in the future .... It is the paramount duty of governments and of politicians to secure the well-being of the community under the case in the present, and not to run risks overmuch for the future.
>
> (Keynes, 1904, quoted in Skidelsky, 1983)[13]

Such evident appreciation of the difficulty of prediction continued to find a place in the writings of Keynes as in his views on the uncertainty of all economic decision-making and especially investment decisions. For example, Keynes, quoted in an essay of Shackle's, declared 'unequivocally that expectations do not rest on anything solid, determinable, demonstrable; "We simply do not know"'. Shackle presents Keynes not as many of his followers became, a believer in the rationality of economic affairs. Shackle's scepticism is based on his thesis that 'tomorrow's new knowledge' destroys and renders obsolete and can destroy all our present ideas (Shackle, 1973a: 516–19). This view has been criticized as making the mistake of conflating knowledge with certainty and arguing that since certainty is not attainable, neither is knowledge; the assumption seems to be that we can either know everything about the future, omniscience at one extreme or omni-nescience at the other. 'Most of the real world lies well between the two' (Hutchison, 1986: 131; Coddington, 1983, Chapter 1). What this amounts to saying is that although we can never be sure of our predictions, nevertheless we should keep trying; such advice may be too weak to counteract the tendency of governments to go in for enormous schemes based on their predictions, which history shows have often been disastrous.

THE SOCIOLOGY OF KNOWLEDGE

The sociology of knowledge, or 'sociologism' seeks to explain ideas by the influence of the social systems in which they appear. Thus, Marx finds the explanation of ideas that have appeared in particular periods of history through the prevailing class structure. 'Sociologism' argues that all knowledge is relative to the class or religion or other social context of the observer or discoverer of that knowledge. If this is true, then there is no possibility of purely objective knowledge and this must have the most serious consequences for our understanding of society. The most well-known and effective attempt to refute the sociology of knowledge is that in Popper's *The Open Society and its Enemies*, 1966, vol. 2. The sociology of knowledge argues that scientific thought, especially on social and political questions, is always socially conditioned. Furthermore, the observer of social, economic, or political matters can never rid himself of the influences that are inseparable from his own preconceived attitudes whether religious, political, or class based. Thus many things are taken for granted by him – whole groups of ideas with which he is endowed by his social position and that he accepts as self-evident and unqestioned, because of his own 'total ideology'.[14] How then, can it ever be possible to see through the fog of the various competing ideologies? The way to true knowledge lies in standing above the battle by unveiling unconscious assumptions. The outstanding contemporary example of this line of thought is what Popper refers

46

to as 'Vulgar Marxism'. This is the belief – which he takes to be a perversion of Marx:

> that Marxism lays bare the sinister secrets of social life by revealing the hidden motives of greed and lust for material gain which actuate the powers behind the scenes of history; powers that cunningly and consciously create war, depression, unemployment ... in order to gratify their vile desires for profit.
>
> (Popper, 1966, vol. 2: 100)

Any disagreement by an opponent can always be explained in the sociology of knowledge by reference to his class bias or his total ideology. Thus a crude example might be the case of an objector to Freudian psychology being told that his very objections are rooted in his childhood experiences or his sexuality; in the same way any view of society offered by a politician must *necessarily* be coloured by his economic position and class. Such a procedure, because it cannot be refuted, is not scientific (on Popper's definition of science).

At 'a joking level', Popper shows how all this is easily dealt with. Assuming the theory of total ideologies is true, how can anyone, including those who claim to be able to pronounce upon the ideologies of others, rid themselves of their own ideological baggage? Clearly there is no possible way in which we could ever be convinced: '... we could even ask whether the whole theory is not simply the expression of the class interest of a particular group ...' (Popper, 1966, vol. 2: 216). Hayek's criticism of the claim of a particular group to know the 'real' truth is that it is self-contradictory. It asserts that we know more than we do know, which is nonsense as it implies the existence of people with superminds – 'a free-floating intelligentsia' (Hayek, 1979: 158).

It must however be conceded that we are all, scientists included, bound to be influenced by our own preconceptions to varying degrees. So how can science ever be objective? How can scientists purge themselves of prejudice and attain scientific objectivity? Two aspects of the method, at least of the natural sciences, provide possible answers. One is the public character of scientific method. Scientists put forward theories, confident of their truth, but which are then subjected to the most rigorous examination and criticism by other scientists: everything may be challenged without fear. Another aspect of science that is important is that scientists try to express their theories in such a form – using language known to other scientists – so that they can be tested and possibly refuted.

Scientific objectivity is thus a product of the 'social or public character of science' (Popper, 1966, vol. 2: 220). 'Science' here refers not only to the natural sciences but to the social sciences and especially to economics. Once again there is some disagreement here between Popper and the Austrians. Popper advocates a 'unified method' for natural and social science, whereas the Austrian attachment to subjectivism rules this out.

The idea that sociological studies of prejudices is the way to get rid of them is mistaken. For, as Popper says, many who pursue these studies are full of prejudice. Also, there are repeated examples of the way in which science 'can look after itself' as in Einstein's questioning of the very foundations of classical physics or the entirely different conception of matter that is now widely accepted in the light of what we now know about subatomic particles. Such fundamental shifts owe nothing to any process of 'socio-therapy' and everything to scientific method.

HISTORICISM

'Historicism' in the sense in which the term is used by Hayek and Popper, is the view that historical events are determined by inevitable *laws* that history aims to predict. It involves a particular view of the concepts we have been discussing, especially holism and the possibility of identifying and predicting social 'forces', 'movements', and 'trends'. To Popper, historicism is the belief in laws of historical development such as those propounded by Hegel, Marx, Comte, and Toynbee.

Hayek's opposition to historicism as a method of study lies in his contention that:

> human history, which is the result of the interaction of innumerable human minds, must yet be subject to simple laws accessible to human minds is now so widely held that few people are at all aware what an astonishing claim it really implies.
>
> (Hayek, 1979: 129)

These words undoubtedly still contain much relevance to the world today, forty years after they were first written. The evidence of the pervasiveness of historicist preconceptions haunts the pronouncements of politicians, trade-union leaders, and leading figures in industry and commerce with their unthinking talk of 'stages', 'movements', 'forces', 'systems', and 'trends'. Evidently, for example, many on the Left of politics believe in some phase called 'late capitalism'. Of course, it can be argued with much justification that the capitalism of the end of the twentieth century is greatly different from, say, that of the 1880s, but the adjective 'late' contains the implicit (Marxist) unwarranted assumption that capitalism may be seen as part of a historical process and that it is near the end of its life. Of course, this may well be true, but I mention it as an example of that historicist frame of mind that subtly but strongly forms the attitude of many people to current social and political events. 'Late capitalism' is accepted almost as axiomatic.

So-called historical theories are more properly regarded as interpretations rather than theories of history. When such theorists find confirmation of their doctrines by sifting through history, they mistake this as proof of their ideas. Such a procedure, it has been shown by Popper, cannot lead to a proof since this could only be the case if it could be shown that the theory could be falsified by reference to the evidence. In many cases, historicist theories are not falsifiable and cannot thereby be tested. This does not make them necessarily untrue; it is simply that they cannot claim the status of science as defined by Popper's criteria. In fact many of Marx's predictions derived from the historicist theory of economic determinism have been refuted by the subsequent course of history.[15] Marx has been defended against Popper on the grounds that he was, in fact, truly scientific in the sense that he first put forward the theory that the dominant forms of production, technology, and property ownership determined the institutional framework – the systems of law and government. Changes in the underlying productive system would lead to tensions that could only be resolved by changes in the institutional superstructure. He then studied history to find evidence for his theory and predicted that given certain conditions – such as the growth of unemployment due to overproduction and the falling rate of profit consequent upon the accumulation of capital – the socialist revolution was inevitable. 'This is neither historicist nor deterministic.... It was not he who was holistic and Utopian; it was the Utopian socialists whom he criticised....'[16] Popper recognized that 'Vulgar Marxists' have misinterpreted Marx in the sense that Marx saw in things such as war, depression, and unemployment not the result of a conspiracy on the part of 'big business' or 'imperialists' but simply the unintentioned results of the social system. Nevertheless Marx did write the following, which seems to deserve to be described as historicist:

> even when a society has got on the right track for the discovery of the natural laws of its movement – and it is the ultimate aim of this work to lay bare the economic law of motion of modern society – it can neither by bold leaps, nor remove by legal enactments, the obstacles offered by the successive phases and its normal development. But it can shorten and lessen the birth pangs.
>
> (Preface i, to *Capital*)

Surely, it may be objected to the Popper/Hayek attack on historicism, no-one could deny the existence of trends in social change. Popper's answer is that trends are not laws. A trend may even last for thousands of years without becoming a universal law. Scientific laws can be expressed as negatives such as 'You can't keep water in a sieve' or 'You cannot build a perpetual motion machine' (Popper, 1960:61). Popper regards the search for laws of evolution as unscientific, whether in biology or sociology. The evolution of life on earth or human society is a unique historical process that is governed by all kinds of laws – of physics, genetics, etc. It is not a law 'but only a singular historical statement' (Popper, 1960: 108). Universal laws make assertions covering all processes of a certain kind and any such law must be *tested* by new instances before it can be regarded as being scientific. The tendency to confuse trends with laws inspired the historicist doctrine of the irreversible 'laws of motion' of society.

Hayek's arguments against historicism have been very similar to Popper's though less detailed or analytical and he has himself been accused by Robbins of falling into the error of historicism in his earlier writings on political philosophy, when he predicts that social disintegration must follow from the extension of the welfare state – as in *The Road to Serfdom* (Hayek, 1944).[17]

To sum up: between them Hayek and Popper have managed to shake the foundations of historicism as a method of studying society, and because of them its grip is now less dangerous than it was. Those people who still like to use, in discussing political and social questions, terms that have been lifted from their proper place in the natural sciences – such as forces, dynamic, movement, velocity, evolution, etc., must if they have read Popper and Hayek, tend to be less assured and more self-conscious about what they are doing.

50

Part II

MARKETS

Chapter Three

THE NATURE AND FUNCTIONS OF THE MARKET

DEFINITION AND ORIGINS

Words used in political economy are potentially ambiguous and signify different things to different people. Notorious examples are: freedom, equality, democracy, and socialism. There is rarely, in such terms, a one-to-one correspondence between the word and the underlying concept.[1] 'The market' is one such term, often to be found qualified in various ways such as: 'the free market', private enterprise', 'the price mechanism', 'the price system', *'laissez-faire'*, 'capitalism', 'capitalist system', etc. Such expressions, although they are generally employed as synonymous with 'the market' should not be considered in isolation but only by taking into account their context and who is using them.

'Free' markets clearly raises the complex issue of what we mean by freedom.

'Capitalist' and 'capitalism' are too near to being terms of abuse or contempt in some political glossaries to be used lightly.

'Price mechanism' sounds neutral and innocuous enough yet might well offend the desire for precision for those who believe that the market is not remotely to be compared to a mechanism – Austrians who stress the subjective nature of individual action.

'Price system' may be misconstrued as implying that the market was *created*, as in 'tax system'.

'Exchange economy' seems a nicely neutral term but does not fully describe the social institution that is the subject of this chapter, since it could apply to a barter economy without money prices.

For immediate purposes I shall nevertheless use the term 'the market'. This should be understood as standing for 'capitalist free

53

market' – referring to a society in which there is private ownership of property, freedom to carry on exchange using money, and the right to accumulate capital.

The market is a human social institution that may evolve to resolve certain economic problems. Markets are *one* way of discovering what individuals prefer to spend their income on. They then transmit these preferences to producers of goods and services and resources are thus allocated between competing uses. Through the 'rewards' of profits and wages, markets provide the incentives, the fuel as it were, that energizes the whole complex web of relationships. In short, markets co-ordinate the wishes of millions of individuals. These are broadly the functions of markets. To quote from the inside front cover of the publications of the Institute of Economic Affairs: markets are 'technical devices for registering preferences and apportioning resources'. The theoretical and technical aspects of markets form that division of economics in general designated microeconomics.

There is little room for doubting that markets originated quite spontaneously – that they *evolved*. However, some critics of the market, those who find the disadvantages and 'unfairness' repellent, often tend indirectly to imply that somehow or other the capitalist system was imposed on an unwilling mass of docile workers. The use of the word 'system' is the key to this implication, suggesting as it does a prior act of creation by some agent or group. Even Marx, although he saw in the capitalist organization of industry, the rise of the middle class, and the industrial wage-earning class inevitable mutual antagonism rather than the harmony that free-marketeers claim as a major virtue, depicts the market as an evolutionary process. However, he is unimpressed by the fact that markets may have evolved out of human interdependence and interaction. He has no reverence for traditional elements in human institutions merely because they happen to be old and customary. The Austrians and especially Hayek, on the other hand, see social and cultural institutions – the market as well as other developments such as language and law – as embodying the same fundamental principle of natural selection found in the mechanism of Darwinian evolution. Not only that, but Hayek sees such evolutionary processes as yielding immense and unappreciated benefits to humanity that are not realizable through deliberate action.

Throughout his writings, Hayek has propounded his belief, not only in the spontaneous nature of cultural and social structures, but also in the beneficial nature of such processes as opposed to planned arrangements. The origin of the market is depicted as spontaneous and as the unintended result of human actions. Hayek contends that a proper understanding of these principles was first properly realized by Bernard Mandeville, who, in 1728, in his second edition of the *Fable of the Bees, or Private Vices and Public Benefits* conceived the idea of the spontaneous growth of orderly structures. For example, the growth of law is seen as 'reconciling men's divergent interests ... not through the design of some wise legislator but through a long process of trial and error' (Hayek, 1978: 260).

Max Weber saw the origins of capitalistic markets in the influence of the Protestant ethic in the sixteenth century, deriving its impetus especially from the stricter sects such as the Calvinists. Benjamin Franklin, American statesman and scientist (1706–90), is cited by Weber as an example of that 'peculiar ethic', which became the maxim for the conduct of life – in which all actions are coloured with utilitarianism and in which the piling up of money becomes an end in itself. Franklin's father, a Calvinist, had drummed into his son the biblical precept: 'Seest thou a man diligent in his business? He shall stand before Kings' (Prov. xxii 29).

It seems that Hayek, although indebted to Weber for some of his methodological insights,[2] says little of his theory of the importance of religion in the origins of Western European and American capitalism.

Adam Smith's judgement is clearly evolutionist:[3]

This division of labour, from which so many advantages are derived, is not originally the effect of any human wisdom, which foresees and intends that general opulence to which it gives occasion. It is the necessary, though very slow and gradual consequence of a certain propensity in human nature which has in view no such extensive utility; the propensity to truck, barter, and exchange one thing for another.

(*Wealth of Nations*, Chapter 2)

DIFFERENT CONCEPTS OF THE NATURE OF THE MARKET

The mature Austrian view of markets and its divergence from that of 'mainstream' economics is to be found throughout Hayek's writings; indeed the process of the market is a theme that permeates much of his thought, being first expressed in his essay 'The use of knowledge in society', 1945 (Hayek, 1980). It is remarkable to what extent this now famous essay foreshadows the subsequent development of his political and economic ideas.

Economics, as it was generally understood in 1945 (and as it still is according to those economics texts that take no account of uncertainty) is seen as the study of optimizing given resources. Until fairly recently, the essence of neoclassical theory was solely that: assuming tastes, resources, and the state of technology as given, then equilibrium prices and quantities are determinate. Hayek argues that such a concept is emphatically not the economic problem. This is because the necessary information concerning costs and prices on which the economic calculus is based, is never realizable in a form in which a single mind could work out an optimal solution. The real importance of the market is not the achievement of equilibrium – seen at its most extreme and unconvincing in the model of perfect competition – it is its function as a transmitter of knowledge. Through the market we have achieved, not only division of labour, but also a division of knowledge. Furthermore, the price system is one among many of those structures in which the individual makes constant use of formulas and rules and inarticulable knowledge without having to understand the meaning of them. Although Hayek makes a great deal of this argument – that the market is the institution best fitted to transmit knowledge of other people's actions and preferences – there are some kinds of information for which it is far from perfect as a transmitter. It breaks down in the theoretical model of the prisoner's dilemma. But more practically the market has limitations in health care; although the 'consumer' is a patient, it is doctors who 'demand' the resources needed for hospitals.

Apart from its neglect of this knowledge – generating aspects of real world market process – Austrians have criticized the neoclassical neglect of the role of the entrepreneur. The latter, who has been seen as a mere receiver of income or as an exploiter, Kirzner has elevated to a much more important position. He is seen as 'the prime mover of economic progress'. Kirzner acknowledges his debt to others such as Mises who, in *Human Action* (1966), emphasizes the role of the entrepreneur as, through his constant alertness to the changing possibilities presenting themselves in the market, is a crucial force in the process by which resources are used. One problem in envisaging the entrepreneur in the modern world is the prevalence and importance of the giant, often multinational companies. Where are the entrepreneurs in these organizations? Can a subcommittee of a board of directors be imagined in the same role as that occupied in the past by the individualistic pioneers of industry or today's small new ventures of which Mrs Thatcher is so proud? Nevertheless, whether firms are large or small, national or multinational, responses to changing market signals are constantly being made somehow or other, and profit is the measure of entrepreneurial success. Furthermore, there is the important fact that not only is entrepreneurial flair essential for the efficient working of free markets, but that only free markets 'breed' entrepreneurs.[4] Where all the facts are fully known to a single mind (e.g. a central planning committee) the problem of how to allocate resources becomes one of maximizing output; this is the picture of the economy as presented by the mainstream theoretical neoclassical models. It ignores the importance of markets in discovering the necessary facts on which judgements can be made and action taken.

This process can, according to the Austrian view, only go on when market agents (consumers, firms) and especially entrepreneurs are free to act according to their own assessments of the kaleidic[5] economy facing them. Rothbard compares the attempt by a central planning board in its decision-making – without market prices on which to base its calculations – as being in the same position as a large firm that is vertically integrated to such a large degree that market prices can be disregarded. There may still be calculations, but not under the discipline of the market. Whenever such a firm supplies the output of one department as an input to another department instead of selling in the market at a competitive price, the problem of artificial transfer prices arises, which are necessarily quite arbitrary.

Now to summarize some of the most common criticisms of the market and possible 'answers'. Critical reservations about the beneficence of markets may be grouped under the heads of efficiency or morality; and in some cases it is not possible to place them firmly in one category or the other. Market efficiency is often challenged, using such rhetorical expressions as: 'the wastes of competition'; 'production for profit, not for use'; 'monopoly profit'; etc.

As a preliminary to this discussion it should be noted that there has, in the last few years, been a marked shift of emphasis in the general critical view of the market economy. The contention that markets are inherently inefficient – unreliable and wasteful – as allocative systems, has moved from its former prominence in the Left's critique of capitalism;[6] the direction tends now to be that markets promote selfishness and inequality, hence stifling 'true' freedom. Indeed, so far have the present leaders of the Labour Party proceeded in this direction, desperately anxious as they are to shed those parts of currently practised municipal socialism, which they evidently consider to be certain vote losers, that they have almost redefined socialism. It is no longer denied that markets are for many purposes the most efficient institutional arrangement for providing people with what they want, although there is a strong line of criticism that rests on the proposition that people are persuaded against their real interests into regrettable consumption patterns. There is, however, one important area of alleged market inefficiency that has received increasing attention to the recent past: the whole complex of problems associated with externalities and economic growth (see Chapter 9). This question has received publicity and political influence through the activists of the Green and Ecology movements, although E. J. Mishan had first sounded the alarm in his *Costs of Economic Growth* in 1967, against the currently fashionable view that economic growth should be promoted as a cure for nearly all ills without much thought for the consequences. Another aspect of efficiency that is still very much alive as part of the critique of the market is the Keynesian proposition, which dominated policy from 1945 to 1980, that a free-market equilibrium is no guarantee of full employment and the 1980s rise in unemployment is seen by many observers as supporting this contention. The Austrian view is that the unemployment of the 1980s was to a great extent a consequence of the ill-conceived policies of 'Keynesian' governments of the 1960s and 1970s and not to market 'failure'.

As the questions of economic growth, externalities, and unemployment are discussed elsewhere, what remains now to mention briefly in the context of 'efficiency' are the questions of monopoly, the role of profit, and the manipulation of consumer preferences.

In standard economics textbooks the model of monopoly predicts that output will be smaller and prices higher than in a competitive market. That such a situation is assumed to be undesirable is demonstrated through a simple theorem in welfare economics, based on utility theory, apart from its common-sense appeal. It is widely accepted that it is perfectly reasonable for the government to seek to 'control' monopolies. How is monopoly to be identified and its extent in a particular industry measured? Apart from the rather arbitrary rules of the Monopolies and Mergers Commission, the perfect competition model may be used as a yardstick by which to judge the extent of a given monopolistic industry. The Austrian objection to this is threefold. First, that the perfect competition model is itself erroneous and misleading;[7] second, the discovery process, which Austrians see as the essence of free markets, has to be undertaken by the monopolist as well as the competitive firm. Third, that the state has itself been the main agent of monopoly.

'Monopoly capitalism' might have been expected to appear first in the country that pioneered the industrial revolution – Britain. This would be predicted by the Marxist doctrine of the concentration of industry that rests on the argument that the advance of technology increasingly tends to favour economies of scale and the consequent elimination of the small firms throughout most of the advanced economies. The extent to which larger firms have attained a dominant position in the last hundred years is not in question. But it is often exaggerated and ignores the phenomenon of the proliferation of rising small enterprises often in hitherto undreamed-of industries. One has only to think of the possibilities of the developments brought about by the rapidly expanding technology of information systems or the servicing of leisure, financial, and sporting interests. Of course, such activities may not constitute what have been thought of as the 'commanding heights of the economy' but some of these erstwhile heights nowadays have shrunk to less formidable hills.

If it were the case that the 'evolution' of capitalism and technology led inevitably to monopolies, then the fact that Britain's economy was, by 1900, less monopolistic than the economies of Germany and the USA, even though the British system had had longer to develop such 'inevitable' symptoms, leaves something to be explained. In fact, the far more monopolistic economies of Germany and the USA were a direct result of the protectionist and regulatory policies of governments (Hayek, 1944, Chapter 4).

The contention that one example of market failure is the 'manipulation' of consumers by powerful persuasive advertising is difficult to refute only if it can be proved that what the consumers eventually choose is in some way not what they 'really' wanted. The fact that much advertising may strike the sensitive intelligence as banal, trivial, and generally deplorable is beside the point. The trouble with the 'manipulation' argument is that human beings are, in a general way, being 'manipulated' from birth onwards – by parents, husbands or wives, teachers, friends, books, films, universities, etc.; 'manipulated', that is, in the sense of being 'influenced by'. It is difficult to see why advertisers have become singled out for special hostility. Also there would seem to be something in the idea that no amount of seductive advertising will, for long, maintain the sales of an unsatisfactory product. Furthermore, consumers can try out products by direct test. They buy a certain brand of margarine and do not like it, so they do not buy it again. This contrasts sharply with the political process in which choosing (voting) politicians is conducted with no possibility of direct tests of success or failure. In the absence of such tests the voter may well choose those politicians who 'sell' their product most convincingly. The average voter will find it difficult to discover the mistakes of politicians. The great inflations of the 1960s and 1970s caused by governments were frequently blamed by politicians on trade unions, or speculators, or black marketeers. The ordinary voter has no way of testing the truth of this sort of propaganda (Rothbard, 1977: 20).

The well-worn objection that production in capitalist markets is for profit, not for use, is, of course, based on a misunderstanding. Of course production is for profit – that is the incentive in markets to produce anything. But it does not follow from this that goods or services that have been produced by someone trying to make a profit are not for 'use'. In fact, without the profit motive they may well not have been produced at all. Furthermore, consumer choice directs producers to offer things for sale that people are expressing their preferences for, unless of course Galbraith is right in his contention that large modern firms do not 'wait' for consumers to express their wants, but that the firms themselves deliberately 'create' such demand through powerful advertising. Some critics see the whole ethos of 'consumerism' exerting pressure to make people buy things they would probably be better off without. The social pressures are strong. For example, people who do not aspire to owning a television set or a motor car are sometimes thought to be rather odd. Such considerations as these raise questions about the morality of markets.

Chapter Four

MARKETS AND MORALITY

UTILITARIANISM[1]

In order to judge the desirability of proposed actions it is first
necessary to agree on some general principle by which such actions
shall be appraised. Utilitarianism is one of the most discussed of such
theories of human conduct; and although it has been much criticized,
utilitarian kinds of assumption will often be discovered to be present
in arguments and 'philosophies' of what action is desirable in
particular circumstances and in answering political or economic
questions. Although the public policy of governments is where
utilitarianism has chiefly seemed appropriate as a criterion, the
principle has relevance also for other institutions and individuals. It
is obvious that decisions to act in one way rather than another –
whether by single individuals or groups – are frequently based on
some theory of what constitutes 'good' conduct. Pragmatists urge
that lines of action should be based on the facts but in practice what
happens is that their actions are based on different *theories* of
conduct in each case and are thus fluctuating and unpredictable.

Utilitarianism is an ethical theory that offers one answer to the
question of how to achieve the kind of world we think is the most
valuable, whatever that happens to be. The answer of utilitarianism
is 'Act so as to bring about the greatest good possible'. Utilitarianism
is a consequentialist theory; that is to say, it argues that particular
actions will promote end results that are themselves good. The
market may be defended on this basis – that it ensures efficiency or
increases total utility or freedom. An alternative to consequentialism
is to start from the proposition that people may be seen as having
fundamental 'rights', which require no justification. The freedom to

engage in market transactions may then be seen as the exercise of such rights and the merits or demerits of market activity are irrelevant to any defence of the market as an institution. For the most part, economists have judged markets on their results; rights are seen only as part of the institutional background to market transactions.

Jeremy Bentham (1748–1832) is chiefly associated with utilitarianism although he attributed his initial insight to reading David Hume. Bentham proposed that the 'ultimate good' was the achievement of the greatest good of the greatest number; the morality of action is not to be judged by concentrating on the actions themselves but by assessing their effect on general happiness – *act utilitarianism*; it raises many ethical problems. Consider two possible examples: should promises be kept only when I believe they will do most good? Why should not a promise be kept because it is a good thing in itself? Supposing two people are in danger of drowning in a river; one is your brother and the other an eminent heart surgeon. According to utilitarianism, the decision on which person to save first should take account of all the lives and reduction of suffering that would be lost if the surgeon is not given priority in the rescue. Most people would find such principles unattractive as guides to conduct, not to say ludicrous.

In order to avoid some of the difficulties there is a modified principle at hand – *rule utilitarianism*. This follows the precept that we should not judge the morality or goodness of a particular act by its consequences, but by the consequences that follow from adopting chosen rules. This gives rise to injunctions such as: never take a human life, or never tell a lie. Clearly, with the possibility of so many qualifications to such rules, finding the most beneficial ones will be very difficult and will raise all manner of controversies.

Both these types of utilitarianism judge behaviour by the results; they are both consequentialist. But theories of conduct might well be based on ethical principles that do not consider results, such as to be against killing simply because it is *wrong*. Benthamite utilitarianism can be criticized on logical grounds, quite apart from the difficulties of measuring 'happiness'. The phase 'the greatest happiness of the greatest number' has been criticized by Peter Geach for its use of two successive superlatives (with support from Fowler, *Modern English Usage*). He suggests that although utilitarianism is very vulnerable to reasoned criticism, the secret of its appeal lies in the fact that it 'arouses a feeling of concern for the broad masses rather than some privileged class'[2] with its phrase 'greatest number'.

Apart from the target that utilitarianism offers to criticism on the basis of its contradiction and illogicality, there is an older alternative theory of human conduct – that people have certain 'natural rights' that are superior to and antecedent to questions of the consequences of our actions. Such rights are derived from the concept of the existence of 'natural law' (as opposed to positive or man-made law): 'The natural liberty of man is to be free from any superior power on earth, and not to be under the will or legislative authority of man, but to have only the law of Nature for his rule' (John Locke, 1632–1704).[3] Bentham attacked this natural rights theory in two main ways.[4] First, that the idea of a natural right independent of human law is nonsense. There can be no way of objectively deciding whether, for example, a man has a natural as distinct from a legal right to freedom of speech. (The idea that everyone has a right to work would have seemed to Bentham even greater nonsense.) Men speak of their natural rights, said Bentham, when they wish to get their own way without having to argue for it. Second, the idea of natural nonlegal rights can have no meaning unless we are advocating anarchy. Anyone who objects to some particular law of a sovereign government could simply claim that he is absolved from obedience by virtue of his inalienable right to some benefit that is antecedent to, and superior to the law in question. On the other hand, if a right is claimed as something never to be touched except by due process of law, the 'right' becomes an empty and useless concept.

Bentham's critique of natural rights became widely approved in the nineteenth century by English political philosophers. J. S. Mill, however, although a utilitarian, concluded that without the recognition of moral rights, over and above ordinary law, there could be no real justice. Mill tried to reconcile his utilitarianism with his desire to support natural rights, by the device of arguing that individual rights in themselves are an 'extraordinary' kind of utility. The right of an individual to have his freedom preserved is a utility that is a more important utility than any other. The weakness of this position is that it is self-contradictory. Utilitarianism advocates maximizing the total welfare of society as a whole but if natural rights are to override this principle, as in Mill's belief in the importance of the liberty of the individual, then there is a clear and unresolvable conflict. This problem is still very much with us today.

The present balance of opinion, at least in the western democracies, has now clearly tended to move towards a rights-based political philosophy.[5] Utilitarianism is seen to imply that individuals are of no value in themselves. Today, the idea that the state has a right to demand individual obedience to its laws without some prior establishment of basic human rights is widely regarded as irrational, and unjust.

It is interesting to note that utilitarians have been attacked from both ends of the spectrum: from the Left for being insufficiently egalitarian, and from the Right for being too much so. In Samuel Brittan's view, 'the principle of utility does not have much to contribute to the distributional question, one way or the other' but he argues that in spite of its faults it has the merit of 'asserting that actions should be guided by their effects on the welfare of individual persons' (Brittan, 1983: 31). This seems difficult to reconcile with the aggregative precept of Bentham's utilitarianism.

The appeal of utilitarianism to many economists has been that it fits well into what Sen has described as the 'engineering' approach; in this, the ends of human life are taken as given and the object of economic analysis is to find the optimum means of achieving them. Sen argues that 'modern economics has been substantially impoverished by the distance that has grown between economics and ethics' (Sen, 1987: 7). This can be seen in the development of welfare economics. When all ethical considerations have been jettisoned, what remains is the idea of Pareto optimality. A social state is described as Pareto-optimal if no-one's utility can be raised without reducing the utility of someone else. It does not tell us very much; a society may be Pareto-optimal with one half of the population starving while the other half is very rich. Sen sees this as 'a legacy left by the earlier utilitarian tradition' (Sen, 1987: 33)[6]

Utilitarianism is seen as reaching its greatest triumph in economics in cost/benefit analysis in which all values are reduced to a common measure: 'reaching, it is felt, particularly repellent extremes when the value of a human life is calculated as something to be set against the extra goods achieved by a motorway. . . .'[7] However Bentham argued that such examples prove, not that the principle is wrong, but that it is misapplied.

Karl Popper has suggested that the utilitarian formula 'maximum happiness' should be replaced by the formula 'minimise suffering', since reducing suffering is a much more urgent task than maximizing happiness. From the moral point of view pain cannot be outweighed by pleasure, and especially one man's pain by another man's pleasure. Popper points out the analogy between this view of ethics and his scientific methodology claiming that it is better in ethics to formulate demands negatively, just as he has advocated the elimination of false theories in scientific method (Popper, 1966, vol. 1: 284–5).

AUSTRIANS ON UTILITARIANISM

Bentham had viewed man as a pleasure seeker. Neoclassical economists see him as a maximizer of utility with a consistent and stable set of preferences: 'Humans are deprived of the capacity for spontaneous action . . . reacting creatures who are incapable of having independent aims unable deliberately to scrutinise their positions and to alter their expectations and actions accordingly' (Grassl and Smith, 1986: 170).

In the Robbins picture of economic reality, man is confronted by the 'economic problem': the never-ending conflict between ends and scarce means. This Robbinsian economic problem has calculable solutions. 'To the Austrians . . . what we have here is not a problem with a calculable solution, but the very stuff of meaningful existence' (Grassl and Smith, 1986: 171). The significance of this assertion is to focus attention on the way Austrians see the market, not as a mechanism driven automatically, but as a spontaneous system in which people do not simply react to 'data' (costs, prices, etc.) but act purposefully and learn by experience. According to Grassl, 'The Austrian approach rests upon an image of man in complete opposition to the anthropology of the utilitarians' (Grassl and Smith, 1986: 147). Yet Rothbard tells us that Mises, for example 'was indeed' a utilitarian in ethics (Dolan, 1976: 104). Mises' view is that human action is always rational. No-one is qualified to declare the ultimate ends of action of another person as being irrational. This is because no-one can put himself in someone else's shoes completely. No-one can say what would make someone else happier. No doubt this assertion could be accepted by most people. Can one judge another person's *means* for the attainment of his ends as rational or irrational? Mises' reply seems ambiguous. He grants that the critic may well approve or disapprove of the method (means) used by someone to attain a given end – whether it is 'best suited' for the attainment of that end. If, however, the means employed turn out to be a failure, the critic cannot pass judgement on the rationality of the action 'so long as they did their best' (Mises, 1966: 20). The praxeological method does not judge the ultimate ends of human action. Economics, which Mises sees as part of a general theory of human action, takes the ultimate aims of acting man as 'given'. Thus, in economics ethical considerations are to be entirely ignored. If utilitarianism says that utility should be (or is) the ultimate aim of human beings, this must be accepted. The science of human action 'is indifferent to the conflicts of all schools of dogmatism and ethical doctrine' (Mises, 1966: 22). Thus Mises writes approvingly of Bentham: 'he does not care about preconceived ideas concerning God's or nature's plans and intentions forever hidden to mortal men; he is intent upon discovering what best serves the promotion of human welfare and happiness' (Mises, 1966: 175). Mises firmly rejects the widespread idea that utilitarianism appeals only to man's baser instincts in some satirical comments on Romanticism in literature. Writers such as William Morris, Shaw, and Wells produced travesties of the utilitarian idea, and very few of those who read Dickens had the faintest idea what utilitarianism was really about. Dickens, for instance, apparently believed that the utilitarians took no account of the distribution of wealth, whereas Bentham had emphasized that an even distribution of wealth brings more happiness than when there is a great gap between rich and poor. Dickens propogated the idea of the capitalist, Gradgrind, who, because of his fanatical adherence to calculating self-interest, is a typical utilitarian. But, according to Mises, being utilitarian in no way rules out altruism (Mises, 1981: 420).

Hayek's attitude to utilitarianism is based on his explanation of the emergence of the spontaneous order[8] of the market that utilizes the fragmented knowledge dispersed among millions of people, governed by rules that most people follow but few if anyone can state in words. These rules have emerged by adaptation to the environment through a version of natural selection. The Darwinian nature of the way these rules emerge means that some combinations of them produce superior kinds of order that enable certain groups to expand at the expense of others. Thus Hayek's social theory regards tradition – 'the wisdom of our ancestors' – as something to be greatly prized. Successful groups (societies) have emerged from a long process of trial and error and the types of social orders that survive have been selected in an almost biological process. This view is, of course, directed against constructivism – the idea that since man has himself created the institutions of society he must be able to alter them at will so as to achieve immediate purposes (Hayek, 1967, Chapter 4; 1978, Chapter 1). This constructive rationalism was challenged by David Hume and Bernard Mandeville and was developed into a systematic social theory by Adam Smith and Adam Ferguson, the late-eighteenth-century Scottish moral philosophers; Edmund Burke drew out the implications of theory for political policy. These evolutionary approaches, which recognized that many social phenomena were not the result of deliberate human creation, are seen by Hayek as receiving a setback in the form of Benthamite utilitarianism. Thus utilitarianism is a particular form of constructivism. The strict, act-utilitarianism of Bentham is, in Hayek's view 'incapable of accounting for the existence of rules and therefore for the phenomena which we normally describe as morals and law' (Hayek, 1982 vol. 2: 19). He also rejects rule-utilitarianism on the grounds that it fails to account for the fact that rules are made necessary because of our ignorance. 'Man has developed rules of conduct not because he *knows* but because he does not know what all the consequences of a particular action will be' (ibid: 20–1). The notion that rules should be judged only by assessing in some way their usefulness in particular applications is seen as being very destructive of respect for the rules of law and morals. On the question of how, then, should a rule be judged he may be accused of a certain lack of clarity and ambiguity. He argues that although the justification of any particular rule must be its usefulness – this to be judged not by rational argument but by the fact that it has in practice proved itself 'more convenient' than any other – the idea that each and every matter should be so decided by each person involved would imply a society of omniscient individuals in which no rules would be necessary; this is an absurdity (Hayek, 1960: 159). Hayek's view of the function of traditional rules has been seen as not fully consistent with that uncompromising belief in the overriding value of freedom that strongly pervades most of his work (however, we are here concerned with Hayek's attitude to utilitarianism and these wider issues are further discussed in Chapter 5). The core of Hayek's opposition to utilitarianism is that it interprets the rules produced through evolution as being 'designed' as if by a single person with deliberate choice for known ends. However, there are some senses in which he may be regarded as finding a utilitarian approach acceptable and in fact inherent in his fundamental approach to the evolution of the 'rules of just conduct'.[9]

Hayek rejects the idea of a natural-rights basis for policy. None of the rights – to work, to education, and so forth – that we often hear about 'can or ever have been absolute rights that may not be limited by general rules of law' (Hayek, 1982, vol. 3: 110). Furthermore, no list of rights can ever include all the possible rights, especially those unforeseeable ways in which individual freedom may be used. Hayek's attitude to rights is derived from his view of natural law and the unintended consequences of human action. Society does not simply and deliberately create law; the rules of just conduct are not natural in the sense that they in some mysterious way antedate the organization of man in societies. The mistake is, then, to assume that the rules must have been deliberately created; the rules of just conduct have not been handed down by God or Nature, nor have they been deliberately created by man; there is a third and frequently overlooked possibility – the rules and institutions have emerged spontaneously by a process akin to natural selection. However, this does not mean that all such phenomena must be approved of: 'the obligation ... to follow certain rules derives from the benefits we owe to the order in which we live' (Hayek, 1982, vol. 2: 27). The test of time will decide on the desirability (utility) of any particular rule. It is in this sense that Hayek is utilitarian, but this attitude is quite consistent with his opposition to constructivist ideas of the deliberate modelling of laws and institutions to serve particular ends. This brand of utilitarianism is derived from David Hume whom Hayek sees as:

> not concerned with any recognisable utility of the particular action, but only with the utility of a universal application of certain abstract rules including those particular instances in which the immediate known results of obeying the rules are not desirable.
>
> (Hayek, 1967: 88)

The Cartesian tradition and Bentham turned this version of utilitarianism into something quite different: a demand that each and every action should be judged on its foreseeable results. Hayek's approval of Hume's utilitarianism rests on the latter's firm belief in the limitations of human reason.

SELF-INTEREST

The doctrine that the pursuit of self-interest will, through the operation of the 'invisible hand' work to produce the greatest amount of welfare can be justified on utilitarian grounds; it is a consequentialist social theory. Adam Smith, with his famous much-quoted passage concerning the butcher, the brewer, and the baker states his view of the mainsprings of human interdependence: that if one wants the co-operation and help of others 'it is vain to expect it from their benevolence only'. And 'we address ourselves, not to their humanity, but to their self-love' for most of our wants. In this way private interests are harmonized with social interests. This concept, that the spontaneous collaboration of free men creates things that are greater than their individual minds can ever comprehend, was not entirely originated by Smith's *Wealth of Nations*. Joseph Tucker, in 1756, wrote that, 'the universal mover in human nature, self-love, may receive such a direction in this case (as in all others) as to promote the public interest by those efforts it shall make towards pursuing its own' (Hayek, 1980: 7).

The assumption that self-interest is the strongest motive for human action was, of course, not at all a novel idea; it is found in earlier political philosophies such as those of Machiavelli and Hobbes. It was in the eighteenth and nineteenth centuries however, that self-interest became fully elaborated into a utilitarian argument for *laissez-fair* and for the freedom of the individual, as the best arrangement for society as a whole. The eighteenth century witnessed the first application of the methods of natural science to human affairs. Helvetius, in 1758, compared the role of the principle of self-interest in the social world to the role of the law of gravitation in the physical world. The full flowering of the alleged beneficence of self-interest is well exemplified in the writings of Frederic Bastiat especially in *Economic Harmonies*, first published in 1850 but not taken very seriously in histories of economic thought. One historian[10] has described his work as an example of that 'most dogmatic and arid formalism' which found expression more in France than in England, but Schumpeter, although he saw no *scientific* merit in the work of Bastiat, nevertheless considered his 'exclusive emphasis on harmony of class interests ... rather less silly than is exclusive emphasis on the antagonism of class interests' (Schumpeter, 1954: 500).[11] Bastiat was much impressed with the existence of the 'harmonious laws' that Newton had discovered and linked this to his belief in God who unarguably had created man such that self-interest is the mainspring of human nature. This being so, the free actions of men must lead, not to class antagonism as the 'socialists'[12] maintained, but to lasting harmony.

Although Adam Smith was pre-eminently the one who integrated the doctrine of self-interest into a general theory of society, it is a naive simplification to present him as dogmatically consistent. Partial understanding of Smith has probably been caused by concentration on the *Wealth of Nations*, though even in this there is less apodictic certainty than is to be found in Bastiat; the economist Jacob Viner pointed out that theories could be found in the *Wealth of Nations* to suit almost any special purpose.

The theory that self-interest is the most certain and useful one for understanding human nature and society has, of course, frequently been opposed on the grounds that it is too cynical and restricted, and Adam Smith has come to be regarded as the chief architect of that view that appears to disregard many of the 'higher' qualities in human motivation. The association of Smith with a fanatical belief in self-interest is a very incomplete account of his work. In the *Wealth of Nations* alone, there is much evidence to refute the idea that he was blinkered in his view of human nature. And in his *Theory of Moral Sentiments* he writes of those principles in human nature which give rise to fellow feeling – 'sympathy' – for others; and later 'to restrain our selfish, and to indulge our benevolent affections, constitutes the perfection of human nature'.[13] One possible way of resolving the apparent contradiction is to consider the way people must, of necessity, act in the market. It is not possible for us to know all the possible consequences of everything we do and adjust our actions accordingly. Individuals and groups of individuals are always constrained by what knowledge they possess. Thus the advocacy of self-interest is not merely derived from a cynical view of human nature but is simply a recognition of the fact that economic agents can, of necessity, have limited knowledge and hence limited objectives; this certainly does not imply that people must always strive to act *selfishly*.

The economist Philip Wicksteed dealt with this matter as follows:

We enter into business relations with others, not because our purposes are selfish, but because those with whom we deal are relatively indifferent to them, but are (like us) keenly interested in purposes of their own, to which we in turn are relatively indifferent.

(Wicksteed, 1933, vol. 1: 179)

Wicksteed argued that the term 'egoism' is misapplied to market transactions; a man engaged in a market exchange is not likely to be thinking of 'others' but neither is he thinking entirely of himself. He is thinking of the matter in hand, as he would, say, in a game of chess. 'The specific characteristic of an economic relation is not its "egoism" but its "non-tuism"'. It has the same characteristics as a man playing chess or football; he would not be dubbed 'selfish' for protecting his king or his own goal. Market exchanges, following self-interest, cannot be moral or immoral in themselves since they are means not ends. The idea that economic (commercial) transactions are tainted because they are mostly driven by self-interest is derived from a faulty conception of their true nature. But, says Wicksteed, the almost religious awe for *laissez-faire* and the market expressed by writers such as Bastiat, in which economic forces are depicted as inevitably leading to beneficial consequences, is equally fallacious. The point is that market forces are means to ends; it is wrong 'to assume that ethically desirable results will necessarily be produced by an ethically indifferent instrument, and it is as foolish to make the economic relation an idol as it is to make it a bogey' (Wicksteed, 1933, vol. 1: 184). This view that self-interest practised as the guiding principle of economic life tends in itself to foster a selfish spirit throughout society is as widespread nowadays as it was in Wicksteed's time.[14] Critics of the free market have alleged that it trivializes human life, generates greed, and fosters the tendency in people's minds to see themselves only as 'consumers', while nobler and finer ends become increasingly cast aside. On the other hand, it might be held that the welfare state in trying to counter market self-interest throws up a paradox; it removes from the individual much of the responsibility for matters that should be of great concern to him – his family's health care, old age, and education – and leaves him with responsibility for choice only in comparative trivialities or luxuries.

Adam Smith's view of human nature was much less narrow and dogmatic than has been propagated by advocates of the self-interest social theory. It is because of the subsequent influence of this distorted view of Smith's writings that Sen argues that economics tended (unfortunately as he sees it) to distance itself from ethics (Sen, 1987: 27). It is a complete misrepresentation of Smith to think that he believed self-love was a wholly adequate basis for society, and he was far from ruling out collective action (in education, for example). It seems doubtful, however, whether Smith would have supported massive redistributive transfers as on the modern scale (Downie, 1976: 104). Transfers to the poor or unfortunate, whilst they should be encouraged – on the altruistic principle that the giver 'derives nothing from it, except the pleasure of seeing it' – should not be enforced; benevolence must be voluntary (Musgrave, 1976: 301). However, Sen claims that 'there is nothing to indicate that Smith's ethical approach to public policy would have precluded intervention in support of the entitlement of the poor' (Sen, 1987: 27).

Finally, the assumption that economic transactions are necessarily and always inevitably 'non-tuistic' has been challenged on the grounds that it distorts reality. Is it really the case that market participants always drive hard bargains? J. R. Lucas questions the idea that in all exchange the participants have no regard whatsoever for each other's interests (Lucas, 1979: 155–6). Perhaps the answer is that whenever the behaviour of either or both of the agents in an economic transaction shows signs of fellow-feeling, or consideration of the other's interests, then, to that extent, it ceases to be a purely 'economic' transaction; another case of the separation of ethics from economics.

Mises' view of the morality of self-interest stems from his concept that the ultimate goal of human action is always the satisfaction of the acting man's desires. Praxeology, the science of human action, is 'much more than merely a theory of the "economic side" of human endeavours' (Mises, 1966: 3). Mises sees the age-old quests of philosophers seeking laws to explain man's destiny and evolution as doomed to failure until the phenomenon of market interdependence was fully grasped. The mistake they had been making was that of misplaced holism; they were setting up quite arbitrary concepts of social wholes like 'nation', 'race', or 'church'. In order to explain the way in which individuals behaved so as to ensure the achievement of the ends of some social whole, various forces were, at different times, called on stage, such as 'nature' or 'the will of God'.[15] Mises dismisses all such speculation as fruitless because it fails to examine the 'molecules' of societies or nations – the acting individuals. These political philosophers imagined that somehow or other society could be reconstructed or reformed as man pleased. But the discovery of the social theory of the market overthrew such ideas:

Bewildered, people had to face a new view of society. They learned

72

with stupefaction that there is another aspect from which human action might be viewed than that of good and bad, of fair and unfair, of just and unjust.

(Mises, 1966: 2)

Thus praxeology is not concerned with the ends of human action. For example, according to Mises, the moralizers who criticize profit-seeking are missing the point. If people 'prefer liquor to Bibles' this is not the fault of the profit-maximizing entrepreneur, as, 'it is not the business of the entrepreneur to make people substitute sound ideologies for unsound' (Mises, 1966: 300). Mises would evidently regard any enquiry into the morality of self-interested market action as irrelevant; according to him there is a widespread social philosophy that holds that a solution to the repulsive morality of capitalist free markets would be in some way to 'ban' selfish motives such as acquisitiveness and profit-seeking. Mises, of course, is firmly opposed to any attempt to coerce people into behaving better – less selfishly – not only because this would be impracticable – in which his is undoubtedly correct – but that it would strike at the very foundations of freedom in general. Any attempt to suppress individuals' right to choose – whether the good or the bad – would be immoral in the sense that it infringes the even greater good of human freedom. Presumably, however, he would have no misgivings should individuals change their moral values for the better, either voluntarily or through persuasion, and such transformations have occurred in the past – as in the early Victorian emergence of increased social approval towards thrift, hard work, and the growth of a socially conscious middle class. Thus Mises' view of the ethical position of self-interest is essentially similar to that of Wicksteed – that self-interest is a means not an end – but again it must be remembered that it is open to the criticism, from the Marxists and socialists in general, that the very nature of the existence of private property and the promotion of profit-seeking as a force for the increase of the common well-being, in themselves induce individuals to act selfishly; in a 'better system' the people would not be driven to be so acquisitive. The big question, however, remains: is it a moral act to coerce people to behave 'better'; is redistribution of income, for instance, a morally good thing when carried out through legally-backed taxation?

Mises' ethical position is founded on his (dogmatic?) belief that:

73

everyone lives and wishes to live primarily for himself ... this fact does not disturb social life but promotes it, for the higher fulfilment of the individual's life is possible only and through society. This is the true meaning of the doctrine that egoism is the basic law of society.

(Mises, 1981: 361)

The ethical distinction between good and evil can only be applied to ends – not to means. There is no contrast between moral duty and selfish interests.

On the question of the morality of advocating self-interest, Hayek's defence has two strands: on the one hand, as in Wicksteed (1933), the confusion of self-interest with selfishness and on the other hand, his view of the essential limitations of human knowledge. In his essay 'Individualism: true and false', he contends that much of the dislike of individualism arises from confusion over what eighteenth-century writers meant by their frequent use of terms like 'self-love' or 'selfish interests'. These terms did not mean a narrow egotism. Hayek's interpretation is that the real significance of such terms lay in their recognition of the plain, undeniable, fact that an individual's knowledge is limited. Whatever the differences which are conceivable in moral attitudes they are unimportant compared with the fact 'that all man's mind can effectively comprehend are the facts of the narrow circle of which he is the centre' (Hayek, 1980: 14). In other words, we might say that with the best of goodwill the efforts of one person are inherently and unavoidably limited by what he can possibly *know*. The important question, therefore, is not whether a man ought to be selfish but whether he should be allowed to act according to his assessment of the immediate consequences of which he can possibly have knowledge, or whether he should be forced to act in different ways in obedience to some individual or body of individuals ('society') who claim to know better what will benefit people as a whole.

One of the main justifications advanced by Adam Smith and his followers for the beneficence of self-interest is the well-known assertion that each person knows his own interest best and thus in aggregation will total welfare be most efficiently increased. Hayek argues that this assumption is 'neither plausible nor necessary for the individualist's conclusions'. The true basis for allowing individuals to follow their own interests is not that they 'know best' but that nobody can know *who* knows best and therefore everyone must be allowed a free rein to see what they can do; but this freedom is to be circumscribed by voluntary adherence to rules which he finds by experience serve him well but which he cannot *know* to be true and may well be inarticulated.

In one passage Hayek is quite surprisingly uncompromising in his belief in the superior beneficence of the influence of the 'invisible hand' in which he contrasts the moral approval accorded to known specific acts that benefit identifiable people with the unimaginative reaction to the benefits that often flow from self-interested profit-seeking. Apart from the fact that the successful entrepreneur may ultimately choose to use his wealth for charitable ends, the aspect that is frequently entirely overlooked and is of greater importance is that: 'He is led by the invisible hand to bring the succour of modern conveniences to the poorest homes he does not even know' (Hayek, 1982, vol. 2: 145). He is led to benefit more people simply by attending to his own self-interest than if he concentrated his efforts on improving the lot of known persons.

Admiration for the effectiveness of self-interest as a means of improving the human lot has not been confined to Smith/Hayekian liberals. Writing about the 1851 Great Exhibition, Wilhelm Lieb-knecht – a loyal disciple of Marx – after criticizing it as 'no more than a piece of free-trade propaganda' conceded that 'egotism has, albeit unintentionally done more for humanity than the most humane and self-sacrificing idealism'.[16] For a highly analytical formal treatment of the concept of self-interest see Oppenheim (1981, Chapter 7).

ALTRUISM, CHRISTIANITY, AND THE MARKET

The meaning of 'altruism' is having regard for others – as opposed to egoism – having regard for oneself.[17] Whatever kind of society one lives in, and with whatever institutions, there are, as David Friedman has crisply pointed out, essentially only three ways that I can get another person to help me achieve my ends: 'love, trade and force'. Presumably friendly co-operation or anything falling short of complete self-interest is, in this categorization, a form of love. There are degrees of altruism: there is the extreme hypothetical state of affairs in which everyone is *totally* unselfish; clearly the dedicated complete altruist would find no-one to practise on! A more realistic possibility is that a person might act so as to forego his maximum utility for the sake of others. Although this might sound like a benevolent and beneficial course of action, by the logic of free market economics, it has adverse consequences. This follows from the argument that the harder a person self-interestedly strives to earn himself a surplus income or wealth, the better placed will he then be to devote his riches to the benefit of, for example, charities or any other individual. Moreover, a really keen altruist would want to work harder at making himself rich so that his charitable work would thereby be further enhanced. Thus, according to this view, an entrepreneur should never sell below the price he could get since this will lead to a less efficient allocation of resources; while benefiting whoever gets the price reduction he is impeding the smooth-working of the mechanism of consumer sovereignty – resource allocation. Also, the recipients of his own generosity may use their accruals in completely self-interested ways. These considerations also apply to any other form of non-self-interested motivation by businessmen. Firms have, at various times, been exhorted by governments as well as by 'statesmen–businessmen' (sometimes turned politicians) to act not so as to maximize their profit, but for such general aims as incomes policies, some vaguely specified public interest, or 'the needs of society' (Brittan, 1973: 203–7). It should be noted, however, that if profit is made without all real costs being taken into account – such as the adverse effects of externalities – this is an entirely different matter (see Chapter 9 this volume).

Although the 'ideal type' of the competitive market is one in which everyone *should* strive at all times to maximize their utility or profit and will, given certain assumptions, lead to an efficient allocation of resources, it is implausible to hold that individuals or firms *always* do behave like this; 'people don't always drive hard bargains' (Lucas, 1979: 155).

If we accept the logic of the most common theory of the market – that self-interested action through the invisible hand works to the greatest benefit of all – how is the morality of this to be reconciled with the teachings of Christianity? There are, of course, many dreadful warnings in the Bible, concerning the sinfulness of greed and selfishness. R. H. Tawney concluded that the quality in modern life that is most opposed to the teachings of Christ is the assumption that the search for material riches is the supreme object of human endeavour: 'it is the negation of any system of thought or morals which can be described as Christian. Compromise is impossible between the Church of Christ and the idolatry of wealth'.[18] Tawney quoted Keynes in support when he wrote that modern capitalism is 'absolutely irreligious ... a mere congeries of possessors and pursuers'. However, it should be noted that Keynes (1973: 381) also gave his blessing to commercial activity which he described as a comparatively innocent practice and less likely to do harm than politicking.[19] The recent and continuing admonitions by churchmen show that they remain suspicious and doubtful of the benefits of the acquisitive drive and in particular the inequalities of income and wealth thrown up by the market are often depicted in highly dramatic terms.[20]

The New Testament, especially, is full of injunctions against the pursuit of wealth and although various writers have valiantly struggled to find support for free market self-interest in the Bible, there is very little to be found that supports the doctrine of the invisible hand. It is not surprising that the Church has hardly ever been on the side of competitive capitalism and internationally has often given moral support to Marxist revolutionary movements. The great increases in real incomes of most people in the west, which have been largely the result of capitalist free enterprise rather than redistribution, seem to count for nothing with the Christian churchmen. A notable exception is Dr Edward Norman, Dean of Peterhouse, Cambridge, who has written of his regret at the anti-free-market bias of the Churches (Norman, 1977). But for the most part the Churches have always chosen to refuse to face up to the full implications of the (to them) unpleasant reality that it is largely free market competitive self-interest that has not only allowed people to indulge their taste for luxuries – television, alcohol, and tobacco – but has also generated the wealth that is the essential prerequisite for the supply of medical care, adequate nutrition, and housing, without which no amount of Christian goodwill would do the slightest bit of good.

Brian Griffiths, on the other hand, has argued that the capitalistic free-market economy is by no means incompatible with Christianity. He sees nothing in Christianity which suggests that the creation of wealth is undesirable; on the contrary it provides an opportunity for people to use the proceeds of their hard work, enterprise, or good luck in the service of others. However, a defence of the compatability of the market economy with Christian theology needs to be careful to avoid the pitfalls of secularism. By this Griffiths means that it is unwise to base a defence of market morality entirely on such 'ideologies' as the invisible hand or the social Darwinism of Herbert Spencer. The problem for the West is that while free market values of efficiency and freedom are being extended, 'we need to re-estabish certain values'. The 'root of the Western crisis is not simply the erosion of economic freedom but the prevailing philosophy of secular humanism' derived from 'a Renaissance and Enlightenment view of man which reduced economic life to something impersonal and amoral' (Griffiths, 1984: 117). He quotes Solzhenitsyn's acerbic view of modern western man as 'worshipping his material needs ... as if human life did not have any higher meaning'. Solzhenitsyn sees the problem as having its source in 'rationalistic humanism ... the proclaimed and practised autonomy of man from any higher force' (op. cit.: 36).

Returning now to the question of altruism in general: whatever induces individuals to want to practise it, for religious or other reasons, there is a strong common-sense appeal in what the philosopher C. D. Broad has called self-referential altruism – concern for others who are close to one such as one's family or workmates. The commandment to 'love they neighbour as thyself' if it means having a universal concern for everyone is wildly unrealistic and impracticable. A realistic view of people's behaviour is that it usually consists of a mixture of egoism and self-referential altruism and little more can sensibly be expected nor indeed would any other pattern be more beneficial to humanity in general. Paradoxically, a devotion to a group wider than one's immediate circle may make it more likely that dislike of some other group will flourish. 'Wider affections than these usually centre upon some special cause – religious, political, revolutionary, nationalist – not upon the welfare of human beings ... in general' (Mackie, 1977: 132–4, 170).

History – and especially twentieth-century history – abounds with awesomely dreadful examples of men who professed a love for the human race (either now, or those yet to come in some Utopian future) and who committed all manner of atrocities against individuals and groups for the sake of the higher and more distant purpose to which they were fanatically attached.

For it is when people step from the selfish pursuit of their own interests to the propagation of perverted ideals that they become really dangerous .... Such a person is very much harder to argue with than the mere self-seeker.

(Hare, 1963: 114)

78

Although it is very likely that people are, for the most part, motivated by self interest or self-referential altruism, and that there is nothing in a free society to forbid altruistic actions – even though, as we have shown, their effects may not, according to the logic of the market be as beneficial as might be wished – people may *desire* to act altruistically towards more distant groups than family and friends. One criticism of the individualistic free market and in favour of some measure of collectivism is that only a central institution such as the state is capable of organizing this kind of more far-ranging altruism (Bosanquet, 1983).

Hayek's view, it is no surprise to discover, is that the market is the best way by which the individual may serve the needs of hundreds of people whom he does not know of and of whose desires he is also ignorant; but this is achieved, not through altruism, but through self-interest.

One important and convincing objection to market morality comes from particular ideals of behaviour. Two parties to a transaction may both follow their respective interests and apparently, therefore, there can be no objection on moral grounds assuming that they should each be free to act in their own interest. The exchange is, as economists say, not a zero-sum game – both parties to a freely arranged mutual bargain must gain, otherwise they would not enter into the contract. However, what some people find offensive about certain kinds of market transactions lies below the surface of such a calculation of mutual welfare; the condemnation of drug-dealing or the selling of violent or pornographic films or armaments, comes from a feeling that such exchanges are *degrading in themselves.* Such conduct offends against some ideal of how human beings *ought* to behave (Hare, 1963: 147-8).

Some critics of market morality regard its need to applaud self-interest as, in itself, a force that distorts human friendship and genuine sociability. The one objective that the market cannot maximize is altruism; the very ethos of the market erodes feelings of goodwill and social obligation, says Professor Hirsch. To what extent market advocates can answer this type of criticism is difficult to say; certainly there can be no possibility of empirical proof either way.

The same applies to Heilbroner's assertion that capitalism 'in general, corrodes moral virtue'.[21] In this case one can surely retort that there is more than one way of corroding moral virtue and capitalism is a non-starter compared to some of the totalitarian regimes, whether of the Right or the Left, when it comes to the encouragement of nepotism, toadyism and bribery, and suchlike corrosions of moral virtue. The Anabaptists in sixteenth-century Munster established their earthly paradise; everyone was expected to love his neighbour under pain of death or exile. 'The Community became reduced to a state where corruption and bestiality reigned supreme and very soon nothing was left except bones and ruins'.[22] Kolakowski has observed that we might not find western capitalism appealing, based as it appears to be, on greed, but this is still better than compulsory love, for that can only end in the Gulag.

The Austrian contribution to the debate about Christianity and altruism is mostly indirect and follows from their general views on the functions of markets and belief in coercion-free action. Mises in a polemic against the Churches, both Catholic and Protestant, accuses them of originally standing in the way of 'this wonderful new world' of economic liberalism. Although he sees Christianity itself as 'the religion that has its seat in the heart of the individual, which controls conscience and comforts the soul', Mises does not think Christianity can be reconciled 'with a free social order based on private ownership' (Mises, 1981: 382–7).

The Christian Church should, logically, be just as much opposed to those socialist societies in which materialism is dominant but 'many became socialists – not of course, atheistical socialists ... but Christian Socialists. And Christian Socialism is none the less Socialism' (ibid: 382). Mises sees no possible 'third way' between free market capitalism and the horrors of central planning. So long as there are effective laws for the protection of private property this is the only safeguard required to ensure that self-interest works for the general good. He regards the altruistic entrepreneur as doing more harm than good. If the prices he is charging are 'too high' and he is urged or ordered to cut them he may cause hardship to a competitor by forcing him out of business. If, on the other hand, he raises his prices, poor people will not be able to buy. The market economy would, if self-interest were to be eliminated or even tampered with, become a chaotic muddle (Mises, 1966: 724–30). But suppose all entrepreneurs acted 'morally' or altruistically. Why would this be wrong? Mises, with faultless logic – given his initial assumption – advises reformers to address themselves not to profit-seekers but to consumers, for it is they who, in free markets, decide what gets produced. It is not the fault of the businessman if people prefer beer to Bibles. Mises is clearly quite unimpressed by the idea referred to on p. 79 that some ways of making a profit simply offend against many people's concept of how, ideally, a human being should, at least try, to behave; at least he does not refer to this question directly.

In Hayek's writings there is little direct reference to altruism and this is not surprising given his interpretation of the self-interest principle. It is not important to Hayek's view of how the market economy has evolved whether the ends of an individual are egoistic or altruistic. Whatever his motivation, whether he strives to serve himself only or whether he takes a kindly interest in the welfare of every person, he knows the basic fact is that it is impossible for him to know anything but a small fraction of the needs of all men; this reality transcends all talk of altruism versus egoism. In his essay, 'The moral element in free enterprise' (Hayek, 1967, Chapter 16) he considers the relation between freedom and morals. He starts from the assertion that morals and moral values will only develop in free societies and that freedom 'if it is to work well' requires strong moral standards – but of a particular kind. Whatever moral standards we have in mind it is obvious that they must not be imposed – 'obedience has moral value only where it is a matter of choice not of coercion'. The results of freedom must depend on the conduct of individuals and there is no guarantee that a free society will necessarily develop values of which we would approve. Hayek apparently believes that a free society in which immorality is general is preferable to a dictatorship in which no-one has the opportunity to choose their own moral standards. This might be seen to be in conflict with his belief in the importance of traditional rules of behaviour. He admits that a free society lacking a moral foundation would be a very unpleasant society in which to live but even so, better than one that is unfree and 'moral'. The particular strong moral convictions that are required for a free society to be healthy are the belief in individual responsibility and the acceptance of the principle that the material rewards of any individual should correspond to the value his services have for others and should not be based on how deserving he is. It is this view of Hayek's that has been most often criticized. Some have argued that such a view deprives the market of moral legitimacy. I think this criticism partly derives from a superficial understanding of his argument. It is no good berating him for what seems to be his heartless attachment to market morality without an accompanying convincing argument as to why some alternative would be morally superior. In fact, Hayek does not wish to deny that 'personal esteem and material success are much too closely bound together' in modern society. He would prefer a society in which less praise were to be given to the acquisition of wealth. But this is not the fault of the free-enterprise system itself – it is no more and no less materialistic than existing collectivist states. There are as it happens two reasons why a free market economy may be less materialistic. One is that the realization of material wellbeing gives individuals more opportunity to be altruistic or to use wealth for nonmaterialistic ends. Second, in a free society, individuals may themselves choose between material and nonmaterial reward. Paradoxically, if a society makes material reward correspond to merit, it will become more, not less materialistic; in such a society other and more important goals than material success would tend to be undervalued. Hayek concludes his essay by stressing that the free-enterprise system 'only deals with means. What we make of our freedom is up to us'. Although individuals should be free to make money if they wish, their moral merit is to be judged only by what they do with their gains. Does this mean that it is quite acceptable for a man to grow rich through lawful though 'degrading' enterprises so long as he ultimately spends his money on endowing new wards in a hospital? There is also the opposing view that the market ethos tends in itself to create an atmosphere in which self-seeking prevails over altruism.

Rothbard with a characteristically ingenious argument manages to show how a market economy, far from fostering materialism, will tend to work in the opposite way. The more affluent an economy becomes the more it satisfies more of people's desires for exchangeable goods; hence 'the marginal utility of *exchangeable* goods tends to decline over time, while the marginal utility of *nonexchangeable* goods increases'. A growing capitalist economy therefore does not foster 'material' values; it does just the opposite (Rothbard, 1977: 224–6).

A widely held view is that the 'market philosophy' that we have inherited from the eighteenth- and nineteenth-century liberals depends on the existence of the assumption of 'economic man' who always acts coldly and rationally, and that it is a faulty interpretation of real human psychology. This is a misconception of the individualism of Adam Smith and his followers; their 'chief concern was not so much with what man might occasionally achieve when he was at his best but that he should have as little opportunity as possible to

82

do harm when he was at his worst' (Hayek, 1980: 11).

The main reason for being in favour of economic freedom is not based on the belief that self-regard is a good thing in itself but that egoism is a fact whether we approve of it or not. This outlook, for many people, undoubtedly lacks the moral attraction of altruism. There is also a strong appeal to practicality in the precept that it is sensible to give at least as much attention to the powerful human instinct of human egoism as it is to exhort people to be less selfish; altruism should certainly be fostered if possible but should not be depended on. The new thinking in the British Labour Party, although it has managed to welcome market forces as not entirely a bad thing, does not yet seem to have fully faced the consequences for socialist theory of the fact that self-interest is such a dominant motive for conduct.

The market should not be idealized – too much must not be expected of it – but the argument that it is preferable to all alternatives though not emotionally appealing, is intellectually convincing. It is, on the whole, probably true that it is the system under which bad men can do the least harm, and the signs are that the current leadership of the Labour Party in Britain is anxious to be known as conceding that market forces are not without merit.

Part III

FREEDOM AND EQUALITY

Chapter Five

FREEDOM

INTRODUCTION

All political movements claim freedom as one of their most cherished values. 'Freedom' has almost become synonymous with 'blessed' and no politician can be imagined going into an election announcing that they want to reduce freedom in general. Even those political sects that stress the value of 'order' claim that it is a necessary condition of freedom. Certainly since the eighteenth century, freedom has been high on the agenda of most rulers and aspiring rulers whether they be conservatives, social democrats, or communists. So freedom must be something that most people value greatly. Even when other values such as 'equality' or 'opportunity' are desired, they are frequently advocated in the name of freedom – they are seen as necessary conditions of freedom.

It is therefore surprising to find so much disagreement about the meaning of something that evidently everyone strives for passionately. Freedom must be the most important ideal in political philosophy judging by the sheer volume of writing on the subject. There is a suspicion that freedom has become a buzz word inserted into any discussion in order to gain points in an argument, rather like the word 'democratic'. Can there be any precise meaning in such a malleable concept? Evidently there must be some point in continuing to discuss it otherwise many eminent political philosophers must be seen as wasting their time.

Freedom is, in many expositions and discussions, linked with equality, for an obvious reason: any achievement of greater equality can be seen as a reduction in freedom, on the one hand, but as a necessary condition for 'real' freedom, on the other hand; it is impossible to discuss one without mentioning the other. However, in this chapter I shall concentrate most attention on the concept of freedom itself and as far as it is possible deal with equality separately. The outstanding feature of all the discussions of freedom is the widespread disagreement over its meaning. The reason that this cannot simply be accepted in a relaxed way as something inevitable arising from the way in which language is used, is that the differing intepretations give rise to strong, and in some cases, dangerous political passions. The different attitudes to freedom cannot simply be passed over as being nothing to fuss over – they have far-reaching implications for the nature of society in general. A divergence of views about freedom is not to be regarded as merely the same sort of thing as a matter of taste. Neither is it in the same category as such things as disagreements in literary criticism over what constitutes 'good' writing.

The extensive nature of what has been written about freedom – from politically slanted dogmatism to the subtleties of Rawls or Raz – tends to foster impatience and a dismissal of it all as perhaps merely scholastic hair-splitting. Even so, the attempt must be made to assess the controversies surrounding freedom. It remains central to practical politics and what kind of society people live in. However much 'freedom' is in practice distorted and perverted, governments of all kinds continue to claim allegiance to the idea. Furthermore, there is a continual argument between the Left and Right of the political spectrum over who has the real interests of freedom at heart. The Left, have, though with some ambiguity, associated liberty with socialism and the present alleged 'hijacking' of the concept by the Thatcherites in Britain is deeply resented as being a blatant attempt to mask their ulterior motives. The notion that capitalist free markets are on the side of real freedom is derided, especially by the prophets of the 'New Look' Labour party, and the advance of the New Right has received much impetus from the perception of socialism as being incompatible with individual freedom.

There have been, historically, so many oracular pronouncements on freedom that it is difficult to know where to start – which to cite in a restricted account to give some examples of the variety of 'definitions'. Here are a few:[1]

A Free-Man, is he that in those things, which by his strength and wit he is able to do, is not hindered to do what he has a will to do.
(Hobbes)

By liberty, then, we can only mean a power of acting or not acting, according to the determinations of the will.

(Locke)

To renounce liberty is to renounce being a man to surrender the rights of humanity and even its duties.

(Rousseau)

(Rousseau thought that people could be forced to be free.)

Freedom is independence of anything other than the moral law alone.

(Kant)

Freedom is necessity transfigured.

(Hegel)

Freedom is control over ourselves and over external nature which is founded on knowledge of natural necessity.

(Engels)

It is clear that, as a description, 'freedom' may have any one of many different meanings and that, taken out of context, it is impossible to know precisely to what it refers. The literature of political philosophy provides extremely varied answers to the question. Searching for precise definitions is regarded as unsatisfactory by some political philosophers. 'What we require are moral principles and arguments to support them' (Raz, 1987: 15).

There is one way in which it is possible to separate in a rough-and-ready fashion into two categories some of the better known modern writers on the subject. These might be described as, on the one hand, those who contend – to different degrees – that the freedom of the individual ranks very high in most possible lists of characteristics that must be present in an ideal society, having generally a higher priority than equality. On the other hand, there are others who would either be willing to sacrifice some degree of individual freedom for varying degrees of 'social justice' and who often argue that equality is itself a necessary condition for the achievement of freedom. The distinction between the two groups is often expressed as a conflict between the ideas of *negative* and *positive* freedom. It should be understood, however, that by no means all the writers who are now to be listed can be placed firmly, without qualification, in one of the two categories; and there are others to be mentioned later, who do not fit at all neatly into one of these two boxes. These two views of freedom, correspond to the division between Left and Right, though this statement also has often been contested as incomplete.

NEGATIVE AND POSITIVE FREEDOM

Among those who regard freedom as, in general, a supreme good in itself it is natural to start with John Stuart Mill, who defended the supremacy of the individual to be free to do what he wishes unless his action causes harm to others. An individual must not be compelled to do something against his will, even if in someone's opinion it would increase his happiness or even because it is wise or right. 'The only part of conduct of anyone, for which he is amenable to society, is that which concerns others. In the part which merely concerns himself, his independence is, of right, absolute' (Mill, 1982: 68-9). Mill's one qualification – about harm to others – has been the subject of much discussion and criticism because of the difficulties in getting clear precisely what actions of the individual become the province of society in general.

Alexis de Tocqueville understood by liberty the security that the individual must have against arbitrary government; no-one must have absolute power and there must be a plurality of centres of power that balance one another. Tocqueville's emphasis on pluralism as a safeguard of freedom finds a ready acceptance in Oakeshott, but he did not take kindly to the later profusion of controversy:

> the door opens upon a night of endless quibble lit only by the stars of sophistry . . . . We are instructed to distinguish between 'positive' and 'negative' freedom . . . between 'social', 'political' . . . 'economic' and 'personal' freedom . . . there is no end to the abuse we have suffered.
>
> (Oakeshott, 1962: 40)

Nevertheless, he goes on to define freedom as the absence of concentrations of power whether it be embodied in a leader, a 'class', church, or trade union. The English tradition ensures such diffusion of power through the rule of law, private property, parliamentary government, *habeas corpus*, and an independent judiciary. 'This is the most general condition of freedom, so general that all other conditions may be said to be comprised within it' (ibid). Oakeshott repeatedly emphasizes the importance of the continuity of the rule of law as central to the preservation of freedom. If the activity of the government consists of:

> continuous or sporadic interruption of our life and arrangements of our society with arbitrary corrective measures we should consider ourselves no longer free ... the society would be without that known and settled protective structure which is so important a condition of freedom.
>
> (Oakeshott, 1962: 43)

On the question of how these institutions arise, which Oakeshott regards as 'the most general condition of freedom', the historical record points fairly clearly in the direction of evolution – not revolution; the latter has so often produced a new set of oppressors. Freedom arises out of 'a spontaneous construction of the political arrangements which permit constitutional government ... free behaviour has arisen directly out of the character of the people concerned' (Minogue, 1963: 180).

The political philosopher most associated with upholding the virtue of negative freedom is Isaiah Berlin who draws a fairly sharp distinction between negative and positive freedom. Political freedom is only absent if coercion or restraint is applied by other human beings. In his essay 'Two concepts of liberty' he states: 'Mere incapacity to attain a goal is not lack of political freedom' (Quinton, 1967: 142). But Berlin does not want to claim that freedom is the only, or even the most important aim: he accepts the need for all manner of curbs on complete freedom, such as compulsory education.

The philosopher Robert Nozick derives his concept of the minimal state from his doctrine of rights following Locke's dictum that natural law requires that 'no one ought to harm another in his life, health, liberty or possessions' (Nozick, 1974: 10). Nothing here of a 'positive' right to, say, food or medical treatment.

Milton Friedman does not spend much time discussing directly what freedom *is* but it is clear that he is on the side of negative freedom: 'freedom has nothing to say about what an individual does with his freedom' but individual freedom should be 'our ultimate goal in judging social arrangements' (Friedman, 1962: 12). Also Friedman's thesis is that, not only is economic freedom an end in itself, but that without it – and especially including the right to property ownership – there can be no political freedom. The historical record, he argues, shows no examples of societies in which political freedom has existed without the presence of a free market or something like it.[2]

J. M. Keynes although, of course, always associated with the policy of macroeconomic management by the state, undoubtedly believed firmly in the value of individual liberty:

> individualism, if it can be purged of its defects and its abuses, is the best safeguard of personal liberty in the sense that, compared with any other system, it greatly widens the field for the existence of personal choice.
>
> (*General Theory*, Keynes, 1973: 380).

Of course, the phrase 'defects and abuses' could be used to justify all manner of interference with the individual by the state.

These 'negative freedom' philosophers and economists are only a few of the large number who might be listed and we have not yet mentioned the Austrians. The many publications of the Institute of Economic Affairs often contain explicit or implicit evidence of attachment to negative liberty.

Critics of the idea of negative freedom as a supreme good range from Marxian radicals to varying shades of social democrats.[3] Pierre-Joseph Proudhon (1809–65) was an early proponent of positive liberty and that rare phenomenon among socialist thinkers – a real live proletarian who was self-taught. In 1840 he published a book entitled, *What is Property?* and gave the famous answer 'property is theft'. He believed passionately that the poor – in his time the majority – were prevented from using their liberty by inequality and exploitation; liberty for him meant the removal of obstacles that prevent individuals from achieving what they are really capable of.

Marx dismissed Proudhon's ideas as not going far enough; they were 'bourgeois socialism'. He held that the workers could not expect much from any conceivable improvement in the (bourgeois) legal system and arrived at his distinction between *formal* and *material* freedom. Formal or legal freedom is not enough; what matters is real or economic freedom. Underlying economic reality – the type of productive system – is more fundamental than political power. Exploitation cannot be eliminated merely by changing the legal system.

R. H. Tawney expressed the positive approach to 'real' liberty as involving 'the power of choice between alternatives, a choice which is real, not merely nominal, between alternatives which exist in fact, not on paper...'.

Professor Charles Taylor's version of positive liberty includes what he calls an 'exercise concept', meaning that freedom consists in exercising control over one's life. Negative freedom he calls an 'opportunity concept' meaning that there be no obstacle in the way of what we do. This is not, as we have seen, the only possible way of designating negative freedom. Furthermore, Taylor adds to his concept of freedom the anti-libertarian contention that the individual is not the final authority on whether his desires reflect his 'true' purposes (Ryan, 1979: 175–93).[4]

The 'New Look' Labour party of the late 1980s, which is really those members of the Labour party leadership who realize the electoral disadvantage of some of the traditional baggage of Marxian derivation, have, in the question of liberty been anxious to modify and present a different face to the idea of the traditional socialist's derision towards negative liberty. In his Fabian Autumn Lecture, November, 1985, Neil Kinnock stated the most important value that the Labour party stands for as 'not ultimately a question of economic organisation or historical inevitability, but of *moral* choice...'. All the structures of the welfare state have the 'primary purpose' of enhancing individual liberty and giving people greater control over their own destiny.

Similarly, Roy Hattersley (1987) in his significantly entitled book, *Choose Freedom*, speaks of socialism's purpose as being to 'provide – for the largest possible number of people – the ability to exercise effective liberty'. And, following Tony Crosland, he accepts as 'self-evident truth that socialism is about the pursuit of equality' (pp. xvi, xix). Clearly democratic socialists are very anxious to refute the idea that socialism inevitably leads to totalitarianism as argued in Hayek's (1944) *Road to Serfdom* or in Solzhenitzyn's jibe that 'democratic socialism' is in the same category as 'fried snowballs'. Although the democratic socialists of most of Western Europe have managed to shed images of bureaucratic centralism, this is less so in the case of the British Labour party. The modified socialism that the leadership evidently believes in and that the cynical would say they have been forced to believe in by the electors, includes much greater awareness of the unpopularity of the state and state-fostered institutions and greater attention to liberty. A concise and perceptive reconciliation of the aims of positive liberty with the need for safeguarding the (negative) freedom of the individual is given by Professor Bernard Crick. He argues that liberty should not be abandoned as a bourgeois concept: 'But it need not remain in the narrow nineteenth century tradition of "freedom from", simply of not being interfered with by the state or powerful neighbours' (Crick, 1987). However, Crick regards talk of socialist liberty as being completely different from bourgeois liberty as 'melodramatic nonsense'. The kind of liberty he advocates would involve *helping* people to count equally as citizens and, 'above all' they would be 'expected to act as citizens'.

> Liberty in this positive sense of public action does not deny liberty in the more liberal, negative sense of being left alone and in peace: it subsumes, complements and extends it.

(Crick, 1987: 84-8)

A refreshingly simple view of what freedom is and which seems to support the possibility that freedom may, for any particular individual, given the situation in which he finds himself, appear as that particular liberty or right that appears at the top of his priorities and the key to all the others, comes from a dissident group in turbulent Moscow: 'Freedom is the right to be against – we have been deprived of this right since 1917' (May, 1988).

AUSTRIAN CONCEPTIONS OF FREEDOM

Mises starts from the Hobbesian view of 'natural man': 'if there be no Power erected, or not great enough for our security; every man will and may lawfully rely on his own strength and art, for caution against all other men' (*Leviathan*). Mises also rejects the myth of original natural freedom that man is supposed by some to have enjoyed in an age before the establishment of social relations. 'Primitive man was certainly not born free' (Mises, 1966: 279). Only in a social system can the term *freedom* have any meaning. Within such a system a man is free in so far as he is permitted to choose ends and the means of achieving them. In order to prevent the tyranny of the strong over the weak, Mises accepts that there must be 'an apparatus commonly called government'. The function of government should be confined to the restraint of conduct which is disruptive of social co-operation and civilization. Thus he defines freedom as that state of affairs in which the individual is free in the sense of being free to choose between various actions within a market economy. The government is to be confined to the protection of people against the violence or aggression of other individuals. 'There is no kind of freedom and liberty other than the kind which the market economy brings about'(Mises, 1966: 283). Mises gladly accepts the description 'bourgeois' and applauds the negative character of the rights guaranteeing liberty in a market economy; this is true freedom and the only kind worth having. Government always means coercion and is necessarily the opposite of liberty; its role is to preserve economic freedom. Without economic freedom all political liberties and rights are vacuous. For example, a law guaranteeing freedom of the press is meaningless in practice if the government controls all the paper-making and printing plants – and so on for all other rights. Mises is no anarchist, however, as he has no objection to conscription for military service and the levying of taxes to pay for defence. But this is only necessary in a world where free nations are continually threatened by totalitarian autocracies. When socialists have been in favour of abolishing 'spurious' economic freedom and expanding freedom outside the economic sphere they argue fallaciously. The idea that there is a distinction between the 'economic' and the 'non-economic' spheres is false. 'Economics, as a branch of the more general theory of human action, deals with all human action, i.e. with man's purposive aiming at the attainment of ends chosen, *whatever these ends may be*' (Mises, 1966: 285). Evidently altruism is merely part of economic behaviour just as much as self-seeking. Only capitalism can guarantee true freedom and it arose in the process of social development. Before capitalism a man was subject to a 'gracious lord' whose favour he had to acquire. In a capitalist society there is no such relation. The 'cash nexus', which has been depicted romantically as a retrograde development, an abandonment of chivalry and *noblesse oblige*, is welcomed by Mises as a blessed release from bondage. In capitalism 'freedom descends from the sphere of dreams to reality' (Mises, 1981: 171).

Mises' admiration for *laissez-faire* capitalism appears to leave no provision for state welfare for the poor or disabled, but he does have an answer: he looks to charitable work and personal insurance provision. He quite rightly points out, the often overlooked but obvious essential condition for *any* help to be given to the less fortunate, which is the existence of the resources necessary for the task. There has been much misguided moralizing over the lot of the poor and needy before the invention in the twentieth century of the welfare state. Much social history implicitly condemns as heartless and selfish the treatment of the sick and needy. But the point is that even if governments had been endowed with the kindness of a Mother Theresa, economic resources and technology were not up to the task. It is futile, for example, to condemn as incompetence or neglect the lack of clean water in the factory towns of the early-nineteenth century; not until the invention and manufacture of machinery for producing iron pipes cheaply did it become feasible to lay on fresh water supplies to the growing population; such constraints applied equally to kind men and cruel. Furthermore, the question of what kind of social system will best foster the required invention and increased output of goods becomes very important. The answer given by Mises is that capitalism works in two ways to relieve hardship: first through its undoubted capacity to generate wealth[5] it raises all living standards – except in the unlikely event that *all* the increased output goes to a minority of the very rich; second, the increase in affluence makes possible the greater effectiveness of altruism through which hardship may be relieved.[6]

Mises concedes that dependence on charity is shameful and humiliating 'an unbearable condition for a self-respecting man' – a system that 'corrupts both givers and receivers'. From this he draws two conclusions: first, he seems to blame the existence of the need for private charity on government intervention, which frustrates the common man's attempts to provide for his own 'less propitious days' and second, he points to the inconsistency of those who criticize the way in which charity makes the giver self-righteous and the receiver submissive and cringing. These same critics blame capitalism for its callousness, but the personal element that they find distasteful about charity does not exist in market transactions. As to the state's social-security system, he sees the need for it to a limited extent. 'No civilized community has callously allowed the incapacitated to perish.' But 'alms-giving' by the state as a right is not free of the degrading features of charity. 'The discretion of bureaucrats is substituted for the discretion of people whom an inner voice drives to acts of charity' (Mises, 1966: 840). To describe all bureaucratic action in the social security system as discretionary is, of course, a great exaggeration, since most civil servants work to fairly tight rules in dispensing benefits but recipients, for whatever reasons, undoubtedly might well feel degraded.

Hayek on freedom

Freedom is the predominant value in Hayek's social and economic philosophy and it has been subjected to extensive study in many books and essays. The majority of these tend to eulogize Hayek but he has come under some quite fierce attacks from those who see him as a pedlar of old-fashioned ideas that should have been put to rest years ago, and that have been identified as one of the sources of the intellectual justification of the hated Thatcherism;[7] and even among the favourable comments of his followers there appear some reservations about the consistency of some aspects of his work. When a corpus of ideas such as Hayek's is subject to such extensive scholarly scrutiny, it is a sign that we must be dealing with an exceptional talent that places him in the category of Adam Smith, John Stuart Mill, or even Karl Marx.[8] Hayek himself has been a prolific scholar; summing up in a brief space, as I am about to do, his version of freedom, is bound to leave out much of importance. More wide-ranging accounts are given in Gray (1986, see 1984 edn), Barry (1979), and Butler (1983).

Although much of Hayek's work is not specifically concerned with liberty as such (as in his economics, for example) one cannot escape the fact of his concern with liberty; it is a theme that is nearly always present. He makes clear in several works that he holds liberty to be a supreme value as in the quotation from de Tocqueville at the beginning of *The Road to Serfdom*: 'I should have loved freedom, I believe, at all times, but in the time in which we live I am ready to worship it' (Hayek, 1944).

Hayek is quite firmly a proponent of negative freedom, following his mentor Mises, but negative of a particular kind, inseparable from his belief in the rule of law. What is original in Hayek's treatment of liberty is his masterly synthesis, his weaving together of strands from writers who valued liberty: Kant, Locke, Smith, Acton, Burke, Mill, Dicey, and others, most of whom were English or Scottish. Hayek, the Austrian of aristocratic birth, has perceptively recognized the uniqueness of the English concept of freedom under the rule of law. The originality of Hayek also lies in the way in which he has made us aware of the way in which, in the twentieth century, the traditional concept of freedom has been corrupted by the demands of democracy for collective action:

The decline of liberal doctrine, beginning in the 1870s, is closely connected with a re-interpretation of freedom as command over, and usually the provision by the state of, the means of achieving a great variety of particular ends.

(Hayek, 1978: 134)

Hayek's concept of freedom is, he accepts, 'merely negative' and 'rightly so'. It is, in this respect, like peace and justice, the absence of an evil, 'a condition opening opportunities but not assuring particular benefits' (ibid).

The opening lines of *The Constitution of Liberty* are to the effect that liberty means that condition in which 'coercion of some by others is reduced as much as possible in society' or 'independence of the arbitrary will of another' (Hayek, 1960). Freedom assures the individal some private sphere with which others cannot interfere. The identification of freedom with power leads to their being 'no limit to the sophisms by which the attractions of the word "liberty" can be used to support measures which destroy individual liberty' (Hayek, 1960: 16).[9] This identification of liberty as power leads to demands for the redistribution of wealth.[10] Hayek deals with this by simply defining freedom 'from' and freedom 'to' as entirely separate questions; for example, a slave could be kept in the lap of luxury yet not be free in a negative sense. Also we may be 'free yet miserable'. Freedom may mean 'freedom to starve, to make costly mistakes, or to run mortal risks' (Hayek, 1960: 18). As Dostoyevsky puts it: 'What a man needs is simply and solely *independent* volition, whatever that independence may cost and wherever it may lead'.

The benefits of freedom are not confined to the free individuals in society even though the benefits of freedom increase as it is extended to more and more people. This is because previously unknowable patterns and arrangements will flow from the exercise of opportunities by the free individuals. This follows from Hayek's theory of knowledge and the results of undesigned and unforeseen developments whether they are in intellectual or everyday affairs: 'the condition of freedom, namely a state in which each can use his knowledge for his own purposes' (Hayek, 1982, vol. 1: 55–6).

In order 'that men can use their own knowledge in pursuit of their own ends without colliding with each other' it is essential that the institution of private property exists and is protected (by the state). Property 'includes not only material things, but (as John Locke defined it) the "life, liberty and estates" of every individual' (Hayek,

1982, vol. 1: 107). Hayek quotes Lord Acton: 'A people averse to the institution of private property is without the first elements of freedom' and the poet Robert Frost, 'good fences make good neighbours'.[11]

Hayek repeatedly stresses that freedom is not a state of nature (cf. Mises), but that it did not arise from deliberate design. The idea of individual liberty in its modern sense began in the eighteenth century in both England and France. In Hayek's view, the French got it wrong and the English got it right. Nevertheless, the French tradition with its scientistic approach has been gaining in influence in the twentieth century; the less articulate English tradition rooted in the spontaneous development of law and institutions has been on the decline. The intellectual aspect of the 'British tradition' was led by the moral philosophers Hume, Smith, and Ferguson and followed up by their English contemporaries Tucker, Burke, and Paley, drawing on the tradition of the common law; opposed to this British tradition were the Cartesian rationalists of the French Enlightenment. The division is not clearly along national boundaries, Alexis de Tocqueville being nearer to the British than to the French tradition (Hayek, 1960: 54–62).

Hayek's definition of liberty depends very much on what he means by 'coercion' – by whom and for what purposes. It is this aspect of his definition of liberty that is the most vulnerable to criticism. By coercion he means a condition in which an individual is forced by some other person or group of persons to serve ends not according to his own plans. Hayek recognizes that 'coercion is nearly as troublesome a concept as liberty itself'. Although he thinks of coercion as evil it 'cannot be altogether avoided because the only way to prevent it is by the threat of coercion' (Hayek, 1960: 21). In free societies the problem is solved by making the wielder of the power to stop coercion a monopoly – the state. Coercion does not include all possible influences that people can bring to bear on each other; there must be a threat of inflicting harm. The interpretation of Hayek on this point leads to some surprising conclusions. Thus, supposing a noisy factory is built next door to your residence, the fact that this drives you away from your home cannot be said to coerce you. This follows from the requirement that 'coercion implies both the threat of inflicting harm and the intention thereby to bring about certain conduct' (Hayek, 1960: 34). In the case of the noisy factory, intention may well be absent. Nor can it be called coercion if a monopolist refuses to supply me with some goods or services except at a very high price that I am unable to afford, so long as I can do without them. But Hayek qualifies this by adding the proviso: 'so long as the services of a particular person are not crucial to my existence or the preservation of what I most value' (Hayek, 1960: 136). What if, in the case of the noisy neighbour, peace and quiet is 'what I most value?' The power exercised by some employers over their workers is an outstanding example in which critics of Hayek's position have argued strongly that the threat of dismissal and unemployment is just as much coercion as anything done by an overbearing state. Hayek's answer to this is to concede that in periods of acute unemployment the threat of dismissal may well lead to a manager exercising 'an entirely arbitrary and capricious tyranny over a man to whom he has taken a dislike' (Hayek, 1960: 137), but he does not regard this as very likely in a prosperous competitive society. What is to be much more feared is the situation of a fully socialist state in which the government is the only employer and he quotes Trotsky: 'In a country where the sole employer is the state, opposition means death by slow starvation'. Even if one is compelled by the threat of starvation to accept a distasteful job at a very low wage, this is not coercion. This is to be placed in the same category as any natural calamity – a fire or flood. This controversial view follows from Hayek's specification of coercion as including an intention to force an individual to do or not do certain things. The unemployed who must take ill-paid back-breaking work or starve are not regarded as suffering coercion. If liberty is defined so as to include all such possible types of harm that one person can inflict upon another, there is no possibility of achieving it. Hayek seems to be saying that, of course, there are all manner of ways in which opportunities for coercion may arise in the course of human relationships but that in most of these cases there is nothing to be done about it, since any attempt by the state to 'regulate these intimate associations' would produce even greater coercion. The conclusion is that although human relationships are full of possibilities for coercion, as, for example, on board a ship or in personal domestic service, so long as such associations have been entered into voluntarily they are not the concern of the government. There is a certain elusiveness about Hayek's definition of coercion; he seems not so much to be concerned to establish a tight definition but rather to remind us that human life is full of opportunities for coercion, that some forms are worse than others, and that coercion by the state is the worst form and the only one to really worry about. There are many degrees of coercion and whilst we cannot prevent all the harm done by one person to another 'this does not mean that we ought not to try to prevent all the more severe forms of coercion, or that we ought not to define liberty as the absence of such coercion' (Hayek, 1960: 139). Thus, it looks as though the chief divide between the negative and positive liberty proponents hinges on the question of what categories of coercion a government should intervene to prevent.

The main function of the state in Hayek's view is to prevent coercion but only within limits. In order to prevent coercion, the state must itself, through the use of the law, use coercion. But the coercive activities of government are not the only things it should be expected to do; and he supports (contrary to some accounts) the view that the government should care for the disabled or infirm and the provision of roads. Taxation, a form of coercion, is thus acceptable for the finance of such services.[12] As well as violence against property or the person, fraud and deception are to be classed as coercion.

Liberty and law

A theme that pervades all Hayek's idea of liberty is that it is under the law and is controlled by the law.[13] He quotes Locke: '... when there is no law there is no liberty. For liberty is to be free from restraint and violence from others: and is not ... a liberty for every man to do as he lists' (Hayek, 1960: 162). The purpose of law is the protection of freedom. Law is not superior to freedom, and it is important to notice Hayek's conception of the rule of law. It is not synonymous with legislation; it gradually evolves by custom. For Hayek, the rule of law is a spontaneous creation that has evolved as an unintended consequence of human action; 'law' is older than 'law-making'. Long before the modern idea took root that law was something to be altered or invented, there were rules of conduct that made possible peaceful existence. Such rules have *evolved* and through a process similar to Darwinian natural selection the best fitted, the most workable and generally acceptable have survived. The modern idea that all law is the invention of the legislator is seen as 'an erroneous product of constructivist rationalism' (Hayek, 1982, vol. 1: 81). The same applies to the view that all social institutions are, and ought to be, the product of deliberate design. In his essay

'The results of human action but not of human design' (Hayek, 1967, Chapter 6) Hayek writes of the law as being older than the legislator and that the whole authority of the state derives from pre-existing conceptions of justice. For the maintenance of freedom all law must be general and applying to all; this ensures the absence of privilege. This concept of equality before the law is the only kind of equality compatible with liberty; equality and freedom are thus seen as competitive, not complementary as held by the positive-liberty school of thought. The rule of law has been weakened in the twentieth century by the advance of democracy and its accompanying demand for equality. However, although democracy can be a threat to freedom, there are three chief arguments by which democracy can be justified. First, democracy is a better way of settling disagreements than fighting and is 'the only method of peaceful change that man has discovered'. Hayek quotes Mises in support of this and also Popper: 'I personally call the type of government which can be removed without violence "democracy" and the other "tyranny"' (Hayek, 1960: 444). The second argument for democracy is as an important safeguard of individual liberty; democracy is not itself liberty but it is more likely than other forms of government to produce liberty. But democracy is not certain to produce liberty; this will only be so if liberty happens to be the aim of the majority. Majorities could easily vote to extinguish the liberty of minorities. The most powerful argument for democracy is that it is the only effective way of educating the majority; it is, 'above all a process of forming opinion'. Admittedly democracy does not put power in the hands of the wisest and best informed and it is possible that a government by an elite could turn out to be more generally beneficial but even so, democracy wins Hayek's approval because in the long run, like liberty, its benefits will show its superiority.

It might seem that the foregoing defence of democracy is labouring the obvious and that people of many shades of political opinion would find nothing so exceptionally arguable or unique about Hayek's view of democracy. The reason for setting out these views is that certain critics of Hayek seem to be mistaken in their suggestion that he is antidemocratic. This criticism probably originates in reaction to his warning that in some cases democracy may be no friend of liberty. 'Those who profess that democracy is all-competent and support all that the majority wants at any given moment are working for its fall'. (Hayek, 1960). The majority should be persuaded that it is 'not the fountainhead of justice' which 'does not necessarily manifest itself in the popular view on every particular issue'. This is a matter of education: unless a majority of people understand the tradition of the rule of law, neither freedom nor democracy can be preserved (Hayek, 1960: 103–17). In Part II of *The Constitution of Liberty*, Hayek argues for limits on the power of governments – even democratically elected ones. It is this that has given rise to the mistaken assertion that Hayek professes an 'undisguised contempt for democracy' (Hattersley, 1987: 71). Hayek's opposition is to the type of democracy, as he puts it in 'Whither democracy' (Hayek, 1978, Chapter 10) in which 'agreement by the majority on sharing the booty gained by overwhelming a minority of fellow citizens or deciding how much is to be taken from them' is disguised as democracy. This kind of democracy has 'no moral justification'. The crucial difference between Hayek and Hattersley is that the latter believes that redistribution of income according to the wishes of the majority has a moral justification, whereas Hayek sees 'social justice' as involving discriminatory measures of coercion, as 'a moral pretence that can hardly be taken seriously'. Hayek fears that the *unlimited* power conferred on a government elected by a majority is destructive of real democracy and ends in 'totalitarian democracy'.

Is the rule of law a sufficient condition for freedom?

Hayek's apparent reliance on the rule of law (as he defines it) has been criticized as leaving unresolved the conflict between law and individual freedom. There is also some difficulty in specifying what precisely constitute 'rules of just conduct' and who decides which of proposed laws are acceptable as general rules. There is a conflict, in Hayek's social theory, between his devotion to individual freedom on the one hand, and on the other hand, his constant stress on the requirement that individuals must be willing to accept traditional rules that they themselves have had no direct part in formulating. Hayek has been criticized both by collectivists who find his reliance on the free market 'extremist' and by libertarians of various shades – among them his followers in a general sense – who have doubts over how firmly grounded are his concepts of individual freedom.[14]

Hayek's work shows an attachment to what might properly be regarded as two different political philosophies: classical liberalism and a conservative position that stresses the virtue of tradition and the desirability of existing institutions. In the Epilogue to the third volume of his trilogy, *Law, Legislation and Liberty* (Hayek, 1982), he emphasizes his belief that rules and institutions have evolved and that the test of the rightness of such rules is the fact that they have stood the test of a 'Darwinian' process of selection; these rules embody more inherited knowledge and experience than could be known to any single individual. Thus, although Hayek is frequently regarded as a libertarian in that he welcomes evolutionary change deriving from the free spontaneous interactions of individuals, he combines this with what appears to be an insistence on traditional values, very similar to that of Edmund Burke. Hayek's libertarianism is not of the sort that welcomes all degrees of 'permissiveness'. He castigates Freud, and his followers, and deplores all the consequences that have come from his teaching as being among 'the worst things that have come out of Vienna' (Hayek, 1982, vol. 3: 174). He views with distaste and foreboding the 'sixties' counterculture that, through permissive education, 'fails to pass on the burden of culture and trusts to the *natural instincts which are the instincts of the savage*' (Hayek, 1982: 174). Hayek is no moral relativist; he envisages nothing but disaster being the result of abdicating from the task of passing on to the young firm concepts of right and wrong. His libertarianism is not of the anarcho-capitalist, thorough-going sort – the David Friedman and Murray Rothbard variety. To them, Hayek's traditionalism is inconsistent with freedom. This is because of the problem of reconciling his stipulation that people just adopt rules that they have not chosen with his presumption that they should be free to initiate action; how can there be freedom if Hayek's contention is true that human behaviour is mostly outside human control. Human action appears to spring from an evolutionary force. Also, if important ideas simply evolve and are not initiated by individuals, how do we explain the original elements in Hayek's own social theory? To this extent his own theorizing would deny his own theory about human action (Machan, 1979: 274). This criticism is similar to one of Popper's objections to the sociology of knowledge.

The problem of distinguishing those general rules that enhance freedom from laws that curtail it has been the focus of attention of several critics who are firmly attached to negative liberty. Some of these have argued that, in the end, Hayek's system of freedom rests on nothing more secure than the goodwill of governments, and that this leaves quite open the problem of how to limit those powers of coercion that are given to governments in their role as defenders of freedom.[15] Hayek's answer to these charges is to accept the 'sad fact' that there is no way of preventing coercion completely; all he seeks is that it should be kept to a minimum. Only in a society in which each individual observed a strict moral code prohibiting all coercion would it be possible to attain 'a happy state of perfect freedom'. How far coercion can be reduced 'depends in part on circumstances which are not in the control of that organ of deliberate action which we call government' ('Some Comments on a Critique by Mr Ronald Hamowy', in Hayek, 1967: 348–50). On the question of how to prevent coercive laws being enacted by the government, Hayek recognizes that there could be general rules that are oppressive, such as compulsory military service or the prohibition of drugs or alcohol. However, he takes the pragmatic view that so long as such general rules prevent *worse coercion* in some form, then they are justified since 'this principle seems to be as effective a method of minimising coercion as mankind has yet discovered' (Hayek, 1967). This, to utopian negative libertarians, is seen as a falling from grace, yet it has much to commend it as a guide to practical affairs in an imperfect world. There cannot in practice be a hard-and-fast line between general rules and discretionary power, but Hayek's critics have insisted that unless the rule of law secures some guarantee of specific rights then it cannot protect freedom adequately. A Hayek scholar who formerly took this view, John Gray, now regards it as 'an impoverished and mistaken view of the nature of Kantian universalizability in Hayek's jurisprudence' (Gray, 1986: 62). A particular rule should be tested for its appropriateness by enquiring into whether it is compatible with the rest of the accepted system of rules or values. This amounts to saying that in applying it to any specific circumstances, the rule will not conflict with any other accepted rules. The whole system of rules must be free of internal contradictions in the sense that the various actions that the rules permit will not lead to conflict (Hayek, 1967: 168; 1982, vol. 2: 27–9). The evolutionary character in the whole system of rules makes it possible in the course of time to bring about a complete transformation of the whole system. It is through this process that rules have evolved that, over time, have proved workable and are not the product of someone's will. Such general laws as those governing freedom of contract and the right to private property were originally developed because they satisfied the general sense of justice and were not as depicted by the naive constructivist interpretation of the origin of social institutions, the product of deliberation and creation at some definite point in the past. The test of generality – the universal nature of rules of just conduct – demands three attributes: consistency between similar cases, that is, non-discrimination; impartiality between individuals; and impartiality as between the preferences of others – moral neutrality[16] (Gray, 1986: 64). 'If it be once fleshed out in this fashion, it will be seen as a more full bodied standard of criticism than is ordinarily allowed, and Hayek's heavy reliance on it will seem less misplaced' (Gray: 1986).

On the whole, Hayek's unflagging efforts to revivify once more those beliefs in the virtue of the rule of abstract general law that originated mainly in eighteenth-century Britain, and that have in recent times been eroded by over confident constructivism are greatly to be welcomed, even though his social theory contains ambiguities and may not satisfy some as a complete guarantee of freedom; but what system could? Hayek's ideas must not be assessed in isolation. Providing one places freedom as a primary aim of social policy, then Hayek's political philosophy must be compared with others as a means, not of *guaranteeing* freedom, but of minimizing coercion; on this basis it must be highly regarded.

'FREEDOM TO STARVE'

A free market may well be cruel in its effects. In the unrestrained market economy the standard of living of each individual is constrained by his ownership of something that others will buy – whether it be goods he has made or his labour to make goods or provide services for others. Furthermore, those who, through hard work, skill, or luck, or some combination of these, become rich are then able not only to command a greater share of available goods and services but also to bequeath such power to their children who have done nothing to 'deserve' it. Such considerations are the basis of the negative/positive liberty distinction. The chief argument for positive liberty, as we have seen, is the contention that freedom without the means to enjoy its possibilities is mere hot air. This general idea underpins all varieties of collectivist opinion but is most radically seen in Marxist social theory, and although Marx's attitude to individual freedom is of a special kind, dependent as it is on the theory of exploitation and inevitable class antagonism, its uncompromising opposition to negative freedom as a bourgeois illusion serves to illustrate the principles that inform the derision of the cry: 'freedom to starve'. The literature on the matter of Marxist freedom is, of course, enormous in volume and for present purposes an account that is noted for its clarity and enthusiasm by Maurice Cornforth in his reply to Popper's criticisms, will suffice.

'There is no practical sense in talking about "freedom" unless one specifies for whom to do what' (Cornforth, 1968: 292). Marxism is concerned to promote specific individual freedoms. To protect freedom, Marxists agree with Popper (who here will be taken to represent the negative-freedom side) that 'the club must be taken from the bully' but, they would add to the list of those who are strong and who bully the weak, the private capitalist who uses his power to exploit the labour of others. Popper's conception of freedom is similar to that of J. S. Mill who affirmed that the state should only interfere with the freedom of individuals so far as is necessary to stop them from harming one another. But 'harm' is too vague and superficial. This principle assumes that state interference is in itself harmful but Marxists (and other collectivists) reply that this assumes that private ownership of property is untouchable and that the private appropriation of the products of labour does not count as 'harm' inflicted on individuals. Cornforth states that 'we Marxists' demand the right to employment; the security of the use of and enjoyment of personal property – but not the private accumulation of productive capital goods. 'Real' freedom must, to have any meaning, provide the means for the worker to develop his capacities for life and happiness (Cornforth, 1968: 302). Thus the most important element in the Marxist view is that capitalism cannot be consistent with freedom simply because the institutions of capitalism, resting as they must on the protection and encouragement of the private ownership of property, necessarily restrict liberty. Marxist freedom transcends mere negative freedom, which is a bourgeois confusion. However, the record of those states in which Marxism has been adopted or used to legitimize a regime is, without doubt, a wretched one. While we can continue to argue about whether or not capitalist freedom is 'real' freedom there is no question about the universally tyrannical nature of all hitherto existing Marxist regimes.[17] The condition in which only 'formal freedom' prevails is not confined to capitalist states; wherever there is rule by an elite – which is perhaps unavoidable – freedom is to some degree formal. The important thing is that the elite can be changed from time to time by democratic elections; it is in the capitalist states that this opportunity is, as a matter of fact, most often available to the mass of people. It is not that capitalism guarantees this particular freedom. There are many states that are capitalist but lacking in individual freedom – South Korea, South Africa, and certain South American countries; but there is a good deal of evidence to support the proposition that a capitalist private-property system is a necessary, even though not a sufficient, condition for the existence of freedom. The New Left's response to this awkward reality has been to argue that the appearance of freedom in capitalist states is because the system afflicts the majority with false consciousness. Capitalism does this by assimilating its critics into the system. Freedom of speech and assembly, tolerance and democratic institutions are simply ways in which the dominance of capitalist values are perpetuated.[18] Such freedoms assume that change can only come about through the institutions of the existing system. Herbert Marcuse has expressed this concept as using tolerance as an instrument of oppression; the only way to break out is through revolutionary violence. In his essay, 'Repressive tolerance' he makes it clear that his chosen brand of tolerance '... would mean intolerance against movements from the Right and toleration of movements from the Left'. By this means true democracy will be achieved by ensuring that the vast majority will no longer be unable to form right judgements when their minds are no longer deformed by democratic sources of information (e.g. in the education system and the press). All this has been seen as a distortion of Marx, 'a curious mixture of feudal contempt for ... democratic values, plus a nebulous revolutionism devoid of positive content' (Kolakowski, 1981: 410–20).

The 'freedom to starve' charge against the J. S. Mill and Berlin versions of negative freedom encapsulates many and varied suggested ways in which it should be modified to produce 'real' freedom, which do not involve the wholesale replacement of capitalism by an entirely different system. Before mentioning some of these it is interesting to notice briefly what might be seen as representing the opposite extreme to Marxism – what has been called anarcho-capitalism or pure libertarianism. This is well represented in the work of Murray N. Rothbard. He poses the 'freedom to starve' question by considering the extreme case of a man with no savings, no capital assets, and whose labour is a specialized skill for which there is no demand. Does not this call for intervention in the free market? Even in this 'impossible' case the individual is no worse off than he would have been in isolation – he may 'pursue isolated production that does not yield a monetary return' or engage in barter. (It is not made clear how barter would help when he has neither assets nor labour to exchange but presumably he must find some way of producing something first.) Rothbard points out that the ludicrous nature of this example demonstrates one advantage of free markets – people are free to 'drop out' and form their own communities. Rothbard's refutation of the 'freedom-to-starve' argument ultimately rests on his contention that freedom is meaningfully definable only as absence of interpersonal restrictions. Robinson Crusoe on his island is absolutely free since there is no other person to hinder him; he is free though starving. Whether he continues in this unhappy state will depend on his success in grappling with nature. Whether or not a man lives in poverty or abundance depends upon the outcome of the work of himself and his ancestors in transforming naturally available resources into capital and consumer goods. The two problems are therefore logically separate. Crusoe is absolutely free, though starving, while it is possible for someone to be a slave kept in riches. A flaw in this argument is that the current stock of capital we enjoy has been made possible only through social co-operation; from man's earliest beginnings his mastery over nature was the work of groups, not of isolated individuals. Rothbard finally uses his argument as the basis for furthering his support for the free market:

> That a person is 'free to starve' is therefore not a condemnation of the free market, but a simple fact of nature: every child comes into the world without capital or resources of his own. On the contrary ... it is the free market in a free society that furnishes the only instrument to reduce or eliminate poverty and provide abundance.
>
> (Rothbard, 1977: 290)

Rothbard's views on liberty are argued at length in *The Ethics of Liberty* (Rothbard, 1982). Not only does he oppose all forms of statism but he contends that both the Berlin and Hayek positions on negative liberty are unsatisfactory. Berlin he sees as a weak defender of freedom since he confuses freedom with 'opportunity', that is positive freedom. Berlin's fundamental flaw was his failure to define negative liberty as the absence of physical interference with a person's property rights. Rothbard's libertarianism rests on the establishment of human rights. But rights such as freedom of speech only make sense as property rights; when property rights are not used as the basis for rights in general, the latter become 'fuzzy and vulnerable'. To illustrate this, Rothbard offers many examples. One concerns the argument that freedom of speech cannot be absolute. The grounds upon which anyone is refused the right to shout 'Fire!' falsely in a crowded theatre have often been accepted as demonstrating that freedom of speech must be modified in accordance with the 'public interest'. But no weakening of rights results if the question is looked at in terms of property rights. 'The shouter is either a patron or the theatre owner. If the theatre owner shouts he is violating the property rights of the patrons in their quiet enjoyment' for which they have paid him. 'If he is another patron, then he is violating both the property right of the patrons to watch the performance *and* the property right of the owner' (Rothbard, 1982: 114; 1977: 238–40).

Rothbard also finds wanting Hayek's version of negative liberty. The 'fundamental flaw' in Hayek is that his theory of individual rights is not derived from the nature of man himself, but from the rule of law, in other words the government 'creates rights rather than ratifies or defends them'. Hayek's conception of what constitutes coercion is too vague for a libertarian like Rothbard. To admit that taxation, for example, is unavoidable and yet can still be regarded as 'non-coercive' on the grounds that it is predictable shows that under Hayek's abstract rules coercion may still exist (Rothbard, 1982: 226).

In his chapter 'Robert Nozick and the immaculate conception' Rothbard (1982) takes issue with Nozick's justification of the minimal state on several grounds. One of these is that he has no theory of rights. 'Rights are simply emotionally intuited, with no groundwork in natural law – in the nature of man or of the universe'. The evocation of natural law as the starting point for freedom is the unifying thread of Rothbard's work. Although Nozick is regarded on the Left as one of the dangerous arch-priests of *laissez-faire* capitalism, libertarians see his work quite differently; Rothbard concludes that *Anarchy, State & Utopia* as 'the most important attempt in this century to rebut anarchism and to justify the state fails totally . . .' (Rothbard, 1982: 247).

One defence of negative liberty is that it can be shared equally by everybody and it is the *only* form of liberty that can be so distributed; unlike positive liberty it should appeal to lovers of equality since it satisfies the Kantian requirement of universalizability. The fact that opponents of negative liberty portray those measures that grant various positive liberties as *increases* in negative liberty seems to tell us that they, too, regard negative liberty as the supreme type. Some government policies raise conflicts between negative liberty and other values, and are often shrouded in confused thinking. Equal-pay laws that forbid employers to pay blacks or women less than white males for the same work may seem to increase the freedom of these groups. The effects of such laws may not be so clear as they, at first sight, appear. First, they prevent employers making certain offers to the 'protected' group, as well as the freedom of an individual member of such groups from accepting certain offers, and the alternative may be unemployment. Bigoted employers will have higher labour costs – the price they pay for their bigotry, and the market will penalize them through the competition of less-prejudiced employers.[19]

The variety of arguments surrounding the 'freedom to starve' thesis and their attempted refutations tend to lead to the conclusion that 'there are no clear and indisputable distinctions between what is relevant to freedom and what is not' (Allison, 1984: 120). There are innumerable ways of using the word freedom, but the contention that 'freedom from the sovereign acts of the state' for man 'to conduct his life as he chooses' (Allison, 1984: 125) has for liberals[20] always had an appeal as a claim to the primary sense in which the word is used ... for the purpose of many of the most important arguments, whatever side we wish to take ... the focus on the relationship between the individual and the state allows us clear argument' (Allison, 1984).[21]

One approach to the negative/positive distinction is to start from the initial assumption that negative liberty is desirable but that to be of any use to an individual it must be endowed with certain rights, which, to use Joseph Raz's term confer autonomy – the capability for, and exercise of, self-government. In this view, education, for example, is as necessary a condition of an individual's autonomy as is freedom from oppressive laws (Raz, 1987). It should be remembered, perhaps, that education provided by the state implies the compulsory transfer of resources from some individuals to others and that the case for such provision must depend on the judgement that one loss of freedom is more than balanced by an increase somewhere else.

One way of disposing of the negative/positive distinction is to present freedom as a *triadic* relation: X is (is not) free from Y to do (not do, become, not become) Z. Looked at in this way, the contrast between 'freedom from' and 'freedom to' is due to a failure to understand the real nature of the relationship. The distinction between negative and positive freedom as it has been represented has encouraged the wrong sort of questions: questions such as 'Whose concept of freedom is correct?' (MacCallum, 1967). The apparently simple nature of the triadic formula allows innumerable possible combinations of X, Y, and Z. But perhaps the negative/positive distinction is not to be cleared away so easily. Berlin thought it to be an error: 'A man struggling against his chains ... need not know how he will use his freedom; he just wants to remove the yoke. So do classes and nations' (Berlin, 1969: xliii).

LIBERALISM AND CAPITALISM

Liberalism has been used to mean different things and in one case has acquired quite the opposite meaning. Liberalism in Europe has included a general approval of the free market whereas in the United States it has come to be associated with socialist ideas. Schumpeter (1954: 394) describes this transatlantic mutation as 'a supreme if unintended compliment; the enemies of private enterprise have thought it wise to appropriate its label'. 'Liberalism' will be used here in its sense as economic liberalism, that is a preference for free markets and with the state's role limited to maintaining the rule of law and intervention only where the market genuinely fails as in the case of public goods, externalities, monopoly, the provision of education, and some measure of redistribution of income to the poor and needy, and with the proviso that all state action is under parliamentary government. The word 'liberal' first appeared in England in the nineteenth century and was used by the political opponents of the liberals. The Spanish form of the word was used – *liberales* – the intention being to suggest that their principles were unEnglish. The word had been adopted by Spaniards to describe policies that they thought of as *English*. Spanish politicians who followed the principles of John Locke were called 'liberales'. It was, therefore, ironical that the Tory party in Britain regarded the term 'liberal' as something foreign and thus to be shunned. The political systems of Britain, the USA and Western Europe as well as those of Australia, Canada, and New Zealand are liberal democracies; all

112

these are capitalist systems with the principle of widely dispersed private-property ownership. This principle is, however, evidently no guarantee of liberty and democracy. Tsarist Russia, Nazi Germany, in the past – South Korea and some South American countries today – demonstrate that capitalism is not a sufficient condition for political liberty. However, one may confidently assert that liberal democracy has only taken firm root in capitalist states. Or, to put it another way, in those states that have been avowedly anticapitalist, such as the Soviet Union and its East European satellites, democratic liberties have not yet appeared. Socialists have a real problem with freedom, which is doubtless why the British Labour party has recently been making such strenuous efforts to dispel the idea that socialism is incompatible with individual liberty. These efforts rest on getting across the idea that only socialism can create 'real' freedom. The problem with socialism in its Marxist form is that if there is to be freedom within a Marxist state, there evidently must be a significantly large area of private ownership within which people can do what they want with what is theirs. There is no doubt that under capitalism men and women can suffer various forms and degrees of loss of some kinds of freedom, but there is the saving possibility of areas in which genuine freedom may be found so long as the state is not the sole owner of all property; there is always some prospect of making a living that does not depend on politicians. Only in capitalist states has there been any genuine and lasting pluralism.[22]

The traditional liberal case on behalf of free-market capitalism is the core of Ludwig von Mises' *Socialism* (1981) and Hayek's *Road to Serfdom* (1944) and from a methodological base differing somewhat from these, so is Milton Friedman's *Capitalism and Freedom* (1962).[23] The liberal case has a historical basis: the coincident rise of competitive capitalism, political liberalism, and eighteenth-century individualism. It is one of Hayek's main themes that these elements have, in the twentieth century, also been declining together under the impact of constructivism and holism. We have noted the fact that liberalism has been particularly successful in Britain, the USA, Western Europe, Canada, Australia, and New Zealand. These countries have mostly developed liberty or adopted it through evolutionary practice over many centuries.[24] Imitators in other parts of the world have not found liberty as easy to foster as it seems; it is a tender plant and is often attacked from all sides. Many people are afraid of it; surely, they say, if you have too much freedom you risk the horrors of that disorder from which it is the state's chief role to protect us. The answer is that the liberal democracies are open societies in which decisions are made publicly as in parliaments or courts of law; debate and disagreement – the open presentation of all points of view – is second nature. We have acquired a 'taste' for liberty. In the economic sphere competition is similarly encouraged. To some (chiefly Marxists) this is all a fraud – bourgeois freedom; to others these societies lack a sense of community. They are based on heartlessness and greed. But, unfortunately for these objectors, it is precisely in the capitalist liberal democracies where we see the most effective help given to the poor or sick; capitalism creates the wealth and the free flow of debate and persuasion can result in the tangible expression of benevolence towards the needy via the medium of the state. Conversely, it is in the states that have shred their bourgeois 'false consciousness' or who stagnate under the oppressive rule of some religious sect where the poor are worse off than in the capitalist democracies, dominated by 'selfish' individualism.[25]

DO PEOPLE REALLY WANT FREEDOM?

The choices that freedom offers the individual entail responsibility:

> Liberty not only means that the individual has both the opportunity and the burden of choice; it also means that he must bear the consequences of his actions and will receive praise or blame for them. Liberty and responsibility are inseparable.
>
> (Hayek, 1960)

These are the opening words of Chapter 5 of Hayek's *The Constitution of Liberty*. Some people have always preferred a sense of security to the turmoil of the disorderly freedom of the world.

> nothing has ever been more insupportable for a man and a human society than freedom ... I tell Thee that man is tormented by no greater anxiety than to find someone quickly to whom he can hand over that gift of freedom with which the ill-fated creature is born.
>
> (Dostoyevsky, *The Brothers Karamazov*)

While history shows us that men have often preferred security to freedom; they would sooner be assured of food, warmth, and shelter and pay the price in loss of freedom; there are today new forces that appear to be a danger to freedom. E. J. Mishan has drawn attention

114

to the inevitability of loss of freedom as people continue to demand that the state protects them from pollution and destruction of the environment and other hazards. One result of economic growth will be increasing regulation and control, which will be demanded to protect people from its unwanted effects. He sees no escape from a loss of individual freedom as the state becomes more repressive (Mishan, 1986: 192).

'Freedom' is a good thing: nearly everyone agrees on this. But what it consists of is, as we have seen, a matter of tangled complexities. One of the most well-aired complexities is the conflict between liberty and equality and 'equality' has become, in modern times, also a much admired value that, apart from its connection with liberty, has its own collection of ambiguities and problems of agreeing on what it consists of.

Chapter Six

EQUALITY

EQUALITY OF WHAT?

If someone believes or is told that he or she is not equal with respect to someone else, resentment is likely to follow, even though what may be meant is only that they are *different* in an infinite number of their characteristics, abilities, and situations. In science, generally, equality implies measurement; to say that two things are equal is to say that they have the same magnitude, number, value, or intensity. Not so easily quantifiable is the comparison of the hardness of two substances, but a diamond and a piece of steel may be compared in their relative power to scratch a common surface. However, when equality is used in a political or economic context, not only is measurement usually impossible but it makes little sense to talk of equality without specifying in what respects the equality or lack of it exists. Human beings may be said to be equal in that they all eventually die; but this fact need not be stated using the word 'equal'. We could have simply said that the same thing happens to everyone. When we were discussing the concept of freedom it became clear that the idea of freedom has, in spite of all the arguments surrounding it, an immediate and fairly well-understood meaning as a desirable value but 'equality' is more ambiguous and does not have the universal approval enjoyed by 'freedom'. Also it is because of this lack of unanimity that we have the debate about the conflict between freedom and equality. There is a sharp contrast between those who see equality as incompatible with freedom and those who see equality (however defined) as a necessary condition for true freedom. There is much evidence that equality has always been of central importance to the political Left and the British Labour party has made clear its unyielding attachment to the fight against inequality.[1]

The opposition to the socialist campaign for more equality has come from several sources: the Austrians, the Friedmanites, from philosophers such as Robert Nozick, the IEA, and the New Right in general.[2]

It is a necessary first step in defining equality to answer the question: 'Equality with regard to what?' The answer may be political equality, equality of income and/or wealth, equal health care and educational provision, the vague 'equality of respect', or equality of power (Norman, 1987). As soon as equality is, in this way, attached to some specific value or characteristic, we plunge into a sea of controversy.

Another way of looking at equality is to notice the way in which the concept's meaning has shifted through time. Originally, and until the eighteenth century the common belief seems to have been that we were all equal before God and before the law, in those states where the idea of the rule of law took root. From this developed the idea that there should be no arbitrary barriers to an individual's chance to develop his potential: equality of opportunity. Accidents of birth, nationality, race, religion, or sex should not stand in his path. In the twentieth century has appeared the assumption that equality should mean 'equality of outcome'; this necessarily involves action by the state to 'correct' free-market outcomes and hence is potentially more in conflict with the ideal of freedom (more specifically, negative freedom).

Equal opportunity ensures that everyone has an equal *chance* to do what he/she wishes and has the capacity for. The principle rests on the idea that inequalities can only be tolerated if they result from differences of personal effort and merit and not as the result of different opportunities. But what exactly counts as personal effort? Before the abolition of the 'eleven-plus' system, all children had the opportunity to go to grammar schools on the strength of their examination performance, but this in turn was influenced by their home background, the quality of the school, how they were taught, and many other factors. Thus, equality of opportunity depends on making (arbitrary) decisions on what is relevant to 'background'. Although some individual characteristics may, unarguably, be regarded as irrelevant – colour of skin or height, for example – there are obvious difficulties in everyone starting from the same base line even if this is thought desirable. In practice it comes to the question, not of trying to achieve the impossible, but of to what extent governments should try to *reduce* the initial handicaps or inequalities. A frequent complaint of egalitarians is that the libertarian right so often present them as seeking the dull uniformity of complete equality but this, they say, is a caricature of their aims; what they want is to reduce those inequalities that are most damaging to the 'life chances' of individuals and that are within the power of government to influence. The trouble is that those inequalities that are most significant in their influence on the life of the individual – accidents of birth and childhood experiences – are in many ways inaccessible to government action without at the same time producing severe intrusions into individual liberty, which must be weighed against the benefits that it is hoped they will effect.

In addition to improving equality of opportunity, egalitarians now advocate that in certain ways material and other satisfactions – the quality of life – should be equalized. This is described as 'social justice'. 'Social justice' has evolved from the term previously known to philosophers as 'distributive justice'.[3] Social justice today refers to the belief that real income and wealth should be redistributed in a
. . . 'fair' way. The underlying assumption is that free markets produce unfair results and that governments have an ethical right and duty to . . .
'redistribute' benefits so as to reduce inequality. The term 'benefits' embraces not only money income but 'social' services such as access to free health care, education, and subsidized housing. The slogan 'fair shares' has, in the twentieth century, proved extremely acceptable to many people and from it have emerged the vast and complex welfare and social-security institutions common to the western democracies. Redistribution involves extensive government intervention in free market outcomes and it is this fact that has been the source of the worry of liberals that equality and freedom are inevitably in conflict.

In this chapter we shall be considering some of the many arguments for and against equality beginning with those of the Austrian school.

AUSTRIANS ON EQUALITY

Austrians are, naturally, opposed to the idea that governments should be busy promoting social justice and of course they are not alone in this; it is a common feature of the radical Right. The Austrian opposition to government correction of social injustice is

118

based largely on the usual right-wing hostility to government intervention in the market, but it differs from some of the cruder manifestations of right-wing denunciations of state action in being able to rest its case on some of those methodological bases discussed in Chapter 1. For example, the Austrians derive, from the rejection of holism, their view that 'distribution' of national income is largely illusory and quite misleading; there is no large *pot* from which someone is required to give out rewards. Hayek especially, has argued against the idea that income should, in some way, be earned by meritorious work, and his concept of the rule of law would forbid much, though not all, of our social-security and welfare provision. In general, Austrians have seen the threat of totalitarianism waiting down the slippery slope of social justice. They have been much criticized for this view as being exaggerated, bigoted, and lacking compassion. More so than any other right-wing school of thought the Austrian case against egalitarianism stems from their view on how knowledge is acquired; only the free market can reveal the relevant information. Governments are inherently unable to allocate centrally and redistribute resources other than in a quite arbitrary way – they simply do not have the capacity to gather all the necessary knowledge. Because of this feature of governments, their re-distributive policies – usually being on a large scale – often produce very undesirable, unintended consequences.

Mises' opposition to equality is uncompromising and could fairly be said to be rather short on subtlety. His remarks on the subject in *Human Action* (Mises, 1966) chiefly revolve round two propositions: that inequality is necessary for economic growth and efficiency and that equality transfers power from the consumer to the state. He shows very little sign that gross inequalities might be even less desirable than a little less economic efficiency. What follows first is a summary of Mises as found in *Human Action*.

The inequality of 'wealth and income is an essential feature of the market economy' (Mises, 1966: 287). The function of inequality is to provide incentives to the individual to make the best of whatever his abilities and opportunities happen to be. The only alternative to market incentives is to be forced to work at certain tasks by the authorities – the police state.

Steeply progressive taxation is condemned on the grounds that it is against the interests of consumers. The large incomes achieved by 'the most efficient entrepreneurs' are the result of responding to public demand; it follows from this that the public approves of whatever it is they are buying from the entrepreneurs. Here again 'the issue is who should be supreme, the consumers or the government?' (Mises, 1966: 806). The argument that what motivates the rich entrepreneur is the lust for power rather than the lust for wealth, and that therefore his lust for power cannot be weakened by appropriating some of his surplus wealth, is dismissed because it ignores the fact that the power is derived from the wealth. Rockefeller and Ford are offered as examples of very rich men who would not have been able to bring their allegedly great benefits to millions of people had their riches been confiscated by the state. Furthermore, if a relatively poor man by his ingenuity and work manages in some way to fill some consumer want and succeeds in making 'excessive' profits it is of the greatest importance that he should have the opportunity to keep such profits and to plough them back into his business in order to expand. Such expansion of new firms exerts pressure on existing large firms to give a better service to their customers. If 'excessive profits' are taxed away from newcomers, the old firms will never be threatened by competition. The 'nouveaux riches are the harbingers of economic improvement' (Mises, 1966: 808). A further justification of inequality is that the power that the rich individual possesses is always a threat or check to political power. Those states in which autocrats rule, both now and in the past, are the most technologically backward. The rulers of such states justify their oppression of the entrepreneur by the fallacious contention that the rich get rich only at the expense of the poor: the mercantilist or 'fixed cake' fallacy. Despotic rulers are able to harness the envy of the masses in their persecution of enterprising individuals. Equality is a disincentive to saving by individuals. This contention rests on the supposition that if the government takes £1000 from a rich man and redistributes it among 10 poor men then aggregate saving will be smaller since the poor will tend to spend more of each extra pound they receive. The fall in savings will mean less available for investment thus eventually rendering the poor worse off than they would have been in a less egalitarian society.[4] Egalitarians, according to Mises, have consistently undervalued the function of inequality in acting as an engine of capital accumulation (Mises, 1966: 851). There is ample evidence that the inequalities thrown up by market forces have, in many cases, been associated with a *general* rise in living standards in the long run; this is an idea less easily grasped and less superficially compelling than the prospect of relieving poverty *now* at the expense of the rich by redistribution of income and wealth.

The Austrian suspicion of macroeconomic aggregates is again shown in respect of talk of 'distribution' of the national income. 'The concept of national income entirely obliterates the real conditions of production within a market economy' (Mises, 1978: 85). It is very easy to fall into the belief that the national income has some real existence – that it is an entity outside the activities of all the individuals who create wealth. This is again the mistaken belief that there exists a pot of wealth that might well be more fairly shared out. The concept of 'national income' reinforces the Marxian idea that goods are 'socially' produced and then 'appropriated' by individuals. Although it is true that goods and services are socially produced in the sense that production is the result of individuals mutually co-operating, it does not follow from this that there is something called 'national income' that has been produced by the nation. Such a holist procedure puts things the wrong way round, if we are talking about free markets. Each individual's 'share' of national income is determined by what his fellow men, competing in the market, are prepared to pay for his 'contribution'. The idea of 'sharing out' a common pool Mises sees as applicable only to closed, centrally dominated societies such as slave states or army camps. But it is, of course, by no means obvious that *some* degree of redistribution falling well short of the absolute command economy is necessarily equally deplorable unless one believes that it would be the first step on the road to totalitarianism. It is the general *tone* and uncompromising stance of the Mises type of opposition to social justice that has caused social democrats to protest that such a view is a caricature of what they are seeking. Nevertheless, Mises offers a useful corrective to the *unthinking* use of such terms as national income and national 'interest'.

An obvious question arises from Mises' unyielding opposition to redistribution: should not those individuals handicapped by disability or involuntary unemployment be helped in some way by the state? He seems rather reluctant to accept that such misfortunes will ever be a large-scale problem in a properly constituted free-enterprise capitalist society, pointing out also that the very existence of disabled individuals is only possible in a civilized state of material well-being that capitalism has made possible. The channelling of support from the fit to the incapacitated has traditionally taken

121

place, if at all, through charitable funds. As 'capitalism progresses and increases wealth' the greater become charity funds; people are willing, as they become richer, to donate more in proportion to their own improved well-being[5] and at the same time the 'number of the needy drops concomitantly' (Mises, 1966: 837). Mises makes it clear that he believes that it is a mark of a civilized society not to 'allow the incapacitated to perish'. But he does not look with favour on the substitution of a legal right of support for charitable relief. One objection socialists have to leaving the needy to charitable relief has been that it casts the recipient in a mendicant and degrading position. Mises, however, is doubtful whether the discretion of a bureaucrat is a good exchange for the discretion of charity workers. But, of course, the bureaucrat, though he may be given the power to exercise discretion, should be constrained by a properly constituted code of practice laid down by the legislature. It is the consciousness of this that ensures the preference most people would have for the bureaucrat over the charity dispenser. The inequality that results from unemployment is ascribed by Mises to a combination of trade-union and government intervention in the market. He writes that 'lack of wages would be a better term than lack of employment, for what the unemployed person misses is not work but the re-muneration of work' (Mises, 1981: 439). The reason people are unemployed is because 'they are not willing to work at the wages they could get in the labour market for the particular work they are able and willing to perform' (Mises, 1981). The provision of unemployment benefit enables trade unions to keep wages up to a rate at which only some of those seeking work can be employed. Trade unions are monopoly suppliers of the labour services and like all monopolists they will try to force up the price of their 'product'. However, there is an important difference between a trade union and a monopoly producer of goods or services. When the latter raises his prices he will only make more profit if the increased prices are compensated for by a less-than-proportionate fall in demand. In the union case, on the other hand, if a union forces up wages beyond what an isolated individual could command in the market, the loss of 'revenue' will be borne by those excluded from the market – the unemployed. Although it soon became widely accepted, following publication of Keynes' *General Theory*, that Mises' view was wrong – that reductions in wages would, in practice, *increase* unemployment through their effect on aggregate demand – Keynes himself in a

122

self-contradictory passage appeared to agree with Mises. Keynes first agreed that the price of labour had to be accepted as inevitably rigid and second that, even if wage-rates were flexible downwards, this would have the effect of worsening a trade depression. But he also is quoted as writing: ' ... if it were always open to labour to reduce its real wage by accepting a reduction in its money wage.... ' things would be different. This condition assumed, he said, '... free competition among employers and no restrictive combinations among workers'.[6]

Hayek's opposition to egalitarianism has much in common with that of Mises and it is a major theme in his writing on liberty and the rule of law. But he develops from the basis of Mises' work a more wide-ranging attack that spreads beyond the purely economic aspects of the matter. There are hardly any of Hayek's major writings on political philosophy without reference to equality, from *The Road to Serfdom* in 1944 to *The Mirage of Social Justice* in 1976 (see Hayek, 1982, vol. 2). Since much of his previous thought on the subject is gathered together and further explored in this latter work, I shall mainly concentrate on that as a source. Before discussing Hayek on social justice it is interesting to notice his original demolition of the unthinking and widespread use of the word 'social' in an essay first published in German in 1957 and reprinted in translation as 'What is "social" – what does it mean?' (Hayek, 1967: 237–47). There is sadly no reason to believe that the magical power to be derived from prefixing nouns with 'social' has diminished in the twenty-two years since this essay first appeared. It has the effect of being, as Hayek said 'the natural description of good behaviour and sincere thinking'. And yet its precise meaning is elusive. Germans have, for many years, referred to the 'social market economy' in order to avoid having to use the term 'free-market economy', as a sort of deferential gesture to those groups who may be frightened by the word free. This usage has later been taken up in Britain by the Social Democrat and Liberal (now merged into Social and Liberal Democrat) parties. Even the names of these parties hold up 'social' like a talisman lest we think they may be 'socialist'[7] but it is hard to conceive of an *unsocial* democrat or an *undemocratic* liberal. The word 'social' as Hayek says 'has become an adjective which robs of its clear meaning every phrase it qualifies and transforms it into a phrase of unlimited elasticity'. Indeed, there are so many concepts that 'social' is nowadays used to qualify that it has been practically drained of any precise meaning. Hayek fixes the start of its current usage to about the middle of the nineteenth century when the upper ruling class discovered that there existed an 'underworld' of very poor people. Social concern came to mean that the more fortunate rulers should take care of the interests of those who were so ignorant and poor as not to know where their true interests lay – 'a concept which seems somewhat of an anachronism in an age when it is the masses who wield political power' (Hayek, 1967: 239). This new demand for the awakening of a social conscience led to a distinction between the hitherto generally accepted view that a 'good' person simply should obey ethical rules – not to lie or cheat, for example – and a demand for wider responsibilities. What this wider duty consisted of was increasingly to be prescribed by people with greater knowledge than the individual: those who had thought deeply about and studied the greater needs of society or 'the community' than could be accessible to the selfish individual. Thus Hayek detects the sinister consequence of the substitution of 'social' for 'moral' or simply 'good', as one more device helping to foster socialism: 'the desire for a comprehensive blueprint of the social scene as a whole and a code of social conduct based upon it in accordance with a uniform and orderly plan' (Hayek, 1967: 240). Just as terms like 'national income' or 'national interest' have been misused, so 'social' carries with it the presumption that there exists something called 'society', which has interests over and above those of the individuals of which it is composed (once again we see the Austrian suspicion of holistic 'cloudy entities'). In order to gain support for his particular opinions, a speaker will proudly claim that they are 'social' or are motivated by 'social concern' or 'social justice' while those of his opponent are 'antisocial'. Hayek's preference in using 'social' is for confining its use to those rules that have evolved by a process of evolution and selection 'the distilled essence of experiences of which we ourselves have no knowledge': these he would properly describe as 'social growths' (Hayek, 1967: 243).

In short, Hayek's criticism is that not only has the word social often become meaningless, but that two baleful effects have been promoted by its widespread use: the substitution for individual morality of the artificial values of a centrally controlled society and the presupposition that 'society' has real aims superior to those of individuals.[8] Hayek's critics would argue that all this is a piece of misplaced worry over the meaning of a word that is a smokescreen to conceal his underlying prejudice against any action by the state to assist the 'underprivileged'. It is unfashionable nowadays to keep harping on about the meanings of words and undoubtedly there are many other words used in political philosophy, the meanings of which are somewhat elastic, but it may not be very useful in gaining understanding, to first demand in all discussions, clear-cut Euclidean definitions of terms. Nevertheless, the unthinking use of words like 'social' and 'community' has become so widespread and harmful to clear thought that the users should more frequently be challenged to tell us what they mean with a bit more precision. (The current popularity of the term 'quantum leap' by people who have no idea what it means is another example of a term that could soon threaten clarity of thought.) One response to the increase in crime has been to deplore the decline of something called 'social cohesion'; this only serves to obscure the fact that *individuals* commit crimes and to encourage the belief that it is the government's job to make 'society' more law-abiding. Of course, the government has the duty of enforcing the law but this should be applied to individuals, who must be assumed to carry some responsibility for their own misdeeds, rather than trying to explain them in terms of something being wrong with society. An individual who turns to crime may do so for all manner of reasons but the cause will be traceable to the actions of other individuals – parents, teachers, employers, or the state,[9] or even simply him or herself – not to the nebulous concept 'society'.

Hayek writes that 'social' or 'economic' justice is an abuse of the word 'justice', which 'threatens to destroy the conception of law which made it the safeguard of individual freedom' (Hayek, 1982, vol. 2: 62). His objection to the socialist view that the shares of the total product of society should, in some way, be allocated more equally is, first, that one must establish that there exists a moral duty to submit to some power that can arrange things so that a particular pattern of distribution is achieved, and that this 'power' having been seen to be capable of achieving this feat, can then decide on a 'just' distribution. This attitude to distributive justice has called forth much criticism – some of it cool and perceptive, and some indignant with veiled accusations that Hayek's true motives are hidden by a pretence of disinterested scholarship, his real purpose being the legitimation of bourgeois domination and the quietening of the conscience of the rich.[10] A less dramatic criticism is simply for egalitarians to protest that it is a caricature of their true position to argue that they want to make everyone equal; what they are saying is that surely it cannot be wrong to *reduce* some of the grosser inequalities thrown up by the free market. Also egalitarians may argue not that they must justify greater equality but that the liberal-right should be called upon to justify *inequality* (Crick, 1987: 88). But even if it is agreed that great inequality is bad, Hayek's question still stands: who is competent and morally justified in reallocating income and wealth between people?[11] He has no objection to equality as such. 'It merely happens to be the case that a demand for equality is the professed motive of most of those who desire to impose on society a preconceived pattern of distribution' (Hayek, 1960: 87). Hayek's fundamental objections to the quest for social justice are based on his desire to defend his concept of spontaneous order: 'nobody's will can determine the relative incomes of the different people, or prevent that they be partly dependent on accident' (Hayek, 1982, vol. 2: 69). The manner in which burdens and benefits are apportioned by the free market, he admits, would in many cases have to be regarded as unjust only if it were the result of some kind of intended distribution. Because of this unintended nature of the process, the question of whether or not it is just does not arise. At this point we may raise the matter of 'starting-lines' or 'initial holdings'. Surely it could be argued that even an unintended market-driven distribution might with some justification be called unjust if the 'game' gives some players severe handicaps. (This raises the question of the justice of the original state of a person's wealth and circumstances, which we shall return to later when discussing Nozick on distributive justice.)

Socialism was, for much of the twentieth century, characterized by its demand for the 'socialization' or nationalization of the means of production but this was seen chiefly as a means to bring about social justice. In an election in the early 1950s the Labour party's slogan was 'Fair shares for all' and increasingly, during the last forty years, taxation has been the instrument of redistribution, though according to some it has had little effect. Now that the 'public' ownership of industry is seen as an electoral liability the chief line of opposition to the Thatcher governments' 'turning back the clock' has been to attack the immorality of inequality. Also Hayek noticed as long ago as 1976 the way in which social justice has been embraced by the clergy; this is even more evident in 1988. 'The commitment to "social justice" has in fact become the chief outlet for moral emotion' (Hayek, 1982, vol. 2: 66). But the fact that a certain belief is widely accepted does not, in itself, establish its validity. Although Hayek sees it as unattainable, the striving for it has produced many undesirable consequences such as the giving to governments powers with which to satisfy the claims of all the special-interest groups who invoke social justice.

Most people are strongly moved by the seeming unfairness of life; it seems unjust that often the deserving who try hard are dogged by accident and ill luck while others who prosper often seem not to deserve their good fortune. Hayek contends that in such cases 'we do not know anyone who is to blame for it, or any way in which such disappointments can be prevented', by contrast with our attitude towards market outcomes, where we are more likely to blame 'society' and to demand redress from the government. But some of the so-called accidents and misfortunes that are not directly the consequence of market forces may be traceable to original inequality in material goods. A poor family may be forced into all manner of situations that greater wealth would have saved them from. Wealth, of course, can insulate its possessor from all kinds of accidents and misfortunes. Hayek's contrast between these two kinds of 'distribution' seems on closer examination to be far from clear cut.

One of the most contentious aspects of Hayek's criticism of egalitarianism is that he does not argue that market forces are just. Those people who are most meritorious, who have done the 'right thing', are not necessarily those who earn the largest incomes. Incomes will be the result of how much an individual's services are valued in the market by others. 'It is not good intentions or needs but doing what in fact most benefits others, irrespective of motive which will secure the best reward' (Hayek, 1982, vol. 2: 72).

Several thoughts occur on this matter. First, the notion that the market does reward 'merit' – that the good, hard-working, or inventive – will be rewarded has a long history as a justification for the morality of markets and Mrs Thatcher seems to believe this to be the case. The abandonment of the merit argument for free-market outcomes, whatever its logical soundness, makes the task of explaining to people why the market is a good thing that much more difficult. Second, the enormous salary increases paid from time to time to chairmen of private and public enterprises[12] are hard to explain in Hayek's terms of how market forces work. While it may be true that no single mind or even group of minds can fathom the complexity of how the market 'allocates' material rewards it is difficult not to conclude that some benefits are quite unrelated to market forces and owe more to social connections and opportunism. It must, however, be stressed that, assuming free-market forces have made possible some high rewards to certain individuals, the argument that they do not need *that* much income to retain their services is mistaken. While it is quite true that all but the marginal sellers of a service will make a gain in excess of what was necessary to induce them to sell their services, this is to be accepted so long as there is competition and free entry to the industry. Strangely, as Hayek rightly notes, most ordinary people seem to have less of a grudge against the high earnings of pop stars, footballers, or boxers than they have against the large, but comparatively modest, earnings of industrial tycoons. People are especially suspicious of any above-average remuneration received by so-called speculators; this is simply due to ignorance of the useful function of speculation in free markets.

My final point is: assuming that market forces *are* the main determinant of incomes and that this produces inequality, then whether or not one is prepared to accept that inequality depends on whether one regards the benefits of the market as compensating for any inequalities that one may find distasteful. The essence of Hayek's position is that any tampering with the market to redress inequality will create much worse evils, while the (moderate) egalitarian reply is that it is paranoiac to oppose some redistribution having the modest aim of redressing those gross inequalities that, apart from their offensiveness to anyone with any idea of fairness, do not seem to have any vital economic function.

Hayek is concerned that people in general should not be persuaded of the virtues of the market by using the argument that it rewards the deserving. If this is to be a major defence of the free market then he doubts whether it will survive.

The rise in the belief in 'social justice' roughly coincided with the decline in religious belief. Although, as Nietzsche claimed, God may be dead, perhaps people have clung to the idea that someone somewhere must be responsible for the varied fortunes and accidents of life. Perhaps this is an example of what Nietzsche meant by 'the shadow of God'.[13]

An ancient but illusory quest has been the search for a way of setting wages and profits according to their 'value to society'; the history of this idea extends from the medieval insistence on the 'just' price to more recent attempts to establish 'prices and incomes'

128

policies, which are now widely discredited as being largely unenforceable or harmful. Such mystical nonsense is not quite dead, however, as shown by a recent case in which the House of Lords felt competent enough to adjudge the work of a woman cook in a shipbuilding firm to be equal in value to the work of male engineering workers in the same firm, astonishingly in the name of equality of the sexes in work. How the 'value' of the different work was measured is not clear.

Hayek's reply to those who agree with him that although we cannot know what 'social justice' is, we can identify 'social injustice' and strive to reduce that, is that there is no test by which we can discover what is 'socially unjust'. This is because 'there is no subject by which such an injustice can be committed.' It would be like looking for a 'moral stone' (Hayek, 1982, vol. 2: 78).

A fundamental misunderstanding of how markets work is the idea that the incomes received by the resources employed in production are, or should be, rewards for services rendered, and that these benefits are, or should be, decided by someone. The earnings of labour and other factors of production are derived from the demands for the goods and services that they co-operate to produce. They are not rewards but signals thrown up by the market that indicate where factors of production may be most profitably employed; that is, where they are of most material value to other people (ibid: 80). The now-common belief that differences in earnings must be 'deserved' in some way arises partly from the fact that many people work in large organizations paying trade-union uniform rates. This may be why when earnings are paid by the largest organization – the government – there is the most talk of justice or fairness; as in the case of nurses or teachers. If, however, we live in a command economy, then the demand for equality in distribution between individuals does become reasonable, but not in an open free-market society.

There is one form of inequality between occupations that strikes many people as being particularly worthy of the description unjust. These are the often great differences between the earnings of those in dirty, unpleasant, but quite essential jobs – such as sewer workers, refuse collectors, and street cleaners – and other more fortunate individuals who enjoy high earnings doing jobs that they enjoy: television or film producers, actors, journalists, lawyers, and medical specialists. Hayek's case against the assertion of injustice here is that while it may be a 'misfortune' to have been born and bred in an environment in which one's opportunities are limited to unpleasant jobs it does not make sense to describe this as unjust. 'Who is supposed to have been unjust?' (Hayek, 1982: 93). This answer will only completely satisfy those who prize the virtues of the free market over other values and raises the matter of equality of opportunity and the education of children, which we shall refer to on p. 134.

Hayek concludes that the term social justice and its use as a justification for equality is not only 'intellectually disreputable' and vacuous, but dishonest: 'the mark of demagogy or cheap journalism' (Hayek, 1982: 97). It is dishonest because it appears to be an innocent expression of goodwill and concern for the unfortunate but it is, in practice, used by pressure groups for purely selfish ends or political advantage. Social justice is also used as a cloak for mere envy 'the most anti-social and evil of all passions' as John Stuart Mill called it. Socialism is based on the 'atrocious idea that political power ought to determine the material position of the different individuals and groups' (Hayek, 1982, vol. 2: 98). The great merit of the market is that it deprives anyone of such power, which can necessarily only be arbitrary. The influence of classical liberalism reduced such political power, but the twentieth-century demand for social justice is threatening to resurrect it.[14]

From what has been said it might be thought that Hayek is in favour of the 'minimal state', and some of his critics portray him as an intellectual lackey of the ruling class. But he has written supporting 'a wide field for the non-coercive activities of government' and has not opposed state help for the 'indigent, unfortunate and disabled' (Hayek, 1960: 257–61). And 'there is no reason why the volume of these pure service activities should not increase with the general growth of wealth'. Governments may also take the initiative in social insurance and education. Also many public amenities such as parks, museums, and theatres may be provided by 'common effort'. On the question of 'social' security the government may, without there being any threat to liberty, provide against 'severe physical privation, the assurance of a given minimum of sustenance for all'. Where Hayek would draw the line is where the safety net grows into government coercion to redistribute income more equally. The way in which this infringes liberty and the rule of law is that it requires discrimination between different individuals and unequal treatment 'to insure that particular people get particular things' (Hayek, 1960: 257–61). In practice it must be the case that the line between government help to the indigent and active income re-distribution must surely be difficult to identify.

One probable consequence of the policy of rushing in to correct all manner of perceived inequalities that is not generally appreciated is that the 'single-channel development toward which impatience and administrative convenience have frequently inclined the reformer', which has become characteristic of the welfare state, tends to stifle the emergence of (possibly more effective) alternative solutions provided by the efforts of individuals or groups outside the government's control (Hayek, 1960: 260).

SOME ARGUMENTS FOR EQUALITY

Attitudes to equality do appear to distinguish fairly well between the political Left and Right, though like most categorizations in political economy this division is not nicely clear-cut; there are, for example, many Conservatives who favour a policy of distributive justice. Although the arguments for equality are many and varied, there is one contrast between them and the Austrian view that stands out. Most of the arguments of the egalitarians are prefixed by the pronoun 'we' as in 'We should not allow people to starve', or 'We should introduce a minimum wage'. These statements always contain a presumption, the justification for which is seldom spelled out: this is that there is a stream of income and a store of wealth that should be 'distributed' by some agency standing above the battle. The staffing of this agency is to be drawn from people who do not question this principle; it is taken for granted that all decent people are in favour of it. There is a sharp contrast between this presumption and the Austrian presumption. The latter *starts* not by assuming that there is a 'social pot' to be distributed but by accepting free-market outcomes. Egalitarians question such outcomes not only because they are currently inequitable but because the participants in the 'race' are not equal when they begin, because of accidents of birth and inherited wealth. Austrians accept the distribution brought about by market forces for all the varied reasons we have discussed, whereas egalitarians in general urge that morality requires the action of some degree of central redistribution to correct market inequity. Making a fuss over the use of the pronoun 'we', which occurs in articles on equality, may appear unduly pedantic and a point of criticism that has little substance. After all, what writers who use

131

this form are conveying, by a conventionally accepted usage, is something like 'the institutions and practices of government in a good society should treat people. . . .' In other words, 'we' means not only 'we individuals in our dealings with one another' but 'a government that, conscious of certain moral values, treats people in certain ways'. But this quite justifiable demand for governments to be bound by the rule of law and to treat people *equitably* can slide imperceptibly into the unwarranted presumption that 'we' doing something to promote equality may include the government 'distributing the social product'. I do not wish to labour this point but it seems worth keeping in mind when considering the various arguments for equality.

There is general agreement that people should be treated equally in some respects. Free market proponents believe all men should be equal under the law and so do egalitarians. The latter, however, are not content with this 'formal' equality; as well as legal equality they want more economic equality, not only for its own sake but, as they have quite rightly observed, a rich man has a great advantage over a poor man when he is involved in the courts of law. I think that one of the most disturbing features of the capitalist democracies and one that is not given enough attention by the Austrians and other anticollectivists is this very serious disadvantage suffered by the poor. Even their access to the law in their own defence is gravely blocked by lack of money to pay lawyers. Of course, worse things may happen to the poor and underprivileged where the law is under the arbitrary control of a despotic state; political influence and 'connections' are substitutes for riches in totalitarian systems; also the market offers insurance schemes to cover possible legal expenses.

Since all people have in common their 'humanity', it has been argued that if they are to be treated unequally, then some justification must be given for this. In other words people should be presumed to be equal and the burden of proof as to why they should not ought to be borne by those who support inequality. This involves the concept of universalizability: that like cases should be treated alike. If my fellow human is in need and I do not help him when I have the power to do so, then I am failing to recognize our common humanity. This argument is the basis of the moral fervour that fuels the justification of 'aid' to the Third World. But although there may seem to be nothing but good in giving tractors to a poor country in order that its ability to feed itself may be improved, such kindnesses may achieve short-run benefits but with long-run harm (Bauer, 1982).

Another principle of equality is 'equal consideration of interests'.[15] This is the proposition that we must regard the interests of all people as being equally important; I should show equal concern for all beings who have interests. The merit of this principle lies in its insistence that everyone's interests should be given proper consideration – that there are no groups whose interests are always overridden. This is unquestionably an essential characteristic of any just society. But it can slide into supporting the idea that everyone is as *good* as everyone else; no matter what I do I am as good as you.

A long-standing and influential utilitarian argument for equality is based on the proposition that everyone experiences diminishing marginal utility. This is to say that an addition of £1 to the income of a man whose income is £20,000 a year yields less 'satisfaction' or utility than £1 added to someone having £1,000 a year. This principle is used to justify progressive taxation of income. Although this policy is widely accepted as a 'fair' one, it is not possible to rigorously defend it by reference to the diminishing marginal utility theory. There is no way of objectively determining utility and therefore interpersonal comparisons of utility are impossible. One might, of course, hold the opinion that A's needs are greater than B's but there is no objective basis for deciding between conflicting views on the needs of A and B. Hayek's view is that the general acceptance of diminishing marginal utility theory as a justification for progressive taxation is based mostly on a wish to reduce income inequality. This economic theory has given 'quasi-scientific sanction ... to a dangerous instrument of policy'.[16] It is interesting to note that Rothbard (1970: 187) accepts that the marginal utility of money income declines as income increases but condemns progressive taxation on the grounds that 'it is not so much the progressivity as the height of his tax that burdens a rich man' (Rothbard, 1970: 805). For example, one society, A, may require everyone to pay 50 per cent of their income in tax; in another, B, tax rates may range from one-quarter to 1 per cent for the poor and 10 per cent for the rich. The rich will prefer B, the one with the progressive tax.

John Stuart Mill regarded progressive taxation as 'a mild form of robbery', but egalitarians have supported progressive taxation as an effective and justifiable policy both on the basis of economic theory and of morality. In 1848, Marx and Engels proposed 'a heavy progressive or graduated income tax' as one measure by which the proletariat will wrest 'all capital from the bourgeoisie' (Hayek, 1960: 517). The main difficulty from the egalitarian point of view is that marginal utility theory suggests that inequality is bad because it reduces the *sum total* of happiness but it is no protection to the inequality suffered by particular individuals.

Progressive taxation is widely cherished, however, and supported as a method of reducing inequality. The deep attachment to the principle was shown by the howls of disbelief and anger from opposition MPs that greeted Chancellor Lawson's proposal for a reduction in the top rate of tax in 1988 from 60 to 40 per cent. The argument that lowering rates produces a higher yield of total revenue through economic growth, which is then available for spending on social services and the poor, cuts no ice with those who see rich men as a moral affront. This has been critized as mere envy, but it is perfectly possible to disapprove of great inequality as a moral 'bad' in itself, without the motivation of envy; opposition to great income inequality needs no further defence – you are for it or against it.

EQUALITY OF OPPORTUNITY

The idea that equality of opportunity is something that any decent society should have as an important aim is generally agreed; but there is comparable disagreement over what it is. Even the causes for the existence of equality are by no means clear cut, and what should be done about it, if anything, is a central theme of political controversy.

The word 'opportunity' must mean opportunity to do something or become something; all the possibilities that an individual might (or should) have as summed up in the phrase 'life chances'. Superficially, it may not sound too difficult to ensure that everyone is given an equal opportunity, but closer examination reveals that the concept raises many problems; although it must be stated that egalitarians get quite tired of pointing out that in this, as in other aspects of equality, they do not imagine that we can have perfection, as some market-liberal caricatures like to depict them. They only wish to see equality of opportunity *increased* for those who start, as they see it, so relatively badly handicapped in their life chances. If, by equality of opportunity, we mean that everyone should have an equal chance to do what they wish, then we would be arguing for an obviously impossible society in which everyone had an equal chance of becoming an eye surgeon or an outstanding footballer, irrespective of mental or physical endowments. Equality must, therefore, necessarily mean that opportunity is open to all those *capable* of achieving some desired end. Thus criteria must be used to select people for the desired ends. Only 'relevant differences' between people are to count for there to be equality of treatment. Colour of skin, or sex, for example, should not be considered relevant in selecting people to be doctors. The trouble with this lies in deciding which differences are relevant. Utilitarian arguments may be used to justify treating people differently. 'Apartheid in South Africa is justified precisely by a theory of relevant differences which suggests that the separate (but equal) development of national cultures is in the interests of the majority of people in the Union' (Allison, 1984: 83). Also such situations cannot be laid at the door of capitalist market forces. The privileged position of party members (the *nomenklatura*) in the Soviet Union is justified on the grounds that it is necessary for the achievement of communism – which in turn is for the greater benefit of everyone. 'In short the concept of equality of treatment is wholly incoherent' (Allison, 1984: 84).

Literal equality of opportunity is, of course, impossible. Children are not only born with different physical and mental qualities but are born in different environments and to different families; their starting opportunities must inevitably differ. However, although it is impossible to equalize children in these respects, education has been the hope of egalitarians as the way to compensate for such unequal starts in life – to provide children with the opportunity to develop their potential aptitudes. Although Hayek favours the government provision 'on an equal basis the means for the schooling of minors who are not yet responsible citizens', he recognizes that this would be far from creating real equality of opportunity even for persons having the same abilities. 'To achieve this the government would have to control the whole physical and human environment of all persons'. This would be 'apt to produce a nightmare' (Hayek, 1982, vol. 2: 84–5).

Ever since the establishment of compulsory state education there has been a trend towards providing opportunities for naturally able children to rise through the educational ladder. This encouragement of the more able fits in well with the market-liberal admiration of competition. The state selective grammar-school system enabled many working-class children to rise into the middle class, but it came under increasing fire from egalitarians as failing to deal with the roots of the problem of the initial inequalities associated with their backgrounds. The currently held view typical of a socialist moderate is stated with characteristic vigour by Roy Hattersley (1987: 32–44) in *Choose Freedom*. The essence of the case is expressed as follows:

> the many travellers must set out from the nearest to a common starting line that society can organise. That requires an assault on environmental deprivation, inadequate housing, domestic poverty, second rate health care, and overcrowded primary schools, which imperfectly teach English as a second language.
> (Hattersley, 1987:36)

The question of what should be done and by whom remains the great divide between socialists and free market liberals. The Hattersley view follows Tawney, who compared society to a family: a good father, although recognizing that his children are differently endowed, would not lavish family income exclusively on his healthiest son. 'That is how we distribute our resources and esteem within society' (Hattersley, 1987: 41). The key phrase is 'we distribute'. It is the implication of this on which the divide rests between individualists and collectivists. In the use of the word 'distribute', we have again the presumption that society owns all the resources that it allots to individuals. 'We' introduces an air of omnipotence. The case against collectivism rests partly on the contention that nobody can be trusted to rearrange society in the way collectivists wish. As J. R. Lucas has said, 'The intellectual limitations of our rulers are of immense practical importance'.[17] Furthermore, liberals see the possibility of Hayek's 'nightmare' of totalitarianism in the drastic social engineering required by the socialist vision. 'If we insist on the state's being answerable for all the arrangements of society, we implicitly concede to it absolute power'.[18] Such views are derided by the Left as mere casuistry, the true purpose of which is to frighten people with mythical terrors, so as to protect the status quo; the accepted social order and the privileges of the establishment.[19] The difficult question is to decide who has the best case.

SOME RECENT DEFENCES OF EQUALITY

New books that defend egalitarianism from its denigrators are constantly being published and a variety of arguments have been used. To some extent such writing shows evidence of having been provoked by the success of the New Right in its attack on socialist verities. Until about fifteen or so years ago the intellectual case for egalitarianism and the need for social justice was more taken for granted than it is today; the need to defend it was less urgent. The influence of Hayek, the IEA, and other free-market proponents has caused egalitarian intellectuals to re-examine and restate the fundamental principles on which their beliefs rest. An excellent, concise, and in some respects original contribution to the socialist case for equality is that by Professor Bernard Crick (1987). This short book poses some intelligent and forceful challenges to the more abrasive proponents of the New Right, and the reader may, in a relatively short space, obtain a good picture of what the moderate wing of the Labour Party now see as important about equality. Many new ways of justifying equality have emerged and there is a clear desire to rebut the charge that equality is incompatible with freedom. What follows is an inevitably restricted account of some of these. We begin with the eminent political philosopher whose theories have been attacked from both Right and Left but who, it seems to me, should be included among those who see real meaning in the term 'social justice' as being an identifiable condition.

John Rawls

In 1971 Rawls's work culminated in the publication of his substantial finely argued book, *A Theory of Justice*, in which the implications of what he calls the 'Main Idea' are fully developed. It must first be admitted that writing a brief note on Rawls is bound to fail to convey much idea of why his work has engendered such a massive volume of comment. H. L. A. Hart has described *A Theory of Justice* as 'the most important work of political philosophy written in English since John Stuart Mill' (Hart, 1983: 194). Another example of approval – perhaps rather surprisingly in an IEA publication – is the assertion that 'I think we are all Rawlsians now'.[20] But another contributor to the IEA remarks 'Nor shall we ever understand the tickertape reception accorded to an extraordinary ill-constructed and

unarresting book'.[21] Robert Nozick, although he remains uncon-
vinced by Rawls, agreed with Hart that Rawls's theory is a powerful,
deep, subtle, wide-ranging, systematic work in political and moral
philosophy which has not seen its like since the writings of John
Stuart Mill . . . a fountain of illuminating ideas' (Nozick, 1974: 183).
Hayek, in a preface 'after careful consideration' concludes that the
difference between himself and Rawls 'seemed more verbal than
substantial' (Hayek, 1982: xvii), and even Rawls's use of Hayek's
anathema, 'social justice' is passed over quite casually as 'a fact which
I regret and regard as confusing'. But he has no 'basic quarrel' with
Rawls. This is because in Hayek's view, the latter recognizes that the
design of political institutions should be just (Hayek, 1982, vol. 1:
100).

Rawls's theory begins as a critique of utilitarianism on the basis
that it does not take seriously the distinction between persons and he
argues that there must be, in any society claiming moral legitimacy
for its various institutions, protection for certain basic rights of the
individual. Other political philosophers also have employed rights-
based theories against utilitarianism.[22] Such modern defences of
rights should not be confused with the seventeenth-and eighteenth-
century natural rights. The establishment of specific rights has been
seen as an essential safeguard against man's inhumanity to man –
especially in the twentieth century – and the movement for human
rights has had practical outcomes in the United Nations Charter and
the Helsinki Agreement. Rawls's 'Main Idea' is that the principles of
justice are those that would be chosen by free and rational
individuals if they had to choose behind a 'veil of ignorance'. This
means that in choosing, they must make an imaginative leap
inasmuch as they must assume that they do not know in advance
what their own abilities or status will be in the imagined society.
Rawls maintains that certain principles would be agreed on by all
rational people of goodwill. In the question of distributive justice
they would agree that the higher expectations of the better situated
are just if and only if, they work as part of a scheme that improves
the chances of the least advantaged members of society. In other
words inequality is only justified if it results in the poor becoming
better off – the Difference Principle. Both the political Right and the
Left have found support in Rawls's ideas from one point of view
whilst deploring them from other angles. His anxiety to see less
disparity in the distribution of property and wealth is naturally

applauded by socialists, but at the same time they warn that free-marketeers will misinterpret Rawls as supporting inequality, on the grounds that it indirectly helps the poor. Rawls's assumption that rational self-interested individuals in the 'original position' would in fact choose as he suggests has been widely questioned. If they were bold gamblers, they might choose from behind the 'veil of ignorance' a state of affairs in which the most intelligent or the strongest had the greatest privileges and status. It has been argued against Rawls and his egalitarian followers that his basic premiss that a social order can be considered just and legitimate only to the degree that it is directed to the correction of inequality has, in spite of all the controversy, hardly ever been seriously questioned: 'The thesis is not considered controversial' (Kristol, 1978: 172). At least one philosopher has since remedied this omission with great vigour. The main thrust of Antony Flew's critique of Rawls revolves around first, the assumption that the principle of equal distribution 'is so obvious that we would expect it to occur to anyone immediately' and second, his implicit presupposition that all the goods and services are there to be 'shared out' equitably – 'the enormous socialist assumption'.[23] As for the individuals who, from behind the 'veil of ignorance' and in the 'original position', find egalitarianism 'so obvious', they are dismissed by Flew as 'blinkered and de-individualised zombies'. His central criticism of Rawls's device of the 'Main Idea' is that it ignores people's deserts. He contends that justice is an essentially backward-looking notion that should take account of the varying backgrounds of individuals and their differing deserts and entitlements. Although there will be many conflicting ideas on what these entitlements ought to be, the Rawlsian kind of justice, which is not concerned to enquire into backgrounds – how given individuals got into the situation they are now in and to 'render each his due' – is seen by Flew as a deplorable evasion and sad departure from the classical concept of justice. Rawls gives comfort to the social engineers and wielders of public power.[24]

Citizenship theory and equality of power

The attacks of the New Right on the concept of distributive justice and one of its main features – the welfare state – have stimulated egalitarians to some thoughtful and well-argued defences, which are worthy of much more consideration than I am able to provide here.

Citizenship theory is based on the proposition that society is not, as the Hayekian liberals present it, atomistic – a multitude of jostling, self-interested individuals. Our membership of 'community' is like being a member of a family. 'Members of a family have claims on others and duties towards them' (Harris, 1987: 152). Just as with a family, one receives a range of benefits from society. Society provides infrastructure.

> It is this general 'social' contribution which helps undermine the argument that one has an untrammelled right to use and dispose of as one sees fit whatever one has acquired through action within the terms specified by one's property rights.
>
> (Harris, 1987: 153).

In this view, if some individuals are luckier or more successful than others through a 'social process', which makes others worse off, 'compensation' to someone who, 'through no fault of his own' remains poor is justified. Thus Nozick's contention that taxation is theft is dismissed on the grounds that individuals do not have an entitlement to keep full control over what they earn; we have an obligation to others. How this obligation is to be implemented is made clear. The state is to claim back 'that portion of wealth which state institutions have created' (Harris, 1987: 117). Thus, in spite of much thought-provoking and intelligent argument fuelled by high moral purpose, what it comes down to is that some individuals (elected representatives, civil servants, workers' councils, or whatever) are morally justified and have enough knowledge to redistribute things between other individuals so as to reduce inequality.

When considering how benefits should be given, there is a principle that would seem to be merely common sense – that only those who need them should get them. There would seem to be little point in giving rich people benefits (provided by poorer people) that they can afford to pay for. There is a strong case for selectivity both on the grounds of morality and efficiency. To use the family analogy: one would not expect a poor father to give money to his rich son. Citizenship theory is apparently rather uncertain on this matter. 'Universal services in kind may help to create a sense of community membership'. On the other hand, 'A flexible and pragmatic approach ... needs to be adopted'. Selectivity should not be ruled out. Such dogmatism has harmed citizenship theory' (Harris, 1987: 150–1).

Citizenship theory rests on a commendably optimistic view of human nature that, if true, should gladden one's heart and Harris's book ends on a hopeful note. 'As the dusk falls on Thatcherism, social democracy spreads it wings'; this was published shortly before the third successive general election victory of the Conservatives in 1987.

Professor Richard Norman contends that equality of power is more basic than equality of wealth: 'causally more fundamental'. In the final chapter of his book, *Free and Equal* (Norman, 1987), he makes what he describes as 'some utopian speculations'. These interesting ideas are presented as various alternative institutional forms. Each of these, in different ways, is intended to enable everyone to share equally in the power to control the activities of their own society. The aim is to transform the relationship between freedom and equality from conflict to complementarity. What is required is for power to be shared more equally through 'direct' or participatory democracy rather than the present system in which ordinary people simply elect others to exercise power on their behalf. More areas of social and economic life need to be brought under democratic control, ideally through co-operative ventures such as citizens' assemblies controlling the activities of the local community, and workers' councils controlling the activities of the workplace. Norman at once admits the practical difficulties: workers' councils are impossible for running a large firm; most people do not have time to devote to such activities; in any case most people prefer to spend their time on other pursuits and the making of policy is likely to fall into the hands of an articulate well-informed minority. Five possible ways of extending democracy and creating co-operative institutions are then suggested. Of these the extension of the jury principle to political and economic matters would seem to be the most original and promising. As in the present jury system every citizen would get their chance to take part in decision-making such as planning application public enquiries. The author concedes that such schemes as he suggests may seem wildly utopian but that they are no more so than the theories of the 'individualistic liberal' school such as Nozick's, which presuppose a world 'which is entirely remote from anything we can recognise' (Norman, 1987: 172). Norman criticizes Nozick's world for, among many other things, the picture it presents of production owned by individuals, whereas in the real world corporate bodies are the typical units. This is only part of Norman's critique of Nozick which, since it occupies twelve pages, cannot adequately be discussed here. I shall only mention one major point of criticism. This is that in Nozick's theory of justice the central place is given to the individual's basic rights, which must not be violated by arguing that do so is justified by the achievement of some greater good. Norman disagrees: 'rights are not basic, they derive their importance from other more fundamental values such as the value of freedom, or the value of individual autonomy or the need for respect' (Norman, 1987: 148).

CONCLUSIONS

The most fundamental difference between egalitarians and the political Right – especially the Austrian branch – lies in their respective attitudes to the possibility of creating human institutions that have the necessary wisdom and knowledge and can be trusted to make moral choices. There is a long-standing belief that the Left is composed of impracticable idealists, or optimists about the possibilities of improvement, and that the Right are tough realists who are cynical as to the innate 'goodness' of human beings. A strong theme in socialist beliefs has always been that *nurture* is more important than *nature* and hence the moral argument for providing better houses, schools, and hospitals. This involves distributive justice as a means to greater equality.

Another divide between Right and Left is over the question of whether freedom and equality are necessarily conflicting aims. Distributive justice inevitably implies state coercion but the Left reply is that the poor are coerced anyway – by employers, for example.

Equality of opportunity raises all kinds of conceptual and practical problems. In discussions of equality of opportunity there is often an implication that life is like a race in which we all compete and some receive better prizes than others. But the radical Right[25] contend that life is not like a race; there is no central authority giving out prizes according to individual merit. Socialists evidently think that there should be. But in that case they are saddled with all the old problems of adopting criteria on which to base redistribution. A persistent and ancient assumption on the Left, which is not always made explicit, is the belief that the free market is a zero-sum game: that if greater ability or effort or just luck enables some individuals to get more, then others must be worse off. But, of course, the efforts of the outstandingly successful individuals do not only benefit themselves.

An element of great controversy in the liberal-market case against equality, is that some individuals begin their lives with appallingly 'unfair' handicaps that are not their own fault. The liberal-market view is that the only acceptable view of justice is based upon what Nozick calls the 'entitlement' theory. This is that any principle of distributive justice that specifies some desirable pattern for the way in which wealth and income are distributed, whether it be according to 'needs' or even according to people's deserts, is to be rejected: 'our objection is against all attempts to impress upon society a deliberately chosen pattern of distribution, whether it be an order of equality or of inequality' (Hayek, 1960: 87). Nozick points out that although Hayek rejects a patterned conception of distributive justice, he welcomes a pattern that he approves of: distribution in accordance with how others value an individual's services. Nozick simply rests *his* case on the proposition that so long as initial holdings have been justly acquired, then any voluntary transfers must themselves be just and any interference with such transfers constitutes injustice because it violates people's rights. Against this it has been held that rights are not basic and that they derive their importance from more fundamental values, one of which is individual autonomy or equality of respect (Norman, 1987: 148; Raz, 1987).

Finally, it must be noticed that many of the arguments surrounding freedom and equality proceed too much on an all-or-nothing basis. Egalitarians, instead of trying to persuade us that liberty without equality is not true liberty, would be better advised to concentrate on marginal cases. It might well be argued with conviction that the loss of liberty or violation of rights that occur when a rich man is prevented from having *full use* of his property is smaller than the gain that goes to those to whom a modest proportion of his resources are transferred.

There are many aspects of equality that have not been specifically mentioned in this chapter. Property rights, for example, have been challenged by egalitarians. Some have argued that the assumption that the individual has a right to do what he wishes with his own property, which is the bedrock of market liberalism, is merely arbitrary and has no firm moral basis. But what alternatives are there from which to begin the discussion and which do have a better moral basis? Nor has there been space to explore some of the wilder manifestations of the obsession with equality and the modish fears of élitism that emanate from the legal measures against 'discrimination'. The effects of these practical applications of the doctrine of equality, although they may have suppressed overt bigotry, cannot, with certainty, be said to have increased 'equality of respect' between individuals and may have made matters worse.

Another preoccupation of egalitarians – 'aid' to the Third World – has not been mentioned, but for those readers who may think that it is an unmitigated blessing the work of Professor P. T. Bauer is recommended, especially his *Equality, The Third World and Economic Delusion* (Bauer, 1982). This book and Bauer's other writings on this subject demonstrate the way in which unintentioned and unwanted consequences may flow from well-meaning but loosely thought-out schemes whereby governments take money by force of law from their citizens and give it, in many cases, not to other individuals but to other governments.

On balance the liberals have the best of the argument, if only because they are less likely to instigate grandiose projects of social engineering with all their potentially dangerous and unforseeable consequences. The free marketeers are, though not perfect, less dangerous than the egalitarians, and even on the Left, the 'new look' spirits of the British Labour Party of the late 1980s have made plain their desire to be seen to have shed some of their traditional attachment to equality of misery.[26]

Part IV

PRACTICAL POLITICS

Chapter Seven

THE WELFARE STATE

The welfare state is an obvious and important arena of potential conflict between freedom and equality.

In a novel published in 1887, *Looking Backward*, by Edward Bellamy, there is a Rip Van Winkle character who goes to sleep in 1887 and awakens in the year 2000 to discover a utopia that promises security 'from cradle to grave'. This, according to Milton Friedman, may well have been the first use of this famous phrase. The main categories of the welfare state today are health services, education, housing, and social security – a huge and varied sector of state activity. In this chapter there is first a discussion of the welfare state as a principle of social policy. At the time of writing, major reforms of housing and education are on the statute book but state health services have hardly felt any of the free market zeal that the Conservative governments of the 1980s have directed at other entrenched institutional vested interests. Judging from present press comment it looks as if the government may be preparing to do little to disturb the status quo. The second part of this chapter briefly considers some of the alternatives now being canvassed by Austrians and other free market advocates.

ORIGINS AND JUSTIFICATIONS

The welfare state's origins reach back to the 1870s, although the term 'welfare state' was not in common use in English until after the Second World War. It probably derives from the German *Wohlfahrtstaat* which was put into practice by Bismarck.

From the middle of the nineteenth century numerous Acts of Parliament were passed designed to ameliorate living and working conditions: Factory Acts, Public Health Acts, Mines Regulation Acts, Education Acts. *The Economist* commented in 1895 that 'the fabric of State expenditure and State responsibility is built up like a coral island, cell on cell'. What was emerging, suggested Sidney Webb, was the 'unconscious socialism' of a 'housekeeping State' (Bruce, 1968: 140). The reports of Booth and Rowntree on the state of the poor provided a mass of shocking detailed evidence. One manifest-ations of poverty rather than occasioned by any underlying political philosophy or social theory. Lloyd George's National Health In-surance scheme of 1911 was carried forward on 'a tide of social pity' (ibid: 140). The reports of Booth and Rowntree on the state of the poor provided a mass of shocking detailed evidence. One manifest-ation of the stirring of the consciences of the middle classes was the University Settlement movement, which brought young, well-to-do, educated young men among the poor; William Beveridge became subwarden from 1903 to 1905 at Toynbee Hall, Whitechapel, which was the first of these Settlements, founded in 1884. Another who was later to be one of the main builders of the welfare state was a Conservative barrister, C. R. Atlee, who was Secretary at Toynbee Hall in 1910–11. All this and many other 'stirrings of conscience' were the driving forces of the Liberal reforms of the Edwardian period. Although the motives for reform were generally pragmatic, the gradual building of the welfare state fitted in well with Fabian political philosophy and enjoyed growing support from a large-enough cross-section of influential writers, academics, and poli-ticians for the idea gradually to take firm root, and grow, as sub-sequent twentieth-century developments showed, in spite of some setbacks in the years of interwar economic depression.

The main foundations of the present welfare state were firmly laid under Attlee's Labour government of the late 1940s after it had been swept to power in response to a national mood that was very sympathetic to egalitarianism, but the welfare state's underlying philosophy owed much to the work of Keynes and Beveridge, who were more liberals than socialists.

What began with the modest aim of ameliorating the lot of the poor, the unemployed, the sick, and the children in an age when general living standards were one-quarter of today's level has, paradoxically, grown to account for half of total government expenditure in an age of unprecedented affluence.[2] It is manned by strongly organized and powerful professional and bureaucratic vested interests. Such a massive involvement by the state has fuelled criticisms from the various strands of the New Right and corresponding answers and justifications from the Left. The need for state intervention in the form of social security, medical care, and housing is now less obviously justifiable than it was in the early-twentieth century when the poor were far more numerous and consciences could be awakened by disturbing evidence. Even though poverty is a relative concept, the fact of our contemporary general affluence and raised average levels of consumption means that proponents of the welfare state have been forced to base their arguments on different grounds than by simply appealing to the rich to help the poor. Although such appeals to conscience are still employed, the dominant theme in today's defences of the welfare state has tended to shift to the concept that we share a common humanity, we are all 'citizens' and have a duty to care for one another just like members of a single family. The state makes the expression of our 'caring' for others possible with greater efficiency than does the free market or private charity.

The citizenship principle

The idea that the welfare state is an expression of our natural desire to express mutual generosity has been passionately expounded by, among others, R. H. Tawney, R. M. Titmuss, and P. Townsend; such views have become the basis of the defence of state welfare.[3] The recommendations of these advocates have been felt by some to require more rigorous analysis in order to establish them on a firm moral basis that might effectively demolish the liberal-market critique. Such an approach is that of Harris (1987). He aims to rebut those familiar criticisms by the market liberals that were mentioned in Chapter 6 on 'Equality'; such as the idea that social justice is a mirage, that the welfare state is coercive, and that taxation is a form of theft. The dominant theme of his approach is that social justice consists in protecting the status of individuals as full members of the community; this is what is meant by 'citizenship'. Social policy must not be confined to 'mere' need; it must provide the material basis for participation in the 'way of life of the society' (Harris, 1987). The preference for universalist welfare policies referred to in Chapter 6 is to protect the indigent from being branded as a public burden. Harris shows his awareness of the dangers of 'traditional bureaucratic

Fabianism'. Welfare services must provide 'opportunities for participation in flexible and decentralised structures rooted in local communities' (Harris, 1987: 146). The reply to Nozick's assertion that taxation is theft is to argue that it is justified on the grounds that the state is merely claiming back that portion of wealth which state institutions have created. 'My suggestion is that we do not have an entitlement to full control over what we earn'. We have a duty to compensate those who bear the burdens of insecurity in the market (Harris, 1987: 118). Taxation is seen as morally justifiable as noted in Chapter 6, because it is a form of 'compensation' which is owed by the successful to those who, through no fault of their own, are pushed down below some generally agreed level: they have 'a claim in justice to be raised up to it' (Harris, 1987: 163). An interesting qualification to citizenship theory is offered in the case of those individuals who, though in need of help, are personally responsible for their own condition, for example, where illness has been caused by smoking or alcohol abuse; in these cases, treatment can only be seen as an act of charity and cannot be demanded as a right. The obvious objection to this is to consider whether this would apply to overeating, or skin cancer caused by too much sunbathing. A free-market approach on the other hand, would give the individual the choice of harming himself and then paying for it, either from his own income or by the use of state vouchers. In either case he is not forced to accept charity.

The citizenship defence of the welfare state demands a wider moral vision than prevails in today's social services. Such a reformed welfare state would rely heavily on a 'sense of duty or community' to prevent or minimize abuse of the system; it implies a belief in the innate decency of individuals once they are given the right setting. This is in sharp contrast to the free-market approach relying as it always has on harnessing, not the 'best' of human motives, but the strongest – self-interest. This is the deep division that separates the idealistic socialist from the more sceptical (realistic?) market liberal.

The public-good hypothesis

Some defences of the welfare state rest on the hypothesis that its very existence is explained as a reflection of the human desire to care for others. This hypothesis can be supported by arguing that there is much evidence of altruistic concern for others among small groups, as when a disastrous accident occurs locally. By analogy there is some justification for having a third party, an agency that links the 'concern' of one group for a distant one – the state being the obvious 'third party' (Bosanquet, 1983). A more 'hard-headed' version of this is the argument of some economists that the relief of poverty is a public good. The existence of people in need of help distresses the more fortunate, therefore they benefit by its alleviation. We might then be willing to contribute to the relief of poverty provided everyone else did (the 'free-rider' situation).[4] It may come as something of a surprise that Milton Friedman 'accepts . . . this line of reasoning as justifying governmental action to alleviate poverty' (Friedman, 1962: 190). The mechanism he proposes to take account of this is negative income tax. Friedman's 'public good' argument leaves untouched his attachment to the belief that individuals are the best judges of their own interests. The public-good theory can be used to justify most parts of the welfare state, but it has been contended that it fundamentally rests on the fallacy that the individual receives equal benefit from giving to a charitable cause whether he or someone else does the giving.[5]

Egalitarianism

State-provided welfare services are often justified on the basis that inequality of treatment is irrational. This has been especially applied to the provision of medical attention: 'the proper ground of distribution of medical care is ill health: this is a necessary truth', says Bernard Williams.[6] Although this may well be a desirable ideal, it ignores the problem of where the resources to meet 'needs' are to come from or who is to allocate them. From the liberal standpoint individuals' rights to dispose of their own justly acquired property should also be the object of rational thought (Nozick, 1974: 233–5).

There is, however, a widespread belief that the welfare state's major justification is the pursuit of equality; but there is evidently some disappointment over the success achieved. J. le Grand in *The Strategy of Equality*, 1982, deplores what he regards as the inherent inability of public expenditure on the social services to achieve equality; the forces that perpetuate inequality, he claims, are too strong to be overcome merely by expanding public expenditure. He argues for a more radical approach that attacks inequalities at their source. Hindess (1987) presents some evidence which suggests that egalitarianism has not been as important as it has been made out to be. This is particularly so in the case of the National Health Service. In so far as the medical profession supported the new service in 1948, it was on the grounds that it would provide a more rational and efficient form of organization. Although egalitarianism played some part in its formation, much of the support for the NHS came from a diversity of other interests and motives such as the desire of consultants to have access to the most advanced medical technology (Hindess, 1987: 91–3).

Marxism and the welfare state

Although it would be the task of a lifetime to know in detail all the multitude of variants of original Marxist thought on most subjects, the generally accepted Marxist view is that it is wrong to regard the welfare state as an expression of the concern of the state for the welfare of its citizens, as in the egalitarian or citizenship explanations. The true state of affairs is that the welfare state serves the capitalist economy. Marx himself had argued that the Factory Acts served the capitalist class by preventing the exhaustion of the labour force. The state in a capitalist economy merely plays a part in the class struggle on the side of the ruling class. The state health-care and education services are there to serve the interests of the capitalist class; the NHS is for keeping the labour force in good condition so as to work efficiently and the function of education is to shape the young into the right habits of work and give them the appropriate skills to serve the requirements of capitalism. The intellectually unsatisfying nature of such an explanation for the welfare state accounts for the endless disputes among Marxists as they struggle to reconcile the contradictions thrown up by their basic theory of the structure of society. Much of the trouble arises from the attempt to explain all political and social and economic phenomena in terms of the class struggle: 'To treat the forces engaged in promoting social change ... or in preventing it, as if they were classes, is at best allegorical ... and at worst thoroughly misleading' (Hindess, 1987: 119). In terms of Austrian methodological individualism the root cause of the lack of rigour of the Marxist explanation thus lies in the holistic attribution of a collective will to 'classes'.

AUSTRIANS AND STATE WELFARE

There are several elements in Austrian political philosophy that generate scepticism concerning the beneficence of state welfare. The attachment to individualism as against holism as a reliable tool for the explanation of social reality has been discussed in Chapter 1; in addition there are the beliefs that the relevant knowledge cannot be gathered centrally by one mind or group of minds (the *synoptic delusion*); the dangers from monopoly in state services; the inevitable coercion; and the stifling of the competitive process – the only reliable method of allowing the market to discover the relevant knowledge and yield a true measure of efficiency. All this is not so very different from, say, the Friedmanite Right, with which much of the Austrian diagnosis agrees. The differences lie mainly in the Austrian emphasis on the undesirability of the welfare state as an example of governments' pretensions of knowledge and the fact that neo-classical economists take insufficient account of the market as a discovery procedure; the market is not only for using resources efficiently. In contrast to the Austrians there are, for example, many economists who, although they are critical of the efficiency of state welfare, would not propose any radical dismantling of state health care, in favour of private provision.

We have already met the *synoptic delusion*, 'the fiction that all the relevant facts are known to some one mind' derived from Cartesian scientism and constructivism as developed by August Comte. Plans made centrally assume away the central problem; the apparent beauty and orderliness of such plans are owed to the planner's disregard of all the facts he does not know (Hayek, 1982. vol. 1: 14–15). The use of computers does not remove the problem – the computer cannot *discover* the relevant facts.

Hayek's generally critical view of state welfare as we have mentioned in Chapter 6 is tempered by a humane and common-sense acceptance that there are some common needs that can be satisfied only by collective action (Hayek, 1982, vol. 2: 87; 1960: 285). He distinguishes between two conceptions of social security. First, 'a limited security which can be achieved for all and which is, therefore, no privilege, and absolute security, which in a free society cannot be achieved for all' (Hayek, 1960: 259). The welfare state is inspired by the desire to achieve a more equal distribution of goods and involves treating people unequally;[7] it aims at 'social justice', is coercive, and 'is bound to lead back to socialism' (Hayek, 1960: 260).

The welfare state prevents the emergence of alternative solutions that might have been more effective. Like all state monopolies it stifles those very forces – the discovery process – which lead to the future growth of knowledge.

The arguments for the state taking sole charge of such services as health care, education, or housing can be very persuasive but the result is a form of paternalism in which whole professions in medicine or education become 'unitary bureaucratic hierarchies' and the decisions of authority determine what people get.

Democratic control of the activities of the administrators of the welfare state is a myth. An administrative apparatus given exclusive power to carry out the instructions of a legislature 'is the most dangerous arrangement possible' (Hayek, 1960: 261). It becomes increasingly what Mises describes as a 'hegemonic system'. People having chosen such subordination 'no longer act for themselves, they are taken care of' (Mises, 1966: 196).

Finally, where private initiative cannot be relied upon to provide certain services, Hayek favours action by local authorities, which, he says, have fewer dangers arising from coercive action of government, as well as permitting some degree of competition between rival authorities: people have the freedom to move house to a different local authority.

Hayek's acceptance of the need initially to provide for the unfortunate through state compulsory social insurance is qualified by his fear that what began as humane help to the 'deserving poor', inevitably becomes a tool of egalitarian redistribution, and loses whatever resemblance to insurance it may ever have had. In private insurance schemes the individual is offered a choice as to how much protection he wants – as in house, life, or car insurance. The state, on the other hand, having no fear of competition, can safely discriminate between groups, though all pay the same premiums. State social insurance is not really insurance at all; its purpose is different.

The complexity of the rules and regulations of the social security system render it incomprehensible to the ordinary person and even those who administer it are, in practice, often ignorant of all the fine details; thus it escapes real democratic control. State social security produces the paradox that the same mass of people who are assumed unable to make their own choices are entrusted with voting for governments that decide how to spend their incomes on their behalf.

In Hayek's view, the power of the state has been used to buy votes:

'Dispensing gratuities at the expense of somebody else *who cannot be readily identified* became the most attractive way of buying majority support' (Hayek, 1982, vol. 3: 103). Such a government becomes vulnerable to the blackmail of pressure groups.

THE BRITISH NATIONAL HEALTH SERVICE

Clear-headed, rational public discussion on this subject has become difficult in the face of people's apparently strong emotional attachment to the NHS. Alternative suggestions to free medical services for all are regularly howled down as being 'uncaring' and even the supposedly 'radical right' Conservative government elected in 1987 has felt compelled to declare its purity. ('the NHS is safe with us') and periodically to 'find' extra millions to try to still the clamour from the NHS unions supported by much of the media (even the dreaded 'Tory press'). The simple facts of economics: that resources are scarce and have alternative uses – both within the medical services and in relation to other nonmedical purposes – tend to be lost in the general uproar. The ample evidence from the academic research that is available on the economics of medical provision seems hardly to get a mention on television, in Parliamentary debate, or in the newspapers. This is true of other issues, of course, but the NHS in its present form does seem to be relatively more protected by a magic circle that forbids the introduction of much realism into any public discussion. The NHS is regarded as the jewel in the crown of the welfare state. However, the conclusion that the general public approve of the NHS in its present form has been challenged as being based on faulty opinion polls. Five surveys conducted by the IEA between 1963 and 1987, designed so as to present respondents with questions in which alternative costs and tax implications were specified have led the researchers to conclude that there exists a substantial desire for choice outside the state system.[8]

The argument that the NHS cannot meet all the demands made upon it because the services are free to the individual at the point of consumption does not lead socialists to the conclusion that the NHS should be privatized; it becomes an argument for the view that society must distribute these limited resources in accordance with social justice. If medical resources are inadequate one reason is that the state has decided to allocate its revenue to some other 'less essential' purposes.

In the arguments over health services we have a very clear example of the fundamental moral divide between Left and Right. On the one hand is Hayek who tells us that collective majority decisions to take from the rich and give to the poor are immoral; on the other hand is the socialist belief that all human beings are equally valuable and that consequently society has an 'obligation to provide them with as equal a share of society's benefits as it is possible to distribute', it being admitted that there is no way of logically justifying this belief – to socialists it is self-evident (Hattersley, 1987: 92). As we have mentioned before, the Hayekian attitude to the succour of the needy is not quite so 'uncaring' as it is often made out to be and there would remain many awkward problems even in a society committed to the socialist principle of equal treatment.[9] There is obviously no logical method of deciding between these two views of the moral foundations of how medical services should be allocated but the debate about the NHS is not concluded merely by insisting on the ideal of equal treatment for all without regard to ability to pay; there are other problems. How should the resources *within* the NHS be allocated between competing ends? Does the NHS as at present organized serve the cause of equality or is it dominated by middle-class interests? How is the efficiency of a state monopoly to be assessed? These, and related questions would remain to be answered even in the socialist ideal of a system that aims to give equal treatment to all who need it, irrespective of wealth. But at the same time there is very little support for a wholly market solution. Even IEA publications support *some* degree of free, state-provided medical care: 'the government should protect the poor, so that no-one is denied essential health care due to their inability to pay' (Green, 1986: 101).

The 'York school'

This is a group of economists who have specialized in the study of health economics at the University of York and have, over the past few years, produced a great deal of rigorous analysis[10] and recommendations for reform. In spite of the diligent research and the abundance of proposals for reform from the York economists (and others) the relatively insignificant results in terms of actual changes in the NHS are a tribute to the public affection it seems to enjoy and the consequent reluctance, even among the 'Thatcherites' to change anything. As Arthur Seldon said in 1980 the NHS is 'virtually irreversible except by political earthquake'.[11]

The York economists, though critical of the NHS, remain committed to its ideals and do not believe that a free market in health care would solve all the problems. Three main difficulties, however, are inherent in the economics of health care, whether supplied privately or by the state. First, the demand for health care comes, not from 'consumers' but from doctors; second, whether health care is paid for by private or state insurance there is no incentive for doctors or patients to economize resources; and third, the monopoly power of the medical professionals who are expected to act in the best interests, as they see it, of their patients, but who act against a background of ignorance since little scientific evaluation is carried out of the effectiveness of their therapies. Neither are they required to be much concerned about the cost-effectiveness of what they are doing, despite the fact that there are wide divergences of practice as between different doctors and hospitals.

The 'York' analysis concludes that, despite the considerable expenditure on state-provided health services, which increased by 30 per cent in real terms between 1982 and 1988 and the staff of which has doubled in numbers in the last 20 years, the health status of the population has not changed rapidly in the last three or four decades, and such changes as have occurred have been caused by factors other than medical attention. Maynard's evidence from international comparative data tends to refute the common assumption propagated by health-care pressure groups that an increase in health care necessarily produces an increase in health status. Many medical services are devoted to caring for people who are likely to die from the effects of their lifetime behaviour. Therefore, it is argued that expenditure on educating people in such things as road safety and reducing tobacco and alcohol consumption, and getting people to adopt better diets and to take more regular exercise would do more to reduce premature death rates in the long run than such expensive medical technologies as the glamour-medical specialisms such as organ transplants or 'test-tube' babies. The 'York' alternative to more expenditure within the NHS is logically persuasive, yet has made little impact on policy. Evidently there is a widespread and grateful acceptance of the view that the NHS is always *there*, to comfort and relieve disease and pain even if it is one's own fault; education in health care is unpopular because of the rejection of paternalism.

Nevertheless, economists should continue to point to the realities of the present system if only in the hope of influencing efforts to improve its rationality and efficiency.

Reform of the NHS

One of the most prolific sources of suggested alternative possibilities is to be found in the numerous IEA studies. These are mostly regarded by socialists as right-wing polemics, yet some of their criticisms are directed at the failure of the NHS to achieve some socialist ideals; middle-class interests prevail over those of the poor and inarticulate; through reliance on taxation less of UK national income goes towards health care than in the USA or Europe; its paternalism undermines the capacity of people to control their own destinies and induces in patients over-reverence for those who decide for them with a minimum of consultation or participation. These are all the kind of ideals that citizenship theory supports, yet radical reform of the NHS in the direction of granting the individual greater autonomy is usually viewed with suspicion or bigotry by socialists. The fact that there may be those on the Right whose true motive is to grind the faces of the poor should not be used to justify a total refusal to discuss alternatives.

In his latest IEA publication, *Everyone a Private Patient* (1988), Dr David Green argues that without radical reform the NHS will continue to be plagued with problems: it suffers from rising demands from the professionals for expensive equipment and drugs coupled with the underfunding, which is a consequence of over-reliance on taxation. In an earlier study Green took issue with the York economists on the grounds that they fail to take enough account of the market as, in Hayek's words a 'discovery procedure'. What he describes as Professor Maynard's 'sticks-and-carrots' approach presumes that governments are able to know in advance how best to spend money on health care. But in fact the best combinations of medical practice, the most able doctors, and the most cost-effective methods of health-care supply cannot be known in advance as they are always changing; only a market can generate the relevant knowledge (Green, 1985: 26–7).

In *Everyone a Private Patient* (Green, 1988), it is argued that the health-care services would be improved by changing to an insurance-based system. The root of the trouble is that government has, for 40 years, both financed and produced services through the NHS; since there is no pricing of services, demand exceeds supply and resources are arbitrarily allocated. Merely throwing more money at the NHS misses the real problem. Green's solution, contained in a set of specific proposals, is to move to an insurance-based system. The NHS should continue to be financed by taxation but people who are dissatisfied should be allowed to choose private insurance cover and take all or part of their tax payments with them. The egalitarian argument that queue-jumping is reprehensible can only be justified if there is some reason to suppose that the supply of medical services is, in some way, different from other services in being completely inelastic. They may be in the short run, but the fact that in Western Europe and the USA, a larger proportion of GNP goes on health-care than in the UK, suggests that supply would respond to the increase in privately financed demand in the long run. One of the strongest arguments against present single schemes of state 'insurance' is 'that their introduction is the kind of politically irrevocable measure that will have to be continued, whether it proves a mistake or not' (Hayek, 1960: 298).

It is widely believed that the British NHS compares favourably with the American system of health care in which the poor, it is alleged, may be left to die while the better off are often brought to bankruptcy by the inflated bills from doctors performing un-necessary operations. Even the critics of the NHS admit that there is some truth in these allegations. But the conclusion that this is just what you would expect with a free market in medicine may be too hasty. It may have more to do with the monopoly power of the medical profession conferred upon it by state or federal government that stifled competition. The monopoly power of the American Medical Association extended to prevent competition between private medical insurance companies, as well as to restrict entry to the profession and control fees. In the past decade the market in American health care has been greatly extended by pro-competition measures enforced by the Federal Trade Commission. Health Main-tenance Organizations of various types have been encouraged, which market themselves as cost-effective suppliers. These depend for their success on being able to offer comprehensive medical services at a competitive price by searching out cost-effective suppliers (see Green, 1986). Even supposing, however, that competition would greatly improve efficiency and shift the balance of power more towards the patient, there remains the question of what should be done to ensure that those unable to afford it get the medical treatment they may need. The free-market solution is to provide the poor with vouchers sufficient to buy specific health services through health-purchase unions who would be responsible for getting the best deal for their members.

All these kinds of suggestions are anathema to collectivists but whilst the citizenship or communitarian ideals are quite noble in their aspirations, they fail to convince that they face up squarely to the implications of scarce resources, the monopoly power of the professions, and that the present system fails to give the individual power to spend more on health care than the taxed-based system permits. Furthermore, even if state expenditure continues to increase there can be little confidence that the money will be spent according to any rationally derived criteria.

The reluctance of British Governments to tackle reform of the NHS is the fear that we may end up with a two-tier system with people who are poor and chronically ill left in the state system and the rest going private. But there is already a two-tier system with 5 million people in private schemes. The attempt to reduce waiting lists within the NHS is likely to fail; as more resources become available 'free' there is greater incentive for private patients to transfer back to the NHS. Simply 'making more funds available' from the Exchequer cannot be regarded as the *only* sensible option.

CONCLUSIONS

The debate on the welfare state is the outstanding example in social policy of the clash between freedom and equality. The individualist assumes that free enterprise can best effect social aims; the collectivist denies this. Citizenship theorists would like the social services to be, not regrettable necessities, but something to be proud of, having a function beyond that of merely being a safety net for the casualties of capitalism. In its present form, the welfare state fails to fulfil the aspirations of egalitarians; it has not done much to equalize 'life chances'. The libertarian critique of collectivism agrees with this in one important respect: that the welfare state tends to favour, not the poor, but the middle-income groups. The introduction of compulsory state welfare in Britain was, in this view, only made possible by the virtual destruction of the growing voluntary friendly-society movement and the corresponding granting of increased monopoly power to the doctors and commercial insurance companies. Mutual aid organized voluntarily by the working class thus virtually withered away (see Green, 1982). The universality of the welfare state does not follow Rawls's principle that society should try to maximize the welfare of its worst-off members.

An important aspect of the welfare state that is often overlooked is the incentive effects of some services and grants. For example, the increase in single-parent families may not be entirely due to changes in accepted attitudes to divorce and the removal of the stigma surrounding illegitimacy; there is an economic factor at work. If the state, through its provision of grants of various kinds, renders certain ways of living less unattractive, then there will probably be an increase in the membership of the categories at whom help is directed.

One argument for the abolition of private-health and education provision is that state services would be improved if the middle classes were forced to use the state system. But within a monopoly state system it is the well-connected and influential who are likely to be able to obtain benefits at the expense of ordinary people. In a competitive system the latter, though unable to pull strings politically, have the powerful weapon of being able to transfer their custom. Socialist states are characterized by the existence of privileged services for party members and powerful bureaucrats.

As far as health services are concerned, the Conservative governments of the 1980s have very largely failed to take any practical steps towards breaking the state monopoly. Some NHS services such as cleaning, catering, and laundry have been opened up to competitive tendering. But there is little evidence that the NHS is to be reformed in response to the voluminous criticisms from the economic liberals. It remains to be seen whether the government's White Paper proposals (January 1989), deserve the accolade 'radical', but there are several features that make it hard to forecast the eventual picture. The undoubted difficulties facing the reformer are partly the consequence of the politicians' fears of upsetting the electorate and the existence of what Friedman called the 'iron triangles': 'at one corner are the direct beneficiaries of a law; at a second, the legislative committees and their staffs; at a third, the bureaucracy administering a law. These three powerful tyrannies enforce the status quo' (Friedman, 1985: 46).

Socialists often depict those who advocate a reduction of state monopoly in the welfare state as simply reflecting the interests of the rich and the powerful who wish to return to 'uncaring' nineteenth-century values. But collectivists may be the ones who are clinging to old values. A hundred years ago, the existence of widespread misery among the poor was a strong argument for state welfare. The great increase in living standards means that massive monopoly state welfare is not necessarily appropriate, and that alternatives deserve to be looked at with an open mind.

Chapter Eight

UNEMPLOYMENT AND INFLATION

If he were alive today J. M. Keynes might, at least temporarily, be puzzled by the concomitance of unemployment and inflation and there is the additional question of how high pay rises persist alongside chronically high unemployment. The extent of the scholarly and journalistic debate on the subject is vast, certainly far exceeding the scope of a single chapter to provide more than the barest outline.[1] However, through the thickets, there may be distinguished two main categories in which the many and varied arguments roughly might be placed: on the one hand, the contention that labour is too expensive and on the other hand that the demand for labour is too low. There is a third subsidiary response, which is the belief that the problem is not as bad as it seems because the official figures overstate the problem because of the existence of a significant number of fraudulent claims for unemployment benefit.

No single generally accepted explanation exists for the prolonged rise in unemployment that began in the late 1960s, and the Keynesian v. Monetarism dichotomy is but a crude populist representation of the true nature of the question and is increasingly regarded as leading nowhere.

DEFINITION, MEASUREMENT, AND TRENDS

Discovering the true nature of the causes of unemployment has been much bedevilled by arguments about how it should be calculated, with mutual accusations that governments 'massage' statistics downward and that their opponents exaggerate the true position – 'the unemployment numbers game'. These quarrels are mostly of little value to the quest for an explanation for the unarguable fact that unemployment, however we measure it, began to be a problem in the 1970s, and continued to increase until about the middle of 1986. According to the official figures,[2] in common with many advanced economies, unemployment in the UK stayed low throughout the 1950s and 1960s within the range of 1–3 per cent of total employees; since 1970 there have been three cycles with the peak of each one higher than its predecessor. It reached 5 per cent by the end of 1977, declining a little to 4 per cent through to 1980. In the first half of the 1980s it doubled and reached a peak in 1986 of 3.3 million (11.6 per cent). Since then and up to Autumn 1988 it has declined to 2.2 million (8 per cent).

For the 1970s the average annual inflation rate was around 14 per cent. As unemployment rose so the inflation rate fell steadily through the 1980s: from 18 per cent in 1980 to about 3–4 per cent between 1985 and the beginning of 1988. At the time of writing the rate has started to move up again (to almost 7 per cent) more-or-less in step with the recent downward trend of unemployment. Clearly comparisons of the trends of unemployment and inflation suggest a number of possible explanations. One important view is that there exists for any economy an underlying rate of unemployment that cannot be lowered without *accelerating* inflation. Any attempt to get unemployment down below this rate merely by government spending will lead to accelerating inflation. This rate of unemployment, labelled the 'natural rate' by Friedman, is now known as that strange beast NAIRU (non-accelerating inflation rate of unemployment). It should be noticed that NAIRU is not some sort of official statistic but a purely theoretical concept.

From the strictly economic point of view the search for the 'true' unemployment rate is futile. On the one hand, there are probably some people who at present are not seen as part of the workforce and who might offer themselves for work if the rewards were great enough; on the other hand, some of the unemployed would find work if they were prepared to work for sufficiently low pay.

DEMAND DEFICIENCY OR LABOUR-MARKET FAILURE?

No answer to the problem of unemployment can be found until a deceptively simple question is answered: is it caused by a deficiency of demand or does the main cause lie in labour-market inflexibility? The way in which this question is answered roughly divides

164

Keynesians from the liberal free-market tradition (which includes Austrians). The solution of the Keynesians is more expenditure, whether financed by governments through Budget deficits or by individuals and companies by tax cuts or easier credit. The other school believes that labour costs must be reduced by various methods, including the reduction of trade-union monopolies. There must also be mentioned a fallacy that has deep historical roots, is remarkably resistant to demolition by a consideration of the evidence, and confuses and impedes attempted solutions. This has been described as the 'lump of labour' fallacy. It is especially trotted out whenever any new labour-saving technique or invention appears. This, it is then believed, will lead to an increase in unemployment, whereas the history of the last century shows no evidence to support this view. The fact is that the increased productivity has been associated with an increase in total employment and continued additions to the list of different possible occupations. The liberal free market viewpoint is commonly and mistakenly labelled as 'monetarism'; though the latter is really only a doctrine that advocates a particular technique aimed at controlling money GDP or aggregate demand, and squeezing out the inflation, which is seen as a necessary condition for the reduction of unemployment.

The neo-classical or free market economists see labour as a factor of production with a range of prices for different kinds. If wages are inflexible downward, then a fall in the demand for labour will cause unemployment, because from an employer's point of view his costs of production (the real product wage) are greater than the value of labour's marginal product. Also, relatively high labour costs may lead to the substitution of capital for labour. Wage flexibility is important because of the constant change that goes on in the market economy; the movement of prices serves to reallocate resources and if wages are inflexible, workers will not have an incentive to move from jobs, the demand for which is falling, to those for which demand is rising. The three chief reasons given by the free market proponents for this inflexibility are the influence of trade unions, the tax and benefit system, and the rent-controlled housing market.

The Keynesians, on the other hand, while accepting that wages may well be 'sticky downwards' regard the tight monetary and fiscal policies of the Conservative governments of the 1980s as having been pursued with ideological fanaticism and having resulted in insufficient demand. In this view the way to increase spending and thus to increase employment is to link such expansionary policies with incomes policies to prevent wages 'taking off'.

The conflict between these two opposing views continues in spite of attempts to evaluate the relative importance of the various alleged causes of unemployment, but the Keynesians have undoubtedly been on the defensive since their version of demand management became associated with the alarming inflation rates coupled with the insidiously rising unemployment of the 1970s.

THE FAILURE OF DEMAND MANAGEMENT

Whether or not demand management has in fact really failed is by no means universally accepted as a fair statement of the truth but what can be asserted with confidence is that the conventional wisdom in macroeconomic policy that dominated affairs from the end of the Second World War to the late 1960s began to be under attack by a counterrevolution usually described as 'monetarist'. It is still arguable whether Keynesian demand management was in fact what Keynes himself would have advocated and it is now dangerous, following years of analysis of what Keynes 'really' meant coupled with the subsequent accretion of much scholarly revision and extension of the *General Theory*, to give a modern concise definition of Keynesian demand management.[3] However, the essence of Keynesianism, as it came to be applied after 1945, was the belief that governments could act so as to ensure full employment through increases, when necessary, in total expenditure. Inflation was not for some time seen as a great threat[4] and even when it was, the favoured medicine was incomes policies involving price and wage controls and optimistic arrangements between governments and unions such as the 'social contract'. An important corollary of post-war Keynesianism was that *only* government action could maintain full employment in a capitalist economy, a conclusion that greatly pleased socialists. This was because the *General Theory* implied that the market economy was inherently unstable since the level of economic activity was sustained by private investment; this in turn was dependent upon the fluctuating expectations of entrepreneurs and investors. Such expectations must inevitably be largely guesswork. The state, on the other hand, could compensate for a fall in private investment by expansionary monetary and fiscal policies; thus, could booms and slumps be ironed out. The central task of economic policy was now accepted, with a remarkable degree of unanimity by politicians, civil servants, and economists as being the management of demand. The few voices of dissent were ignored or dismissed as reactionary. Also widely accepted was the view that economic growth would be ensured through such policies because of the constant stimulating effect of full employment. Inflation, should it become a problem, would be best dealt with by incomes policies. In the late 1950s, however, A. W. Phillips' study of the relationship between unemployment and wage-rate changes during the period 1861–1957 generated the famous 'Phillips' curve', which graphically suggested a 'trade-off' between unemployment and inflation. The view then gained many adherents among policy-makers that a price might have to be paid for full employment in terms of some inflation but the idea that a *bit* of inflation might prove unsustainable without consequences for unemployment was not at first apparent. The Phillips curve appeared to provide a neat justification, if one were needed, for macroeconomic interventionism.

By the late 1960s the Phillips curve hypothesis was breaking down in many countries: *both* inflation and unemployment were rising alarmingly. The debate among economists revealed a fallacy at the core of the Phillips' analysis; this was to confuse real with nominal (money) wages. Real wages can remain constant provided nominal wages and the price level are changing at the same *rate*, whether rising or falling. Phillips' apparent neglect of the importance of the price level may be explained by the fact that he was working within the Keynesian system. It was natural for him to follow Keynes' assumptions: first, that prices are rigid in the sense that people do not plan their behaviour allowing for the possibility that the price level might change, regarding changes in nominal wages or prices as a change in real wages or real prices; second, that workers could be persuaded to accept the lower real wages consequent upon inflation, whereas they would have resisted taking wage cuts.[5] The second blow to the original Phillips curve came when a number of attempts failed to find similar results at different times and places. Finally, came *stagflation*, with the concurrence of high unemployment, high inflation rates, and low growth rates – the worst of all possible macroeconomic worlds.

After this, Friedman (and others) reinterpreted the long-run Phillips curve as being vertical, with the 'trade-off' virtually nil – arising from the fact that inflation would be anticipated in the formulation of wage claims. However much inflation might be increased, unemployment would return to the same level – the 'natural rate'. Thus, in the 1980s demand management as pursued hitherto, became unfashionable both in Western Europe and the USA.

Incomes policies

The proliferation of policies designed to apply the necessary curb on incomes implied by Keynesian demand management even exceeded the number of 'national' plans that flowered in the 1960s and 1970s. It was found necessary to call successive ventures by different names in order to allay scepticism born of experience and to whip up enthusiasm for the latest scheme. Thus we had the Macmillan Wage and Price Plateau, 1956; the Selwyn Lloyd Pay Pause, 1961–2; the Guiding Lights, 1963–6; the Wage Freeze, 1966–7; the Stages I, II, and III 'Freezes', 1972–4; and finally, the crowning glory of the Social Contract, 1974–6. In spite of all this activity inflation continued and eventually even accelerated to 24 per cent in 1975, but it is only fair to note that some of this was attributable to the fourfold increase in oil prices at the end of 1973.

In spite of these failures incomes policies still retain some appeal, though nowadays post-Keynesians generally concede that demand-management policies must, to achieve success, be implemented alongside measures to improve the supply side.[6] Demand-management advocates have sought for alternative forms of incomes policy that might avoid past mistakes. One variant is the tax-based incomes policy. In principle this consists of the imposition of a surtax on any firm that grants wage increases in excess of some government guideline. An alternative variant would be to reward those firms granting wage increases *below* the guideline. Apart from the difficulties of administering such schemes their unfavourable effects on market allocative mechanisms must be weighed against any benefits.

Moderate socialists still have faith in incomes policies: 'A national view on the overall level and general distribution of wages must become a permanent part of both our economic and social strategy' (Hattersley, 1987: 241). Socialist incomes policy is thus not only to establish general income and prices guidelines but – a more complicated business – to decide *relative* incomes.

168

LABOUR-MARKET DISTORTIONS

The failures of 'fine-tuning' demand-management and incomes policies have led to the focus of attention shifting to the market for labour, and especially to the role of the trade unions. There are two main ways in which the labour market[7] is distorted, leading to high unit-wage costs: the power of unions to raise wages and the unemployment benefit system. Only a fundamental reform of the labour market can, on this view, reduce the 'natural' rate of unemployment.[8]

Collective wage bargaining

The contention that union-monopoly power prices workers out of jobs is regarded as obviously true, especially by, but by no means exclusively, the New Right.[9] The connection between the traditional concentration of unions on getting the biggest wage rises and the increase in unemployment is deplored even in a book that offers a Marxist diagnosis of the problem, speaking of the traditional union leadership as maximizing 'the earnings of the employed workforce, however small it may become, and however long the dole queue' (Jordan, 1982).

The crux of the matter is the assertion that collective bargaining is the strongest of all the factors that inhibit the operation of the labour market. If the price of labour of a given level of productivity is increased, less of it will be demanded. This produces 'a class of "insiders" – members of unions that have successfully achieved higher rates of pay – and "outsiders" – the unemployed or the low paid' (Minford, 1987: 131). The outsiders are deprived of market power. The only way out is to replace *collective* bargaining by *competitive* bargaining (Minford, 1987: 135). The rapid rises in real wages of the employed – at about 4 per cent per year in recent years – are at the expense of the unemployed. In order to place this thesis on a firm footing the question must be answered: does collective bargaining really raise wages above what they would have been in a competitive market? A number of empirical investigations suggest that trade-union 'mark-ups' in Britain range from 4 per cent for middle managers to 25 per cent of some semi-skilled manual workers (Minford, 1987: 136).

The source of union power in Britain lies chiefly in the legal immunities they were granted under the Trade Disputes Act, 1906.

The legislation of the 1980s, although it has resulted in some significant reforms, has left some important privileges intact. The step-by-step approach to reform of union law of the Conservative governments of the 1980s has made significant inroads into excessive union immunities but for the zealots of the New Right more needs to be done. First, they would like to see immunities removed entirely from unions in essential services, especially where health and safety is at risk; second, employees in such essential services should be required to sign a new contract of employment including a no-strike clause; third, other methods of settling disputes in such services would be provided, as they are now for the police; fourth, all secondary strikes, as well as secondary picketing should be made unlawful. All attempts to reduce the legal privileges of the unions will be weakened, however, if the monopoly 'public-sector' unions are able to pass on to the consumer or taxpayer higher prices or lower quality of service. Thus, for example, trade-union law reform should be reinforced by the introduction of more competition into areas such as education, health care, and postal services.[10]

The 'right to strike' has been questioned as deriving from an outdated concept of the worker as a 'wage-slave' without resources of his own faced by a powerful employer. This picture has been 'undermined by the spread in personal ownership of property, in their homes, pensions, equity shares, and rising incomes and standards of living' (Hanson and Mather, 1988: 28). Various proposals are put forward for reform, the most important being the deregulation and individualizing of the labour market allowing employers and workers to agree that their relationship is one of self-employment, free from the regulations attaching to employment contracts. This could be done by changing the law such that employers and workers have a right to choose a self-employed relationship. Also: benign neglect should be shown by the executive arm of the state towards laws governing minimum wages and employment protection (Minford, 1985; 6).

All these kinds of proposals are naturally regarded by the Left as putting back the clock to the nineteenth century, and leaving the individual worker powerless, especially now that he is often faced with a powerful multinational company.[11] Judgement on the New Right's proposals depends a great deal on the realism of their picture of the modern worker as now a free-wheeling property-owning individual who is quite capable of holding his own, and entering into agreements on an equal basis with his employer under the ordinary law of contract; but Unions must still have a useful role in protecting an individual worker, who through age, sickness, or the obsolescence of his particular skill may be 'picked-off' and harshly treated, even if complete deregulation were to prevail.

The unemployment benefit system

Disincentive effects will, to some degree, be inevitable in any system of benefits. This has been described as the 'moral hazard'. The wages 'floor' is set by the level of unemployment benefits and if the pay of the lower-paid is less than the value of the total package of benefits for the unemployed, vacancies at the bottom end of the wage scale will remain unfilled, while at the same time the unemployed will tend to seek work in the 'black economy'; all this is obvious.[12] The difficult question is how can things be improved? The reforms of the social-security system introduced in April 1988 removed some of the worst features; it is now less possible for someone in work to earn more but end up worse off, but any means-tested system faces the same problem. If the benefits are increased, the disincentive effect is increased, and on the other hand, if benefits are reduced there is a risk of pushing some families into deep poverty. A grave weakness of the present system, it has been argued, is the way in which it penalizes part-time work. Part-time workers may only keep £5 a week after which they lose a pound in benefit for every extra pound they earn. This acts as a disincentive for someone who has been unemployed for a long time to use a part-time job as a stepping-stone to full-time work. The remarkable fact is that there are probably large numbers who choose to work even though they would be better off exploiting the social-security system.

One set of proposals consists of the setting of a maximum statutory ratio ('benefit capping') for total employment benefits to net income in work (say, 70 per cent), making benefits conditional on acceptance of a job after, say, 6 months as in US 'workfare' schemes.[13] The poor in work would be protected by a negative income tax (Minford, 1985: 4–5). Another proposal is to shift the balance from means-tested to non-means-tested benefits. All existing benefits would be abolished: unemployment benefit, personal tax allowances, and mortgage tax relief. Instead, everyone would receive a basic income, free of tax. They would then be able to earn extra but all earnings would be taxed. The poverty trap would go, because there would be no means-tested benefits to withdraw.[14]

An older and more radical solution that would, in principle, solve all these disincentive problems, and some others besides, is the idea of negative income tax as suggested by Milton Friedman (1962: 191–3; Friedman and Friedman, 1980: 150–5). Essentially this would mean that if someone's income fell below a certain level, they would receive a payment from the state (negative tax) and if their income rose above this level they would pay tax as they now do. The advantages of this arrangement are that it gives help to the individual in its most useful and nonpaternalistic form – cash – and it has less-direct distorting effect on market forces. In its 'ideal' form negative income tax would enable the benefit and tax system to be integrated thus slimming down the present large bureaucracy administering all the welfare state's numerous benefit programmes. There are many other advantages such as the fact that everyone would easily be able to see where they stood. At present, the citizen has only the vaguest idea how much he pays to the state in taxes or receives from it in benefit; in many cases he may not even know whether or not he is a net beneficiary or a net payer. Although some disincentive effects would remain, it would be a great improvement on the present position: an extra pound earned would always mean more money available for spending.

Unemployment and the housing market

The privately rented sector of the housing market has, in the past, served the needs of the youngest and most mobile workers but years of rent controls have reduced the number of housing units available to let. These forces squeezing privately rented housing have been reinforced by the tax relief on mortgage interest, and the exemption from capital gains tax enjoyed by owner-occupiers. These reliefs have tended to increase investment in a single main residence relative to other investments. All this, it has been argued, has discouraged the unemployed in one area from moving to where there are vacancies. But it seems possible that even if these distortions were removed, the effect on total unemployment would not be very significant in the short run; people often have many nonpecuniary reasons for staying where they are.

THE RADICAL-LEFT VIEW

A common feature of Marxist-inspired explanations of macro-economic fluctuations, whether of unemployment or anything else, and whether people as a result become materially better or worse off, is that they must be fitted into theories of the class struggle, historical determinism, or conspiracies to serve 'late capitalism'. If the mass of people become worse off, this is 'immiseration'; if they become better off they are being corrupted by 'consumerism'.

The dissolution of traditional Keynesian economics is seen as having given a perfect opportunity to the New Right to propagate free market ideas. Andrew Gamble writing in 1979 on the newly elected Conservative government chose to describe the doctrine put forward by the Insitute of Economic Affairs, Milton Friedman, and economic commentators such as Samuel Brittan, and rather suprisingly Hayek, as the 'social market economy'.[15] The main obstacle to the achievement of the social market by the New Right he saw as organized labour; therefore they would strive to curtail union power. The reforms in labour law (which Gamble rightly predicted) would serve 'in Marxist terms to restore the full operation of the industrial reserve army of labour' (Gamble, 1979: 15). The idea of the 'natural' rate of unemployment he saw as a reborn idea of the 1920s and 1930s: that unemployment was high only because wage rates would not fall far enough due to such 'imperfections' in the market as trade unions and social-security benefits. All this was merely a smokescreen hiding the revival of an 'ancient ideology': that labour is merely a commodity and has its market price. Gamble's conclusion was that socialists must return to fundamentals[16] and rethink their case by reviving Marx's critique of the bourgeois ideal of the market, as set out at length in the *Grundrisse* and in *Capital* (Gamble, 1979: 22).

The existence of large-scale unemployment in the 1980s has given the radical Left a powerful base from which to condemn capitalism, and they are contemptuous of policies that aim to remove labour-market distortions in capitalist terms; not only would these lead to treating labour as just another commodity, but they would also be merely an attempt to reform capitalism, the system that is regarded as the very cause of the problem.

A sociologist wrote in 1982, that only a Marxist analysis offered any hope for the 'bleak consequences' that awaited the British work-

173

ing class 'because the analyses offered them by all the respectable leaders, including Benn, have proved hollow' (Jordan, 1982: 12). He argued that talk of industrial democracy, work-sharing, and other palliatives is useless so long as the capitalist system persists. A socialist government would provide more employment in the social services but the greatest increase in employment would be achieved by 'reductions in working hours, compensated for by increases in the social wage provided by the state' (Jordan, 1982: 242).[17] A socialist government would 'seek to rediscover the spirit of national unity which was characteristic of wartime Britain' as the best defence against injustice and class conflict (Jordan, 1982: 243).

Also, during the 1980s, the radical Left, confronted by the evident rise in living standards of the majority of the population, including the working class, have somewhat shifted their attention to other allegedly oppressed groups such as ethnic minorities, women, and the 'under-class' of the inner cities. 'Late Marxism' must be saved; thus we see a continuing stream of reinterpretations of the master – 'the vast internalised and narcissistic Marxiological literature of the now rapidly ageing "New Left"' (Crick, 1987: 115) – in order to fit the unprecedented events of the real world into the cherished framework.[18]

THE AUSTRIAN POSITION: A SUMMARY[19]

Hayek first showed his scepticism towards the good faith and competence of governments' management of money as early as 1925 in an essay written in German on the monetary policy of the United States: 'This current inflation therefore works like a drug, giving rise not merely to a short-lived increase in well-being but also an extended nightmare later' (Hayek, 1984: 11).

Hayek v. Keynes in the 1930s

The unprecedented high and chronic level of unemployment between the wars, the obvious human misery resulting from it, and the evident failure of the orthodoxy of 'sound' management of the economy to cure it meant that Keynes was easily hailed, fairly uncritically, as a saviour. Economists such as Sir John Hicks, who formerly had supported Hayek went over to the Keynesian 'side'. The widespread and unsympathetic reaction to Hayek's theory of the trade cycle was undoubtedly because the policy implication of Hayek's theories was one of 'hands off', to let the depression run its course. The now-familiar story of the debate between Hayek and Keynes is told in a series of articles, replies and counter replies between Hayek, Keynes, Sraffa, Pigou, and Robertson (Machlup, 1977: 18). Hayek published ten articles on the subject between 1932 and 1936, six of them in English. The story of these events will not be further pursued here,[20] except to note that Hayek's opposition to Keynesianism was sustained throughout the years when he was completely unfashionable and dismissed as an out-of-date reactionary until the horrors of 1970s stagflation began to make his ideas increasingly relevant to the times. Even as late as 1968 one reviewer could write that 'more and more the direction in which he is forced to point is backward to a lost golden age' and that Hayek 'now prefers to speak only to the converted, as represented for example, by the members of the Mont Pelerin Society' (*Economic Journal*, December, 1968, p. 903).

A tiger by the tail

This is the title of the IEA Hobart Paperback first published in 1972 with a 2nd edition in 1983 consisting of extracts from Hayek's writings. It provides a useful and concise compilation of his various analyses of the problems of inflation and recession. The essence of these is that if output and employment is made to depend on inflation in any way, then slowing down the *rate* of inflation will produce recession. (How true this became in the 1980s.) Only by constantly increasing the rate of inflation can recession be averted. This clearly agrees with the Chicago view but it differs from it on the question of aggregation. The 'active' role of money is not denied but the impact of changes in the money supply goes beyond the 'general' index of prices. The latter ignores the dislocating effect of money-supply changes on the structure of *relative* prices; not all prices are affected simultaneously and to the same extent. It is individual price changes that determine production and factor employment. Money is not neutral in its effects; this is what distinguishes the Austrian view from the quantity theory. Everything depends on where the money enters the system. It follows that changes in money supply can affect prices and production even with stable prices. This approach derives from the Austrian distrust of macroeconomic aggregates such as the 'general price level', preferring as they do to work upwards from microeconomic foundations, which follows methodological individualism and subjectivism. The economic system is kaleidic (to use Shackle's term), in a state of continuous change. Monetary expansion dislocates the market forces that achieve the 'discovery process'.

Trade unions

Trade unions are seen by Austrians as monopolies of a special kind that are more dangerous than enterprise monopoly, mainly because of their legal privileges and their powers of coercion (Mises, 1966: 376, 777–9; Hayek, 1960, Chapter 18; Rothbard, 1970; 620–30).

There has grown a widespread opinion among almost all elements of the Right that trade-union reform is essential both for the cause of individual liberty and for the reduction of unemployment. As already mentioned, a considerable degree of reform has been enacted in the 1980s. Hayek's persuasive and unremitting arguments have undoubtedly played a significant part in bringing these changes about.

Hayek is aware of the historical merits of unions and does not question their right to exist as voluntary organizations; he defends the right of an individual to join a union but he would deny anyone the right to force others to do so. Also, anyone should have the right to strike except where this would break a contract, but no-one should have the right to force others to strike. Rather than having been of benefit to workers 'the unions have become the biggest obstacle to raising the living standards of the working class as a whole'. Also, 'they are the prime source of unemployment' and 'the main reason for the decline of the British economy in general' (Hayek, 1984b: 52). They have become the 'chief cause of unemployment'. Since attempts to cure unemployment by adding to the money supply only lead to accelerating inflation, it can only be cured by allowing the labour market to redirect workers to jobs where demand has risen. This requires changes in *relative* wages: some wages must fall and others must rise. Trade unions impede the process by preserving a conventional outdated wage structure. 'The final disaster we owe mainly to Lord Keynes' (Hayek, 1984b: 57). His advocacy shifted responsibility for employment from the trade unions to government. Unions, for 40 years, were allowed to enforce their wage demands disregardful of their effects on employment and the government was expected to increase aggregate demand to accommodate their irresponsibility.

176

'Inevitably the consequence is continuous and accelerating inflation' (ibid: 57). Hayek saw no way out of the problem unless trade-union privileges were revoked.[21]

Privatizing money

Because the root cause of inflation is seen as lying in the power of governments to create money, various suggestions have been made as to how this power might be constrained.[22] The most radical ideas have come from Hayek who has challenged the assumption that there must, within a particular area of the earth's surface, be only one uniform medium of exchange. This has arisen from the unjustified (in terms of individual liberty) practice of rulers insisting on having a monopoly of legal tender. Hayek argued in 1976 for national currencies to be replaced by competing private moneys. Because of the temptations open to politicians, unchecked party politics and stable money are inherently incompatible.[23] The gold standard secured some constraint on governments' powers to create money, and prices were relatively stable from the beginning of the eighteenth century until 1914.[24] Hayek has subsequently given up the idea of the denationalization of money, not because he has changed his mind as to its desirability, but because it seems unrealizable. He has put forward a more modest proposal. For most retail transactions, traders would pay in terms of 'pounds' or 'dollars' but would calculate in terms of a 'Standard' unit of account whose value would be related to a 'basket' of internationally traded commodities and foodstuffs. This would be the first step towards the disappearance of 'the absurd conception of a "national currency" with the eternal temptation for politicians to abuse it', which he adds optimistically, 'will vanish sooner or later'.[25]

CONCLUSIONS

Keynes was right about employment in the 1930s and Hayek has been right since 1960. Given that we have a predominantly market economy then theory and experience suggest that, unless there is some kind of world recession of catastrophic dimensions, interventionism and demand stimulation through repeated increases in the supply of money only serve to end up with both inflation and unemployment.

177

The effects of inflation are not as emotionally charged as those associated with unemployment; unemployment makes 'good television'. But the mass robbery of people on social security and those with small savings such as we saw in the roaring inflation of the 1970s is not as amenable to dramatic presentation. Inflation distributes gains and losses arbitrarily, the strongly unionized gain at the expense of the non unionized; debtors gain, creditors lose, and experience now strongly suggests that even the 'little bit' of inflation designed to increase employment ends in reducing it. Unemployment is regarded by many people as a symptom of an immoral society but inflation is doubly immoral because it robs the hard-working and the prudent saver and ultimately causes unemployment. This is now understood by most policy-makers and aspiring 'policy-makers', although it is to Hayek's credit that his warnings, ignored as unfashionable for years, eventually began to shift influential opinion. Governments, from the days of ancient Rome, have always been tempted to 'print money' and the work of Keynes apparently provided, after the Second World War, an intellectual justification for this tendency although ironically Keynes himself had written that Lenin was right when he declared that the best way to destroy capitalism was to debauch the currency: 'the process engages all the hidden forces of economic law on the side of destruction, and does it in a manner which not one man in a million is able to diagnose'.

Chapter Nine

ECONOMIC GROWTH AND ITS COSTS

DEFINITION

An increase in Gross Domestic Product (GDP) is described in everyday language as economic growth; however caused, it signifies an increase in goods and services and is also used as a measure of the 'wellbeing' or opulence of a population when calculated per head. Some confusion arises from the fact that economists define growth as an increase in the *productive potential* of a country; GDP could, however, have risen simply because resources have become more fully utilized. The growth rate of productive potential can only be measured properly over long periods of time or by excluding the cyclical effects of high and low employment. Most people welcome growth; politicians are fond of claiming credit when they have been in office during periods of growth and most economists have always taken for granted that growth should be an important policy aim because it is regarded as the basis for an increase in individual welfare. Some people, and at least a few economists, such as Galbraith and Mishan, view the preoccupation with growth as a method of increasing welfare as a delusion, and there has been a steady increase in concern for the environment, the destruction of plants and animals, and the depletion of the earth's resources, backed by the 'Green' movements. This chapter is mainly concerned with the question of the desirability of growth as a way of increasing welfare. We begin with some general changes in Britain over the past century.

GROWTH-RATE TRENDS

Between 1870 and 1939 the GDP per head of the UK approximately doubled in real terms, an annual average rate of increase of roughly

1 per cent. Ignoring the years of the Second World War and its immediate aftermath, the period 1950–69 was one of unprecedentedly high growth averaging 2.25 per cent per year, a rate that would double GDP if it were sustained for 30 years. But between 1970 and 1979 the rate fell to 1.9 per cent per year. Since the economy emerged from the recession of 1980–81, growth to the end of 1987 has been at the historically high level of 3 per cent per year. On the basis of this measure it looks as if average material prosperity per head has increased by about four times during the past century. However, there is much more to be said before this statement can be accepted as it stands.

DEFICIENCIES OF GDP AS A MEASURE OF ECONOMIC PERFORMANCE[1]

While it may be reasonable to compare GDP over a period of a few years, it is much less so for longer periods of, say, twenty or thirty years. Goods change in quality; some goods disappear altogether and new ones appear; the increase in leisure is not counted, government 'output' is valued solely on its cost; these are just a few of the conventional reservations to be found in the textbooks. Absurdities exist: increases in cigarette output *and* hospital provision for the care of lung cancer victims both *add* to GDP. In general, the validity of equating an increase in GDP with a corresponding increase in living standards is doubtful. 'Being the denizens of a quantomaniac society, we could easily be also the victims of a statistical hallucination' (Mishan, 1984). Whether or not the 'hallucinations' are large enough to be significant in making generalizations about living standards depends, of course, on what proportion they make up of total economic activity, which is a *genuine* addition to GDP.

THEORIES OF THE CAUSES OF GROWTH

While there is widespread agreement on the desirability of growth, there is less agreement on the right policies to secure it. Adam Smith discussed the accumulation of capital and referred to the people who 'produce nothing'. These were: the ecclesiastical establishment, the royal court and the armed forces who, if they consume too much in one year of the produce of productive labourers, will cause 'next year's produce to be less than that of the foregoing'. Ricardo, Marx

180

and Schumpeter emphasized the importance of technological change, while Rostow distinguished five stages of growth, from subsistence through to 'the take-off into sustained growth' which culminates in the age of high mass consumption. The Keynesian 'revolution' with its promise of greater macroeconomic rigour was accompanied by theories of economic growth from which it was hoped policy prescriptions might emerge for the use of growth-conscious governments;[2] new investment opportunities assumed a crucial role. Although growth theory has attained a higher degree of quantification, the influence on growth of the unquantifiable nature of the social, political, and legal framework probably encompasses the most crucial factors; among these is, as the Austrians have stressed, the extent to which the social climate is favourable to entrepreneurial action.

EXTERNALITIES

The term externalities includes external economies and external diseconomies – conventionally regarded as examples of market failure. The problems only arise, however, when the institutional and legal system fails to ensure that individuals pay the full costs and likewise receive the full benefits of their activities: in this sense externalities are not market failure. External diseconomies are variously described as 'side effects', 'spillovers', 'neighbourhood effects', or 'social costs'. (The term social here does seem to have a real meaning.) Also used is the term 'disamenity', and 'pollution' is the spillover causing most concern, especially since the end of the Second World War in the more affluent countries; the most obvious explanation for this raised consciousness being the increase in pollution associated with rapid growth.

There has been much argument over the question of whether growth is desirable at all in view of these problems. The 'growthmen' defend it on the grounds that it is feasible to correct the spillovers and in fact that only increased wealth provides the means so to do; also, that any free society must accept the consequences of individual choices even if one does not happen to approve of them. The opponents of growth see it as leading to a planet that will not be fit to live on and that far from increasing freedom, the growth of pollution will result in everincreasing government controls. We begin with a very brief account of some of the typical arguments against growth.

THE COSTS OF GROWTH

There is an opportunity cost of growth; it requires investments, often in goods and services (education and health care for example), which do not yield an immediate return in the form of consumer goods. The kind of costs with which we are concerned here, however, are social costs such as pollution of air and water, the destruction of plant and animal species, noise, and dirt. Growth involves change and change means that many people find their settled ways destroyed. Skills that may have been acquired with great effort and sacrifice may be rendered obsolete, and the question must be asked whether the growth is worth these real costs. Many of these costs are virtually unquantifiable and statisticians therefore ignore them – GDP shows rises without deductions for many disamenities. E. J. Mishan, the economist who is the best known for his critique of growth, has questioned whether 'the irresistible spread of steel and concrete ... the plague of motorised traffic, the growing impatience and tenseness of people' is really worth it (Mishan, 1967). Mishan has written extensively in this vein. He is particularly regretful at the disappearance of such pleasures as the ability to stroll in peace along city streets and the transformation of the Mediterranean coast by the mass-tourism industry into a sewage-ridden subtopia. In the twenty years since Mishan went on the attack matters have become worse and in his later writings he is even more pessimistic. The thunderous denunciations of the modern world and the deeply gloomy conclusions of the last chapter of his *Economic Myths and the Mythology of Economics* (Mishan, 1986) are stated with passion and a religious fervour that are very persuasive. There is something of a contrast between these later misgivings and his earlier attitude. In *The Costs of Economic Growth* (Mishan, 1967: 219–20) are to be found many practical suggestions and technical discussions of ways in which social welfare might, on balance, be increased by economic growth, rather than reduced. The recognition of amenity rights, for example, whereby people are endowed with property rights in such 'goods' as privacy, quiet, and clean air is proposed. This would involve, in the case of aircraft noise, the payment of compensation to thousands of people for the 'use' of their right to quietness. But the important consequence of such a change in the law would be that many plans that at present look potentially profitable would not have been started in the first place if proper account had been taken of all social costs. From the point of view of income distribution, many external diseconomies are regressive. A rich person can move to a quieter area; the poor must put up with whatever disamenity is inflicted upon them. One has only to consider the proliferation of urban flyovers and where they were built in the 1960s to see that there is much truth in this. Although economists, in general, would agree with Mishan on the existence of such social costs, their interest in optimality problems arises more from their intellectual fascination rather than to any real concern over what is happening to our environment. Also there is a widely held view that economic growth itself provides the means of advancing welfare (Mishan, 1967: 221). Of all the many sources of 'bads', Mishan puts the motor car among the greatest: 'The common sight today, of street after street thickly strewn with lay-about cars, no longer dismays us'. The car also ensures 'that any resort which became accessible should simultaneously become unattractive' (Mishan, 1986).[3] This kind of 'limit to growth' is the theme of Professor F. Hirsch (1977), in which he argues that many of the goods and services that consumers seek cannot be acquired for all without spoiling them. He advocates collective means to implement individual ends. Certain things must be kept off the market: outstanding natural scenery, historical monuments, and the foreshore that provides access to the sea.

There is certainly growing worry today over the question of the limits to growth. From many sides there are calls for a halt to economic growth and technological marvels. The Green movement, unfortunately, seems to have identified its interests more with the Left than the Right, yet there is no evidence that socialist states are particularly concerned about pollution (Beckerman, 1974: 44-6). Traditional socialism is materialistic: the life of abundance and leisure is sought for all. The apparent obsession with growth of most politicians and people in the already rich west is seen by Mishan as puzzling and he sees our only hope in a change in values to replace the 'spiritual void that is the culmination of 500 years of science and secularisation'.[4] External diseconomies are not, on this view, amenable to correction simply by changes in the law of property rights, but are inseparable from mankind's whole web of cultural and spiritual values. Critics have contended that Mishan confuses the issue by conflating the cultural and economic aspects of growth. This is a very superficial judgement on the sheer richness and depth of Mishan's critique of which I have only been able here to give such a brief glimpse. No-one who may be complacent about the effects of growth, whether from Left or Right, could avoid some awkward and thought-provoking questions after reading Mishan's personal reflections.

THE CASE FOR GROWTH

The argument in favour of economic growth rests partly on the historical record: the vast improvements in living standards, health, personal choice, and leisure now available to millions. Growth is only a bad thing if it can be shown irrefutably that externalities are an insuperable problem, unless of course the Mishan view is accepted that growth destroys so many precious things that correcting for externalities is only, in the end, tinkering with the real problem.

The obvious solution for dealing with such externalities as pollution of the environment is for the government directly to ban those activities that are the cause of the trouble. Such a method has, naturally, most appeal to those who envisage the state as possessing a high degree of both knowledge, competence, and benevolence. More sophisticated approaches have been the subject of much thought ever since Pigou's *Economics of Welfare* in 1920. The common theme has been to accept that externalities are a market failure and that the role of government is to make the polluter pay, either by taxes or by making him pay compensation to the sufferers from his activities. More recently there has developed a school of thought that is much less confident of governments' abilities or good intentions and that advocates the solution in the appropriate application of property rights; were this to be achieved there is no reason, on this view, why the free market would not reach optimal solutions.

Professor W. Beckerman (1974) has cogently argued the case for the adoption of 'pollution charges' against direct controls; his work is a good example of the clarity of reasoning of a good economist compared to the wholly emotional approach of *some* 'environmentalists'. There are two ways of looking at pollution: either in terms of the pollutant 'produced' or, in terms of the clean environment 'used up'. The 'optimum pollution level' is that at which the marginal social costs of reducing pollution just equal the marginal social benefit from doing so. In this sense pollution is simply a problem of resource allocation. Beckerman favours taxes as the method of 'charging for pollution'. The taxes should be equal in value to the damage caused. The advantages of charging for pollution over direct controls are that firms will strive to find the cheapest methods of reducing pollution, and technical progress in pollution control will be stimulated. Beckerman replies to seven commonly raised objections to pollution charges. Among these is the contention that the scheme is unworkable because the necessary data are lacking; but neither are the data available for direct regulation. Another objection is that polluters would accept only very precise measures if they are to be the basis of a tax, whereas they will accept approximate measures used as a basis for direct controls. This is 'manifest nonsense': charges now accepted such as rates, parking-meter charges, telephone calls, and many others are not on finely graduated scales. One argument that has been used against all manner of suggested steps to freer markets is the unemployment bogey. But the fact that pollution abatement might mean a loss of some jobs does not rule it out, unless other methods of reducing unemployment have first been rejected for sound reasons. Beckerman's presumption is that some 'optimum' pollution must be accepted rather than doing without the benefits that would be lost if pollution were to be reduced below this optimum. The misallocations, which is what the pollution problem consists of, are not, in Beckerman's view, caused by economic growth and he argues that growth is the major means by which pollution levels are likely to be reduced to socially optimal levels. As for those who, like Mishan, are hostile to growth in principle, it 'reflects an emotional over-reaction to some of the obvious disamenities of modern life'. It has been suggested, for example, that the hostility to mass tourism is simply middle- and upper-class resentment of the way in which formerly exclusive areas are now overrun by working-class hordes.

Instead of using taxes and/or subsidies to correct divergences between private and social costs, which was the method favoured by the followers of Pigou, Professor R. H. Coase, in his influential 1960 paper, stressed that social costs are not simply a case of restraining A from harming B; doing this may inflict harm on A.[5] The problem could be resolved by direct trading between A and B. If both parties stand to gain from an exchange, then in a free market, trade may be expected to follow. The reason this does not always happen is because of 'transaction' costs. The most important of these arises from the inadequate specification of property rights. 'A clear-cut decision on property rights may be all that is required to resolve the difficulty'; government action would not then be needed. The advantages flowing from a proper specification of property rights are that it harnesses individual incentives; it utilizes the price system as a cheap way of generating and using information and it avoids bureaucratic administrative complexities. Such an approach is advocated by the 'public choice' school of economists,[6] derived from their suspicions that politicians and civil servants will not behave exogenously as disinterested social agencies, and that government intervention often gives rise to costs that exceed the benefits. Furthermore, as the Austrian theory of market knowledge suggests, governments have no access to the relevant facts above that possessed by individuals.[7] It is ironic that pollution is often held to be evidence that the property-based market economy does not 'work'; the truth is 'that high transaction costs make it difficult to *enforce* the private property rights of the victims of pollution' (Nozick, 1974: 80). In spite of the existence of transaction costs, the extent to which the market, in practice, does reflect disamenities has been underestimated by economists, following the theoretical methods of Pigou. Evidence from property transactions for example, confirms that nuisances such as noise and dirt are duly registered in the rents and prices of houses and flats.

THE DOOMSDAY ARGUMENT

Over the past twenty years the Friends of the Earth and other environmental groups have vigorously propagated their unquestioned assumption that the earth's resources being finite, are being used up at an ever-increasing rate and that the 'planet earth' will become uninhabitable. They are particularly strongly opposed to the use of nuclear power. This is rather odd, in view of the death and disease caused by the fossil fuels oil, coal, and gas, and especially in the light of the possibility that the production of carbon dioxide may be dramatically changing the climate – 'the greenhouse effect'. The environmental lobby's beliefs have been challenged, notably by Beckerman (1974), Julian L. Simon, and Maurice and Smithson of the Hoover Institution.[8] The main criticism of the 'eco-doomsters' is that often their statistics are 'guesstimates' and that in their projections into the future, assumed 'bad' trends continue to rise exponentially, while the 'good' variables only increase by finite amounts; it is not, then, surprising that they reach the conclusion that some day the 'bads' will outrun the 'goods'. Beckerman is optimistic that society will respond to the 'bads' – either by automatic market responses or by government policies. The market response is that, as a given good is becoming scarce, the rise in price induces consumers to look for substitutes and to economize in the use of the scarce good, while suppliers are induced to use methods of production and exploit new sources that were too costly to be profitable before the price rise. The 'oil crisis' of the 1970s and subsequent reactions in the market have clearly demonstrated this process. The way in which market forces worked to cause coal in sixteenth-century England to become a profitable substitute for depleted timber reserves is one of many instructive examples from the past.

The environmental pressure groups tend to call for government and international action in order to protect us from the 'ravages' of private greed. Yet it is possible that there is a greater incentive to conserve a privately owned resource than one in communal or state hands; for example the colossal human tragedy of the Sahel region of Africa may have been aggravated by the custom of having communal grazing rights. Private ownership may induce more incentive to conserve a resource rather than use it up to the point of exhaustion.

Even if, however, we accept the arguments of Beckerman *et al.* and take the optimistic view, two matters remain that must give cause for concern. First, the damage now being done by some spillovers may be irreversible: the cutting down of forests and the disfigurement of coastlines, and the possible erosion of the earth's biological equilibrium. Second, as Mishan has pointed out, it is not merely a matter of food or other resources – there is the sheer discomfort of more and more people being compressed into places that are being made steadily less agreeable through the increase in travel. Also, although there are many precedents for the discovery of new substitutes in the past, to be too optimistic because of this would be like 'reminding a sick man of ninety that he also thought he would never recover when he was twenty'.[9]

Both the cases for and against growth deploy sound and convincing arguments. Possibly the best way lies in between the more hysterical of the 'eco-doomsters' on the one hand and the more blandly complacent free marketeers on the other hand.

THE AUSTRIAN VIEW

It seems fitting that the Austrian approach to growth is last in this chapter since, to economists in the Austrian tradition, there is no 'problem' of growth, and the whole concept of an 'economy' growing is fairly meaningless given their methodology of subjectivism and individualism. The 'economics of growth' is seen as an historicist concept expressing a misleading biological analogy, similar to the related terminology of 'developed' and 'underdeveloped' economies (Rothbard, 1977: 236). When we speak of growth in the economy, there is the implied suggestion that the nation is a single unit moved by mysterious external forces. Macroeconomic entities such as the GDP are taking an arbitrarily selected aspect of the market economy as if it were an integrated unit. Macroeconomics is studied as if the actions of millions of individuals were 'the outcome of the mutual operation of one macroeconomic magnitude upon another such magnitude' (Mises, 1978: 83). The Austrian objection to the use of macroeconomic aggregates is based on this tendency to ignore the microeconomic subjectively determined valuations from which they are in practice derived. Also, a preoccupation with aggregates such as growth rates fosters the delusion that the economy can be managed along 'maximum growth paths'. Such practices are examples of what Hayek means by *scientism* (see also Lachmann, 'In criticism of economic models', 1977: 116–22).

Rostow's 'stages of economic growth' theory is sharply criticized by Rothbard as a 'futile search for non-existent "laws of history"' with each stage 'somehow destined to evolve automatically into the next' (Rothbard, 1970: 839) with technology seen as the driving force of all economic development, ignoring the role of individual entrepreneurs who perceived profit opportunities in the use of new inventions.

The Austrian viewpoint on externalities agrees in many ways with those of other free-market theorists mentioned previously, who see the ideal solution, not as any sort of government responsibility except that of maintaining the rule of law – especially the legal enforcement of contracts and the extension and protection of individual property rights. Given this, then individuals may be expected to arrange mutually beneficial agreements in which 'users' of such goods as clean air or water are charged – such charges to be recoverable, like any other goods, through the courts. The 'blame' for the existence of social costs in this view rests on the government's failure to make it possible for individuals to enforce their property rights, not, as the Left put it as a defect in the system of private ownership (Rothbard, 1970: 156). The whole question of externalities is an example of what Mises regarded as a pseudo-economic problem (Mises, 1966: 658).

Where Austrian subjectivism implies a somewhat different approach lies in the specification of costs. 'Opportunity cost', is, of course, an entirely familiar concept in orthodox economics, but subjectivist economics, as well as some alternative possibility foregone, emphasizes that there can never be any objective way of measuring the cost of the foregone alternative. This cost can never be determined by an outside observer because it exists only in the mind of the decision-maker (Rothbard, 1970: 290–4). This view not only has implications for the evaluation of social costs, but also rules out any assessment of the economic efficiency of individual actions. The individual's freely made choice is the only criterion of efficiency. In the matter of externalities the Austrian position is that where no actual contract is made between individuals, any attempt to assess costs is hypothetical and depends on the judgement of some outside observer – such as an economist or the government. But in contemplating a given externality, different individuals would, if placed in the situation, value the loss or gain differently; thus no objective check is possible. Efficiency in an economy is thus a matter of how freely contracts may be made between individuals. Social cost-benefit analysis imputes values that individuals have not expressed in practice in the market: it produces calculations that are hypothetical and of interest only to economists.[10]

The Austrian attitude to conservation is, in general, that there is little truth in the environmentalists' belief that governments must act to protect us from the voracious destructiveness of private enterprise: 'only the wise, providential state can foresee depletion' (Rothbard, 1977: 65). On the contrary, private individuals have every incentive to preserve the capital value of their resources. One aim of conservation laws is to preserve resources for future generations, the state allegedly being more 'far-seeing' than individuals. Austrians see this as showing an unwarranted faith in the state. There are many examples of the reckless exploitations of some natural resource associated with an absence of private-property rights: the slaughter of whales; the depletion of soil fertility by nomadic tribes; the excessive use of western grazing lands in the USA when the government prevented cattlemen from owning the land and fencing it in.

Hayek's analysis of the question of conservation is similar in general to the foregoing (Hayek, 1960: 367–75), except that he does not brush aside so uncompromisingly the conservationist's faith in government. He distinguishes 'fugitive resources', such as fish, water, oil, or natural gas, which no individual exploiter will have any incentive to conserve 'since what he does not take will be taken by others'. In such cases 'we must resort to alternative forms of regulation'. He also has no objection to natural parks and nature reserves being provided by the government, although voluntary bodies like the National Trust in Great Britain are to be the preferred agencies. In general, however, Hayek is not at all in favour of government initiatives to correct externalities, because, in most cases, it will necessarily be ignorant of all the necessary facts, which can only be known to individuals. Also, all resource conservation constitutes investment and should be judged by precisely the same criteria as other investment.

Austrian methodology has been used to illuminate the thesis of Julian L. Simon (1983) in *The Ultimate Resource*, which is seen as a praxeological analysis: cost and price are here taken as defining the scarcity of raw materials. The fact that Simon asserts that 'long before the shelf would be bare' individuals would take steps to hoard materials is seen as an example of the application of Mises' theory of human action (Sinnett, 1987) even though Simon himself seems unaware of this. Applying Austrian praxeology strengthens Simon's case against doom-laden forecasts of raw-material exhaustion.

CONCLUSIONS

Economic growth has been most vigorous in free market economies and the Austrians see no benefit emerging from government attempts to foster growth; if the result of millions of individual actions were to result in zero or negative growth, so be it. Most economists would agree that the doomsday arguments based on fixed technology, though sincerely held, are fallacious. Some objections to growth are based on a dislike of how people use its fruits; there is no guarantee that people left free to choose will, in general, behave so as not to create a world that many will find increasingly unpleasant. Before, however, the conclusion is drawn that the state must control individual freedom, particular sources of unpleasant side-effects (e.g. of road traffic) should be carefully examined to see whether market forces are the cause of the problem or whether state intervention or failure to protect individual property rights is itself to blame.

There is a sincerely held view that the problems associated with growth transcend squabbles between Left and Right – between socialism and capitalism – and that individual human pretensions and values must change. But the question of how, and by what means this is to be achieved receive many competing answers. There are some good grounds for optimism; the very increase in awareness and discussion of these matters are hopeful signs.

Chapter Ten

CONCLUDING NOTES

Many controversial questions have been touched upon in the preceding pages; thus I first select a few of these and oppose brief critical remarks as they might be put by the two most obviously conflicting political ideologies. This is a simplification of some complex questions but the use of 'individualism' and 'collectivism' seems a closer approximation to reality than the misleading 'Left' and 'Right'.

AGAINST INDIVIDUALISM

(a) The principle of private property
The private ownership of property is no defence against tyranny, as exemplified by the case of Nazi Germany. Also, unlimited rights to the acquisition of large individual property holdings may give rise to coercion of others; the state is not the only source of coercion. The libertarian principle that no social goal can justify forcibly depriving an individual of some of his property leads to circular reasoning if the powers of property owners can themselves be shown to reduce the liberty of others.[1] Thus there is a strong case for the redistribution of inherited wealth.

(b) Morality
Individualism is not morally attractive. Most of the New Right arguments ignore the need for shared values; there is too much emphasis on the economic aspect of life. Capitalist societies lack an 'agreed concrete morality'.[2] The Hayekian view is that the market does not necessarily reward merit. Capitalism has undermined all previously recognized moral restraints. The weakest point of modern capitalism is the encouragement of individual greed unredeemed by generosity or concern for others.

(c) Externalities

We have no rational way, within the mechanism of the free market, of dealing with the ever-increasing global 'spillovers' created by new technologies: the destruction of tropical forests, the poisoning of the sea, the 'greenhouse effect', and the extinction of plant and animal species. All these can only be dealt with by governments nationally and internationally.

(d) Cultural standards

The market tends to result in the devotion of most resources to the output of trashy books and newspapers, and radio and TV programmes with mass appeal. Only the state can subsidize such institutions as theatres, art galleries, and free libraries. The establishment of free public libraries, state education, and the BBC enabled millions of individuals to attain cultural levels that would not otherwise have been within their reach. The coming of free market satellite TV will result in a cataract of pornography and mediocrity.

AGAINST COLLECTIVISM

(a) The principle of private property

If the state has great power over individuals' property then they will direct their energies, not to the fruitful acquisition of personal wealth, but to trying, through political activity and lobbying, to persuade bureaucrats and politicians to grant them favours. This behaviour is called 'rent-seeking'. Endless time is unproductively wasted sitting on committees and currying favour with local officials. The inheritance of property is only one way in which children start off their lives unequally endowed; they may inherit greater intelligence or be educated more wisely by their parents, and it is a lesser evil than the alternative ways in which people seek to provide for their children. These cause greater waste of resources and injustice in societies where inherited property is forbidden (Hayek, 1960: 91)

(b) Morality

One of the consequences of increasing affluence in the west has been an apparent increase in the number of individuals who are obsessed with worldly success and all its meretricious trappings. Those on the Left who condemn this selfish behaviour see it as the inevitable consequence of the encouragement of self-interest in a capitalist

193

system, the suggestion being that somehow or other, under socialism, selfishness could be eradicated. The fact is, however, that in socialist societies, the 'selfishness' merely takes different forms. All changes in general morality must come from changes in individual consciences and this may take a very long time to achieve, if ever. 'Better' private morality can only evolve slowly. Such transformations have often been associated with religious revivals. It is interesting to note, in this connection, that Hayek, although himself agnostic, regards the 'symbolic truths' of Christianity as having 'been indispensable conditions of the growth of civilisation' (*The Guardian*, 17 September 1984).

The state's role is to assist those forces that help this process, not to engage in too much direct action. The welfare state, for example, has tended to kill off private philanthropy to some extent.

(c) Externalities

It is simply not true that the seeking of private profit is the main cause of 'pollution'; some governments are equally to blame. Also, although it must be conceded that international co-operation between governments will be required to deal with matters such as air and sea pollution, it does not follow that market incentives, such as the extension of property rights and other measures, are necessarily inferior to 'direct' state action. Paradoxically, it is the very success of capitalism in producing goods in response to individual demands that has not only caused externalities but has also provided the technology for dealing with the problems; some of the worst examples of environmental destruction are to be found in the poorest countries.

(d) Cultural standards

There is too much pessimism among many people – of all political persuasions – as to the consequences of freedom to publish or to broadcast. Just as there are mass markets for consumer goods, often of poor taste and quality alongside specialized markets providing things that appeal to minorities, so will freedom in broadcasting throw up junk and quality provided there is *enough* competition so that it becomes worthwhile for entrepreneurs to provide for small niches in the general market.

One curious contradiction in some collectivist attitudes has always been their rejection of censorship in general (unless it is degrading to some favoured minority) as an infringement of human freedom but their passionate desire to control free economic activity.

THATCHERISM

It is a curious fact that Mrs Thatcher has given her name to this frequently used and increasingly tedious '-ism', an honour (or fate) that has befallen no other British prime minister. To what extent there is any objective reality in the notion that Thatcherism is definable, and if definable that it can stand as a major political creed which is the chief explanation for the changes in British society in the 1980s, is very doubtful.[3] A comparable idea is that the full employment of the two decades after the Second World War is to be explained solely by Keynesianism. This type of history tends to ignore the powerful though relatively unseen economic and technological forces at work; the 'cult of personality' distracts from what is really going on.

Nevertheless there evidently is something in the idea that the governments of Mrs Thatcher's premiership have struck out in new and radical directions. It is widely agreed that Mrs Thatcher has changed the political agenda, causing significant reactions among the moderate Left, as seen for example in their attempts to claim that they are the upholders of 'true' freedom as against the libertarian Right. Whether or not Thatcherism is an identifiable political philosophy and how far it is dependent on a single personality is uncertain. There has been a good deal of myth-making. The return of the Conservatives in three general elections has only been possible because of the disarray and fragmentation of the opposition. It should be remembered that what is now heralded as the dominance of the Thatcher government owes much to this and the British electoral system. No matter whether the term 'Thatcherism' is capable of definition, there is no doubt that the record of the Thatcher years has become the focus for some intense and passionate disagreement. For the libertarian Right, the 'revolution' has been too tame; for traditional Conservatives, change has been too fast and too great. Socialists have viewed with apprehension some of the far-reaching changes and trends in society. Many intellectuals, academics, 'media' people, and actors have reacted with quite astonishing ferocity to Mrs Thatcher at a personal level. There have been many suggested explanations for the dislike of capitalism, which is allegedly evident among many members of the intellectual and artistic classes,[4] but this interesting question obviously cannot be adequately discussed here. All manner of things have been credited to Mrs Thatcher – good and bad – from the extravagant eulogies of some of the newspapers to the dark forebodings of the Left and some bishops, who have described her as 'wicked'. The extremism of these fulminations or glorifications is more likely to be explained in psychological than political terms: perhaps a type of infantilism.

THE BRITISH GOVERNMENT'S RECORD IN THE 1980s[5]

The greatest change from previous governments' policies has been the abandonment of the presumption that the government should seek to 'fine tune' the economy at the macro-level by detailed interference. There has been a marked and welcome adoption of more modest ideas concerning the power of government to 'manage' the real economy beneficially: an end to corporatism by which it was thought necessary frequently to consult and draw into the task of policy-making, huge self-proclaimed representative 'interests' such as the CBI and the TUC. There is some evidence that government ministers have, to some extent, begun to recognize their limitations in respect of the impossibility of possessing superior centralized knowledge: thus there have been fewer exercises in 'directing' investment and 'picking winners'. The record on inflation, the reform of trade-union law, and the privatization programme has been seen as a success story by government supporters, but although the decline in inflation has been significant by previous British standards, it compares much less favourably by international standards. The reform of trade-union law has left some important immunities and privileges untouched. By the end of the Thatcher government's second term of office, about 40 per cent of state industries had been privatized, and there are now plans for the privatization[6] of electricity, steel, and water. Apart from the ideologically inspired objections coming from collectivists, there are several other possible criticisms that can be made of the privatization programme: sometimes public monopoly has been exchanged for private monopoly as in the case of gas; the motives for privatization have been influenced by the revenue-raising prospects; the optimistic forecasts that privatization would give birth to a nation of shareholders have fallen somewhat flat; some very obvious monopolies have tended to be relatively untouched – such as the Post Office[7] and branches of the legal profession. Two benefits of privatization, even where monopoly has been left intact, have been that these industries must now raise new capital in the market, so ending some alarmingly copious flows of taxpayers' money into the hands of state monopolies, and there has been a welcome change in the relationship between the government and the nationalized-industry trade unions whereby the government ceases to be directly involved in disputes, thus taking the 'politics' out of them.

The aim of the Thatcher governments significantly to reduce public expenditure has not been realized. In 1978–9 it was 43.25 per cent of GDP, rose to 47 per cent by 1982–3, and fell slowly to a planned 42.75 per cent by 1988–9 (*The Autumn Statement*, 1987). The government has not reduced its share of the provision of health, education, or social security, the costs of which have been steadily rising in real terms; thus economies have had to be made even to hold public expenditure as a proportion of GDP fairly constant. This has displeased both Left and Right. The Left have campaigned against all economies whether they are reasonable or not and the Right have been disappointed by the failure to reduce the total.[8] The root of the government's dilemma is that it is unlikely to be able to reduce or even to stabilize its expenditure unless it manages to shed some of its responsibilities in health, education, and social security.

Among all the descriptions of the Thatcher governments, 'monetarist' has caused the most confusion and been the least understood. The Medium Term Financial Strategy that was adopted in 1980, began to collapse in 1983 and the 'naive' monetarist view that there is a direct mathematical relationship between the growth of sterling M3 and the inflation figure in three years' time has allegedly been disproved. The reason given is that financial deregulation has made matters much less simple than is apparent in the works of Milton Friedman. By the end of 1988 it looked from one point of view as if the Government had 'lost control' of the growth of credit, failing to compensate for the resulting growth of demand because of its 'ideological' opposition to tax increases. The critics assert that Britain will run into a period of chronic deficits on the balance of payments, a collapse of sterling, and accelerating inflation – just like old times! The disagreement is connected with what is counted as money. Some economists, such as Tim Congdon, have repeatedly warned that inflationary consequences must follow from the Government's complacency in the face of the recent rapid increase in broad money measures (such as bank and building-society deposits). Others, such as Professor Patrick Minford, argue that such measures are no longer money in the proper sense since they depend for their size on their attractiveness to savers and are mostly not used for paying bills. The Chancellor of the Exchequer, Nigel Lawson, takes the more optimistic view that we are in a period of temporary overheating that will be corrected by higher interest rates; direct controls on borrowing are not on the agenda. This view follows from the Government's free-market philosophy: if firms and individuals spend more than their income in aggregate thus causing a trade deficit, this simply indicates their private assessment of the information they have. This mass of knowledge far exceeds that available to any central planner. The government itself has a Budget surplus; only if it were to be in deficit should it increase taxes. Undoubtedly we are now entering a period in which the belief in non-intervention and suspicion of macromanagement, which appear to have had, on balance, such favourable consequences so far, are going to be put to the test to a greater extent than at any time since the first years of the Thatcher governments. The most commendable aspect of Government macroeconomic policy that has been such a reversal of the policies of the 1970s is the apparent recognition that individuals in aggregate really do know more than the central authorities; also, that individuals and firms must bear the consequences of their own mistakes in economic choices.

The Government's recently acquired concern to 'regenerate the inner cities' by pouring vast sums of taxpayers' money into various schemes invites the charge that the government is engaged in a cynical abandonment of free-market philosophy when it threatens electoral success. A likely riposte would be to point out that inner-city dereliction has been mainly the result of municipal socialism and that the Government is bent on correcting *its* evil consequences. Whether this argument is valid must, of course, remain a matter of opinion, but there is something disturbing, carrying an echo of the 1960s, in the untroubled enthusiasm of the 1980s breed of 'redevelopers' and large-scale planners (what makes them so confident *they* will avoid the mistakes of their predecessors?).

AUSTRIAN INFLUENCE ON BRITISH GOVERNMENT POLICY IN THE 1980s[9]

It would be unrealistic to try to identify very precisely the Austrian contribution to the general direction of New-Right thinking since there is some overlapping between Austrian and other strands and

Austrian ideas have been influential relatively indirectly in shaping attitudes to the nature of competitive markets, the case for individualism and the way in which much knowledge is widely dispersed and inherently unattainable centrally.

Competition

In some areas: the abolition of price controls; planning agreements; increasing competition and the abolition of bans on advertising by some professions; the deregulation of public road transport – the Government has demonstrated its belief in the market. There are now plans to introduce more competition into radio and television broadcasting. On the other hand, there is still a good deal of regulation of air fares,[10] the benefits of the abolition of certain restrictive practices in the financial markets have been reduced by some lack of appreciation of the real costs of the subsequent regulatory activities of the Securities and Investments Board[11] and very little has been done to introduce market forces into health and education. There has, however, been a significant reduction in the extent of government involvement in housing markets, except of course for the anomaly of mortgage tax relief and the exemption from tax on capital gains made by owner-occupiers. The idea of encouraging parents to serve as governors of schools so as to increase 'participation' is unlikely to increase competition between schools; what parents should have the opportunity of is more *choice* as between schools, with vouchers for the poor.

The Government's belief that the price mechanism is the rational method of resource allocation evidently does not extend to the use of road space; the Transport Secretary spoke, in September 1988, of road-pricing as a 'deeply unattractive idea' and 'very unfair'.

Trade Unions

Although union restrictive practices have not been brought within the monopoly legislation that applies to firms, the abolition of certain legal privileges, which Austrians regard as the best way of increasing competition, has certainly had some effects on union behaviour, notably in the practice of secondary picketing.

199

Privatization

Privatization has been implemented in two ways: the sale of the nationalized industries to private investors and the contracting out to the private sector of services that were formerly provided by the public sector (such as hospital cleaning and refuse collection). From the Austrian point of view, what matters in judging these measures is not how many new shareholders are created, but whether competition has been increased. The picture is at present rather mixed in this respect, but the important point to grasp is that privatization should not only be judged by the neo-classical economic yardstick of efficiency, but also on the extent to which it facilitates the *discovery* process of the market.

THE LIMITED ACCEPTANCE OF AUSTRIAN IDEAS

Austrian ideas, and especially those of Hayek, have not yet been widely understood even by some of the politicians involved in the 'Thatcherite revolution' and their businessmen supporters. The idea of the market as a self-regulatory mechanism in a free economic order is not widely trusted. 'Do It Yourself Economics', which David Henderson spoke of in the BBC 1985 Reith Lectures,[12] is still very influential in the corridors of power of business and government. The belief that governments are there to 'run the economy' is still widely cherished. There is still much talk of the national income as a holistic entity that it is the responsibility of governments to distribute.

In 1968 Samuel Brittan drew attention to the 'moral inferiority complex' among Conservative voters who were uneasy about supporting what looked like selfishness as against socialist egalitarianism.[13] Although Hayek has fully demonstrated the fallaciousness of this view, it remains influential, but there are signs that it has been to some extent weakened. Public discussion is still frequently pervaded by unconscious holism with much talk of vague concepts such as 'society', 'the public', 'social needs', or 'the national interest'. There is evidently much support for the unliberal notion that the economy should be 'run' by the government. The fact that large and perhaps the most important areas of human life are beyond the reach of governments tends to be forgotten in the face of the politicizing clamour.

The 'Thatcher revolution' is not, as some would depict it, simply a return to *laissez-faire*. It contains too much regard for traditional values for that to be an accurate picture. Yet, it does in many respects profess – and to some extent act upon – those precepts that Hayek once thought conservatives incapable of. 'It [conservatism] may succeed in slowing down undesirable developments, but, since it does not indicate another direction ... cannot prevent their continuance' wrote Hayek in 'Why I am not a conservative' (1960: 398).

It would be fair to say that the dominant movement in the Conservative party of the 1980s has managed to some degree to falsify this prediction, and that a probable reason for this new liberalism owes a good deal to the work of Hayek himself.

APPENDIX

In his latest book, *The Fatal Conceit*, which should be widely accessible, being a pleasure to read, Hayek (1988) has managed with remarkable conciseness and vigour to combine and further develop many of the thoughts of his lifelong studies into an incisive exposure of the fragile intellectual and moral foundations of socialism. His argument is not merely that socialism has been tried and has failed to engender material wealth, but that the collectivist tradition is an obstacle to the development of any advanced degree of any form of civilization: 'an atavistic longing after the life of the noble savage' and 'to follow socialist morality would destroy much of present humankind and impoverish the rest'.

From the richness and depth of this work it is here only possible to draw attention to a few points that struck me as of especial interest.

Altruism is generally regarded as morally superior to self-interest and 'socio-biologists' have even theorized that it is genetically determined, having a biological purpose – it helps the continuation of the species. Hayek's contrary view, which some people may find rather distasteful, is that had humans throughout history treated their neighbours as themselves, the growth of civilization would have been impossible. We should, instead, have remained stagnated in poverty and tribalism.

One of Hayek's central themes is that there is an important aspect of behaviour that is neither instinctive nor based on reason: 'cultural and moral evolution ... is on the one hand ... beyond instinct ... and on the other hand incapable of being created or designed by reason.' This concept, which has been recurrent in much of his existing work, is explored here with fresh erudition and intelligence.

Although himself agnostic, it is interesting that Hayek wishes to acknowledge the debt we owe to religion – though evidently not the Christian precept to love one's neighbour as oneself – especially in its monotheistic variants, in preserving and transmitting beneficial traditions: 'like it or not' we owe civilization in part to the practice of believing things that are not true – not the result of rational discussion. 'As a gesture of appreciation' he describes these beliefs as 'symbolic truths'.

One slight disappointment is that although the problems of pollution and conservation that are now to the fore in public debate have been discussed elsewhere by Hayek (see Chapter 9 of this volume), I should have liked to have read something of his responses to the current surge of concern about 'the planet'. There is a growing danger of the whole matter becoming another stick with which to beat capitalism and of the contrary argument being lost by default.

Although the main themes of this volume will not be unfamiliar to students of Hayek's existing work, it is remarkable for the coherence and subtlety of the analysis in which the 'extended order misleadingly known as capitalism' is decisively shown to have evolved as no part of anyone's intention. One might add that capitalism – the propensity to trade with each other – is what humans do as soon as they have shaken off the oppressions of tribal leaders: individual 'chiefs' such as Stalin, Mao Tse-Tung, or Pol Pot.

NOTES

CHAPTER ONE PHILOSOPHICAL ROOTS AND METHODS

1. See Grassl and Smith (1986) for an exploration of the variety of the philosophical roots of the Austrian school.
2. Whilst mainstream economics regards the need for empirical verification and testing as of first importance, Popperian falsificationism is not always practised even by those economists who profess to believe in its virtue. (See Blaug, 1980, pp. 259–60.)
3. For example: Frank Knight, Murray Rothbard, and Israel Kirzner.
4. 'Positivism' is here being used in the sense in which Lipsey uses it in his famous textbook: 'All that the positive economist asks is that something that is positive and testable should emerge from his theories somewhere – for if it does not, his theories will have no relation to the world around him' (Lipsey, 1983: 7).
5. For an extensive introduction to these matters see John Hospers *An Introduction to Philosophical Analysis*, London: Routledge & Kegan Paul (1956); Eaglewood Cliffs: Prentice Hall (1981), pp. 179–207.
6. See Passmore (1984: 464–5); also Nozick (1977: 362) '. . . it is fair to say, I think, that there are no arguments, generally acknowledged to be compelling against the possibility of . . . synthetic necessary truths.'
   See also Grassl and Smith, (1986: 12–18) on how the work of the philosopher Husserl offers an explanation for what it is for a proposition to be synthetic and a priori.
7. Bertrand Russell *An Inquiry into Meaning and Truth*, Harmondsworth: Penguin Books, 1962; repr. edn 1965, pp. 156–7. An important and rigorous examination of the blurring of the boundaries between analytic and synthetic is given in W. V. Quine (1963) *From a Logical Point of View*, New York: Harper & Row, Chapter 2.
8. See, for example, Hahn and Hollis:

   Similarly, if economic theory can be axiomatized, then its axioms will have to be self-evidently true. There will still be room for dispute about which the basic axioms are to be. But that does not cancel the search for *those axioms which state the real definitions of the basic concepts of economics.* (Hahn and Hollis, 1979: 55).

(My emphasis)

9. *The Counter-Revolution of Science* brings together in one volume essays that were first published in *Economica* between 1941 and 1944 amidst 'the continuous disruption of falling bombs' (Hayek, 1979: 9). Scientism is also criticized in the essays, 'The pretence of knowledge' (Hayek, 1978: 23–34) and 'The errors of constructivism' (op. cit.: 3–22).

10. The question of Comte's subsequent influence on the methods of the social sciences has been largely indirect. See Raymond Aron (1965) *Main Currents in Sociological Thought, I.* Harmondsworth: Pelican Books, and Hayek, 1979: 358–63.

11. See also review article in T. W. Hutchison, 1978 *Economic Journal* 88: 841, December; and Hutchison, 1981: 214–19.

12. The percentage of the UK working population who were registered as unemployed rose from 2.06 to 5.66 per cent between 1974 and 1980. In the same period the annual average inflation rate was 16 per cent. All this, of course, was before 'Thatcherism'.

13. For a devastating and concise exposure of the weakness of Marxian value theory see Nozick, 1974: 253–62.

14. The prices referred to here are relative prices – the prices of goods and services that result from the operation of supply and demand – not the absolute price level as indicated by the Retail Price Index, for which there is every reason to hold the government truly responsible.

15. For a fuller discussion of the implication of the subjectivist position for both demand and cost see Shand, 1984, Chapter 4 and Rothbard in Sennholz, 1956: 224–62.

16. Nagel (1961: 478–85) gives a detailed discussion of some of the problems associated with subjectivism.

17. C. D. Broad (1925) *The Mind and its Place in Nature*, London: Routledge & Kegan Paul, p. 622.

18. See Hayek's reference to Gödel's theorem in this context (Hayek, 1967: 62).

19. BBC Reith Lectures, 1984.

20. Gary Zukor (1980) *The Dancing Wu Li Masters: An Overview of the New Physics*, London; Fontana/Collins, p. 136.

21. For a summary of the Austrian/LSE subjectivist approach to costs see S. C. Littlechild, 'The problem of social cost' in Spadaro (1978).

22. Burman's (1979) essay is a review of John O'Neill (ed.) (1973) *Modes of Individualism and Collectivism*, London: Heinemann.

23. As Blaug (1980:xi) points out, the term 'methodology' is ambiguous – it may be merely a more impressive-sounding word for 'methods'. As used in my text it includes 'study of the methods of' and the implications of these methods for the social sciences.

24. See also, Mises, 1981: 51–7; 1978: 81–3.

25. This analogy may support the contention that collective terms need not

be redefined in individual terms, but it does not refute the Austrian insistence that 'society' is composed of individuals who act purposefully and whose actions are frequently unpredictable.

CHAPTER TWO UNINTENDED CONSEQUENCES, KNOWLEDGE, AND HISTORICISM

1. Menger defined economics and other social sciences as the study of the unintended consequences of human action.
2. See Peter Unger (1975) *Scepticism*, Oxford: Oxford University Press, p. 1.
3. For example: the criticisms by Nicholas Kaldor, Lord Balogh, E. J. Mishan, T. W. Hutchison, and others. To question what one is doing is very desirable but the extent of this among economists suggests that previous certainties have been fatally weakened. The overoptimistic expectations of the public aided by the popular press gave a false impression of the powers and limits of economics.
4. It seems doubtful whether the extent or standard of economic understanding among the general population and even among many of the educated section has proportionately improved in relation to the feverish expansion of economics education during the past twenty-five years.
5. Gödel's theorem is not referred to in *The Sensory Order* (Hayek, 1976), but it figures in Hayek's 1962 essay, 'Rules, perception and intelligibility' reprinted in Hayek, 1967: 62.
6. 'Civilisation advances by extending the number of important operations which we can perform without thinking about them' (A. N. Whitehead quoted in Hayek, 1960: 22).
7. Gilbert Ryle (1949) *The Concept of Mind*, London; Hutchinson, p. 81.
8. Essentially this holds that it is impossible to measure the position and momentum of a particle simultaneously with complete precision. Related to this is Niels Bohr's complementarity principle that argues that an experiment on one aspect of subatomic particles destroys the possibility of learning about a 'complementary' aspect of these particles.
9. Popper (1979: 296) goes further than this; his thesis includes the view that even classical physics is not deterministic.
10. Originally in his paper (Popper, 1950) 'Indeterminism in classical physics and in quantum physics', *British Journal for the Philosophy of Science* (1 and 3) and 'a more satisfactory treatment' in *Postscript after Twenty Years* to his (1959) *Logic of Scientific Discovery*, London: Hutchinson.
11. See Lachmann, 1977: 88–9; Brian J. Loasby 'Economics of dispersed and incomplete information' in Kirzner (1986). Also see the 'non-Austrians': Thomas Balogh (1982) *The Irrelevance of Conventional Economics*, London: Weidenfeld & Nicholson, p. 54 and Kenneth J.

Arrow, (1974) 'Limited Knowledge and economic analysis', *American Economic Review*, LXIV: 1–10.
12. See Beckerman, 1974 for further examples.
13. Part of an undergraduate essay that Keynes submitted, 'The political doctrines of Edmund Burke', written in 1904 when he was 21. The quotation is from Robert Skidelsky (1983: 156).
14. One consequence of the sociology of knowledge is to reinforce the contemporary practice of placing people in 'camps'. 'Ideology is a form of theoretical conscription: *everyone*, by virtue of class, sex, race or nation, is smartly uniformed and assigned to one side or the other' (Minogue, 1985: 5).
15. For example, that the working class must inevitably become worse off. 'The modern labourer ... instead of rising with the progress of industry, sinks deeper below the conditions of existence of his own class. He becomes a pauper and pauperism develops more rapidly than population and wealth' (*The Communist Manifesto 1848*, Section I). It would probably be no exaggeration to assert that the vast majority of the working class are now better off materially than were the bourgeoisie of 1848. Because of this undoubted and awkward fact, modern Marxists have turned their attention to other targets such as the assertion that workers are manipulated into buying things they do not really want. The very increase in working-class material comfort that falsifies Marx's prediction is itself now regarded with suspicion. Also, other forms of deprivation such as 'alienation' have been called up in order to save the ideological picture.
16. Homa Katouzian (1980) *Ideology and Method in Economics*, London: Macmillan, pp. 86–9 defends Marx against Popper. Also see Peter Urbach, 'Good and bad arguments against historicism' in Gregory Currie and Alan Musgrave (eds) (1985) *Popper and the Human Sciences*, Dordrecht: Martinus Nijhoff, pp. 133–46.
17. L. Robbins (1963) *Politics and Economics*, London: Macmillan, pp. 111–12.

CHAPTER THREE THE NATURE AND FUNCTIONS OF THE MARKET

1. See Oppenheim (1981) for an extensive discussion of concepts and their real meaning.
2. For example, on the role of value judgements in the social sciences (Hayek, 1967: 253–4).
3. Adam Smith may well have been influenced by Mandeville (Hayek, 1978: 264).
4. See Shand, 1984, Chapter 6 for a fuller treatment of the Kirzner/Mises view of the entrepreneur.
5. The analogy of economic processes as kaleidoscopic is developed in Shackle, 1972.

6. An example of the 'new' thinking in the Labour Party is found in Hattersley, 1987.
7. Hayek, 1978, Chapter 12, 'Competition as a discovery procedure'.

CHAPTER FOUR   MARKETS AND MORALITY

1. I am conscious of the danger of superficiality in trying to present a brief account of utilitarianism, of which there seem to be as many varieties as there are writers on the subject. My need to discuss utilitarianism arises mainly from its relevance to the doctrine of self-interest.
   Full and valuable examinations of the matter are M. D. Bayles (1968) *Contemporary Utilitarianism*, New York: Garden City and J. J. C. Smart and Bernard Williams (1973) *Utilitarianism: For and Against*, Cambridge: Cambridge University Press.
2. See Peter Geach (1977) *The Virtues*, Cambridge: Cambridge University Press, pp. 91–4.
3. Second Treatise of Government, Section 4.
4. See Hart, 1983, Essay 8 for a full treatment of what follows.
5. See Ronald Dworkin (1977) *Taking Rights Seriously*, London: Duckworth; also Nozick, 1974; Mackie, 1977.
6. The 'utilitarian tradition' may not be so oblivious to questions of income distribution as it has sometimes been depicted. Mises (1981: 421) points out that Bentham maintained with special emphasis that happiness is increased the more wealth is distributed evenly.
7. T. L. S. Sprigge (1987) *The Rational Foundation of Ethics*, London: Routledge, p. 27.
8. Hayek proposed to call this spontaneous order a *catallaxy* to distinguish it from an economy. A catallaxy is simply a complex structure of interrelationships. The term 'economy' would then be confined to mean such organizations as households, or firms, or a society in which all resources are controlled by a central authority; these are bodies that are directed with *known ends* in view; a catallaxy has no known ends. In this sense the British 'economy' (as the term is customarily used) is not an economy but a catallaxy. (It may be an 'economy' in wartime.)
9. For a full account of these matters see the essay by Leland B. Yeager in Leube and Zlabinger, 1984.
10. See Eric Roll (1973) *A History of Economic Thought*, London: Faber, p. 302.
11. Bastiat is not mentioned in Blaug's (1968) *Economic Theory in Retrospect*, (2nd edn, London: Heinemann), perhaps because he is thought not to have made any original contribution to economic theory.
12. To Bastiat, 'socialists' embraced all those advocates of collectivism and planners of 'artificial' social orders such as Fourier and Saint-Simon.

13. Quoted in Wilson and Skinner, 1976: 75. For a full examination of Adam Smith on self-interest see Chapter 3 of this work.
14. 'In Thatcher's Britain greed has been elevated to a philosophy of life ... the social and spiritual desert of Thatcherism, unwatered by the refreshing springs of altruism, generosity and hope' (David Steele, former leader of the Liberal Party, *The Times*, 4 April 1985).
15. Mises evidently has in mind the Middle Ages when ideally, people lived up to the principles of the Gospels, when the canon law decided moral questions, and before the advent of 'bourgeois' morality.
16. See Rosemary Ashton (1986) 'Marx's friends and comrades', *Encounter*, February.
17. There is a third possibility: what J. S. Mill called 'benevolence' when a member of a group regards his own interest as being no more or no less important than that of any other member of the group.
18. R. H. Tawney (1922) *Religion and the Rise of Capitalism*, Harmondsworth: Penguin Books, 1938 edn, p. 280.
19. 'It is better that a man should tyrannise over his bank balance than over his fellow citizens' (*General Theory*, chapter 24).
20. The Bishop of Manchester described the £1 million salaries of some company chairmen, compared with £5000 for student nurses by the now regularly misused word 'obscene' (House of Lords, 24 February 1988).
21. See Robert Heilbroner in Edward J. Nell (ed.) (1984) *Free Market Conservatism*, London: Allen & Unwin, p. 5.
22. See Digby Anderson (ed.) (1984) *The Kindness that Kills*, London: IEA, p. 116.

CHAPTER FIVE FREEDOM

1. See Pelczynski and Gray (1984) *Conceptions of Liberty in Political Philosophy*, London: The Athlone Press: essays on liberty from Ancient Greece to Rawls and Habermas.
2. Far more libertarian is his son David Friedman in *The Machinery of Freedom*, Arlington House: New York, 1978.
3. 'Social democrat', though a considerably vague term, is nevertheless in common usage and refers to those who are anxious to use the power of the state to mitigate many kinds of inequality, but who would not favour the abolition of a private-property-based market, and who shy away from being regarded as 'socialists'.
4. The chief weakness of Taylor's view is that it fails to capture the real objects of concern. When people are worried about liberty, the sort of things that they are worried about are governments arresting and detaining citizens without trial, jamming foreign broadcasts and making it an offence to consume alcoholic drinks in public houses after 11 pm. (J. P. Day (1987) *Liberty and Justice*, London: Croom Helm, p. 224)

I think this tends to show the impossibility of enumerating various 'liberties' and arriving at any useful general conclusion, since what different people value most must vary greatly.

5. With humblest apologies to all readers whose economics is beyond the most elementary it perhaps should be pointed out that 'wealth' means physical resources and the goods and services that they produce. Thus human skill is one kind of wealth.

6. After the 1988 UK budget measure that reduced dramatically the top rate of income tax to 40 per cent, both the Prime Minister and the Chancellor of the Exchequer made speeches reminding the affluent of their now greater ability and responsibility to give their surplus income to self-selected good causes rather than, as before, having it taken from them by force of law. Time will tell whether the rich take notice.

7. A leading Labour party politician once advised Mrs Thatcher to stop listening to the 'mad professor who is constantly whispering in her ear'. He could have meant Hayek or possibly Milton Friedman.

8. The sheer weight of the endless exegesis of Marxism, even after admitting Marx's outstanding genius, seems somewhat disproportionate and to be accounted for partly by the simple fact of the adoption of Marxism by a powerful totalitarian state.

9. Hayek has in mind here arguments such as those in Barbara Wootton's *Freedom under Planning*, her response to the *Road to Serfdom*, in which she argues that 'the freedoms that matter in ordinary life are definite and concrete' and not all of equal value (Hayek, 1960: 423), and John Dewey the American philosopher and educational theorist with his view that 'the demand for liberty is the demand for power' (ibid: 424).

10. 'The achievement of a more equal distribution of wealth and power, and *the resultant increase in the sum of freedom* for the community as a whole, is the principal goal of socialism' (Hattersley, 1987: xviii, my emphasis).

11. There is apparently some evidence that crime in blocks of flats has been significantly reduced simply by modifying their structure so as to remove ambiguity over private domains.

12. For a view that 'taxation of earnings from labour is on a par with forced labour', see Nozick, 1974; 169.

13. An excellent essay on this is by Gottfried Dietze, 'Hayek on the rule of law', in Machlup, 1977: 107–46.

14. It is tempting to conclude, at this point, that since he is criticized from widely separated political angles, then, by analogy with the BBC, which is similarly assailed, he may have got it about right.

15. See R. Hamowy (1978) 'Law and the liberal society: F. A. Hayek's *Constitution of Liberty*,' *Journal of Libertarian Studies* 2: 287–97; Rothbard, 1984; Joseph Raz, 'The rule of law and its virtues', in Cunningham, 1979.

16. The requirement of moral neutrality seems to contain the probability of conflict with Hayek's opposition to some aspects of permissive education.

17. See George Friedman (1986) 'Marxism, violence and tyranny', in E. F. Paul, J. Paul, F. D. Miller Jr., and J. Ahrens (eds) *Marxism and Liberalism*, Oxford: Blackwell; also John Gray, 'Marxian freedom, individual liberty and the end of alienation' (op. cit.).
18. See Minogue (1985) for an account of how only those gifted with 'true consciousness' are able to see the reality and fraudulence of capitalist freedom. Their problem is how to escape the charge that they themselves are only one more manifestation of 'oppressive tolerance'; this book explains how this trick is performed.
19. For a detailed analysis of some of the confusions surrounding various other measures to extend liberty through positive action see Michael Levin (1984) 'Negative liberty', *Social Philosophy and Policy* vol. 2, issue 1, Autumn. Also Thomas Sowell (1977) *Markets and Minorities*, Oxford: Blackwell.
20. The word 'liberal' is well known for having almost as broad a spectrum of meanings in economics and politics as 'freedom'. In the text it is to be taken as including a presumption in favour of capitalist free markets but implying no dogmatic objections to state intervention to deal with externalities, monopoly, and public goods. Some liberals do not regard freedom as an overriding moral value and think that state coercion of individuals should extend to preserving 'the moral fabric of society' if necessary (Allison, 1984). This has much in common with Hayek's support for traditional rules and his opposition to anarchism.
21. See, for example, Robert Heilbroner (1986) *The Nature and Logic of Capitalism*, New York: Norton.
22. At the time of writing we wait with hope and bated breath to see whether Mr Gorbachev is (a) a genuine believer in individual freedom and (b) if he is, what will be the result of his attempts to liberalize the Soviet state and its vast apparatus.
23. Perhaps George Orwell's *Nineteen Eighty-Four* was the most influential book in warning of the processes that produce totalitarianism, though I think that it may now be seen as chiefly inspired by his reaction to Stalinism.
24. The case is not so strong for France and Germany where the peculiarly Anglo-Saxon skill in the practice of liberty has had a much more unstable history.
25. See Kenneth Minogue (1984) 'How critical is the "crisis" of liberalism?', *Encounter*, June, and (1987) 'The idea of liberty and the dream of liberation', *Encounter*, July/August.

CHAPTER SIX EQUALITY

1. For example: R. H. Tawney (1964) *Equality*, London: Unwin Books; C. A. R. Crosland (1956) *The Future of Socialism*, London: Jonathan Cape; Roy Hattersley (1987) *Choose Freedom*, London: Penguin Books.
2. For example: the works of Mises, Hayek, and Rothbard; Milton

Friedman (1962) *Capitalism and Freedom*, Chicago and London: University of Chicago Press; Robert Nozick (1974) *Anarchy, State and Utopia*, Oxford: Blackwell; W. Letwin (1983) *Against Equality*, London: Macmillan.

3. Aristotle's idea of distributive justice rested on the idea of 'proportionate equality', that is the distribution of equal benefits to equal persons. All should be treated according to the contribution they make to society.

4. Of course, if the economy happened to be in a sluggish state at the time of the redistribution, then this would increase aggregate demand and ultimately investment, according to Keynes.

5. See note 6, Chapter 5.

6. See W. H. Hutt (1960) in H. Hazlitt (ed.) *The Critics of Keynesian Economics*, Princeton, N.J.: van Nostrand, pp. 389–90.

7. But one dictionary definition of 'social' is: 'a member of a political party having socialistic views' (*Shorter Oxford Dictionary*).

8. Whether deliberately or unconsciously, Hayek avoids the word 'society' in the title of volume 3 of *Law, Legislation and Liberty* (1982) by entitling it *The Political Order of a Free People*.

9. Perhaps it should be stressed that 'the state' is not the same collective entity as 'society', though some people use the latter when they really mean the former.

10. For example, Hattersley (1987): ' ... Hayek provided a desperately needed intellectual legitimacy for parties and people with a vested interest in inequality' (p. 69). This sentence is prefixed with the saving phrase, 'Whatever his academic intentions ... ' but after this we have the accusation of intellectual dishonesty: ' ... he abandons logic when intellectual rigour becomes inconvenient' (p. 70).

11. If the answer to this question is: 'a democratically elected government' then some explanation is called for as to why politicians and their servants may be trusted to act in a more benevolent and disinterested way than the free market.

12. In 1985, the salary of the chairman of ICI was increased from £3,288 per week to £5,524 per week 'because of his responsibilities'. The Oxford economist, R. G Opie, wanted to know how these responsibilities had suddenly increased by 68 per cent (*The Times*, 23 March, 1985). At the time of writing, the chairman of one company has been awarded £750,000 'in recognition of his performance in improving the business', and it is reported that the chairman of British Gas received a salary increase from £74,000 to £185,000 per year. What is the message these Hayekian 'market signals' are conveying? It is not a sound defence of these increases in pay to dismiss objections as *merely* due to envy. Some of these increases in pay were given to people who were due to retire in the near future; increased pensions may thus have been the aim, not incentives to work.

13. 'God is dead; but given the way of men, there may still be caves for thousands of years in which his shadow will be shown. – And we – we shall still have to vanquish his shadow, too' (Friedrich Nietzsche (1974)

The Gay Science, New York: Vintage Books, section 108). 'What Nietzsche, is speaking of here is ... for people who, from time immemorial have been accustomed to think in terms of theocentric interpretation of themselves, their lives, values and reality' (Richard Schacht (1985) *Nietzsche*, London: Routledge & Kegan Paul, pp. 119–20.)

14. This was Hayek's fear in the 1970s but clearly the years of the Conservative governments of the 1980s have altered the picture to some extent.

15. Stanley I. Benn (1967) 'Egalitarianism and equal consideration of interests', in J. Roland Pennock and John W. Chapman (eds) *Nomos IX: Equality*, New York.

16. F. A. Hayek (1956) 'Progressive taxation reconsidered', in M. Sennholz (ed.) *Freedom and Enterprise*, Princeton N.J.: D. van Nostrand, pp. 265–84.

17. J. R. Lucas (1977) 'Against equality again', *Philosophy*, 52: 255–80.

18. Ibid: 259.

19. The word 'establishment' is commonly used by socialists to stand for the capitalist class and their political and legal minions but it has also been used by conservatives to describe the professional classes who implement socialism through the welfare state as in 'socialist establishment'.

20. Michael Beenstock (1983) 'Ideology in social policy' in *Agenda for Social Democracy*, London: IEA, p. 79.

21. Antony Flew (1983) 'Justice: real or social', *Social Philosophy and Policy*, vol. I, issue I, Autumn, p. 163.

22. R. Dworkin (1977) *Taking Rights Seriously*, London: Duckworth; R. Nozick, 1974; J. Mackie, 1977.

23. See note 21, this chapter.

24. The sincerity of egalitarians has frequently been questioned: ' the "dirty little secret" – the hidden agenda – behind the current chatter about the need for "redistribution". The talk is about equality, the substance is about power' (Kristol, 1978: 224). 'In fact when ideologists talk of freedom, they are usually concerned with power' (Minogue, 1985: 244).

25. Even though the 'Thatcherite' Right may take this view, the British Conservative party traditionally has a strong liking for paternalism; giving out benefits to the poor and needy was seen as not at all against true Conservative principles.

26. Alan Ryan (1987) 'Left rethinking', *Encounter*, September/October.

CHAPTER SEVEN THE WELFARE STATE

1. Also see Bruce (1968) for other historical background in the text.

2. Beveridge envisaged that the demands on the welfare state would diminish as affluence became more widespread.

3. R. H. Tawney (1964) *Equality*, London: Unwin (first published, 1931); R. M. Titmuss (1974) *The Gift Relationship*, London: Allen & Unwin;

P. Townsend (1979) *Poverty in the United Kingdom*, Harmondsworth: Penguin Books.

4. The free-rider problem, according to Rothbard (1970: 88), is based on a faulty analysis of the real nature of the situation.

5. Robert Sugden (1983) *Who Cares?*, IEA Occasional Paper 67, pp. 16–28.

6. Bernard Williams (1962) 'The idea of equality' in P. Laslett and W. G. Runciman (eds) *Philosophy, Politics and Society*, Oxford: Blackwell, pp. 110–31.

7. A welfare system organized according to citizenship principles should discriminate 'against the well-off, the skilled, the person with adaptable talents ... the person in a healthy job ... in favour of the poor, the unskilled, the poorly educated, the imprudent' (Harris, 1987: 164).

8. Ralph Harris and Arthur Seldon (1987) *Welfare Without the State*, Hobart Paperback 26 London: IEA.

9. It would be very useful in deciding on such questions if there were a society somewhere where the socialist principle of medical treatment has been successfully implemented. Sweden is often cited as a good example, but see Peter Stein (1987) 'Sweden: failure of the welfare state', *Journal of Economic Growth* 2 No. 4.

10. A. Maynard and A. Ludbrook (1980) 'What's wrong with the National Health Service, *Lloyd's Bank Review*, October; A. Maynard (1983) 'Privatising the National Health Service', *Lloyd's Bank Review*, April; A. Maynard (1983) 'The production of health and health care', *Journal of Economic Studies*, 10 (1).

11. Arthur Seldon (1980) *Corrigible Capitalism: Incorrigible Socialism*, Occasional Paper 57. London: IEA.

CHAPTER EIGHT UNEMPLOYMENT AND INFLATION

1. An excellent concise account is Samuel Brittan (1982) *How to End the 'Monetarist' Controversy*, Hobart Paper 90, London: IEA.

2. All the changes made in the official way of counting have had the effect of *reducing* the unemployment totals by about 420,000 (1.4 per cent): Lloyds Bank (1987) *Economic Bulletin*, no. 105, September.

3. See *Keynes's General Theory: Fifty Years On*, Hobart Paperback 24, 1986, London: IEA.

4. There is, however, evidence that Keynes himself was soon aware of the dangers and that Hayek saw himself as 'on the same side' as Keynes immediately after the war in the fight against inflation (letter to the author from F. A. Hayek, November, 1982).

5. See Milton Friedman (1975) *Unemployment versus Inflation*, Occasional Paper 44, London: IEA; Friedman (1977) 'Nobel Lecture: Inflation and Unemployment', *Journal of Political Economy* 85 No. 3.

6. For example, see Lloyds Bank (1987) *Economic Bulletin*, January: 'Unemployment in the UK could be reduced by 1m over the next five years, if present policies were reinforced by policies to restrain pay and prices'.

7. The view that labour is just a factor of production strikes many people as ludicrous and even offensive.

8. 'Natural' does not imply 'desirable' or 'inevitable'.

9. The IEA has examined the question of unemployment in 30 publications.

10. Charles Hanson (1984) *1980s Unemployment and the Unions*, Hobart Paper 87, 2nd edn London: IEA, p. 77.

11. The case of the Nissan Company is, however, instructive. At its Sunderland plant only one-quarter of the workforce had bothered to join the union and were evidently happy with the relatively more flexible job specifications (Hanson and Mather, 1988: 23).

12. See Hermione Parker (1982) *The Moral Hazard of Social Benefits*, IEA Research Monograph 37.

13. See *Economic Affairs*, April/May 1988 on 'workfare'.

14. See Peter Kellner (1988) 'The general character of the poverty trap remains', the *Independent* newspaper, 4 April.

15. Hayek had written explicitly in 1957 of his opposition to the description of the 'free market economy' as the 'social market economy' (Hayek, 1967: 238).

16. Precisely what Marxist 'fundamentals' are valid is the subject of endless disputation among scholars who work within a Marxian framework. See, for example, Geoff Hodgson (1984) 'What is wrong with Marxism?' *The Democratic Economy*, Harmondsworth: Penguin Books, Chapter 12.

17. There is some evidence that shorter working hours offer little protection against unemployment (R. Jackman and R. Layard (1987) *Monetarism and Macroeconomics*, IEA Readings 16, pp. 107–11).

18. A Marxist might very well reply that 'free marketeers' have their own utopia and 'biblical' texts. Further discussion of this interesting matter must, regretfully, be deferred.

19. For more detailed accounts see G. P. O'Driscoll and S. R. Shenoy 'Inflation, recession and stagflation' in Dolan, 1976: 185–214; also Shand, 1984, Chapters 10, 11, 12.

20. See Hayek, 1967: 270–99; 1978: 191–231.

21. For a vigorous defence of the idea that unions should be regarded as 'vehicles for anything other than the pursuit of individual emancipation' see Hattersley, 1987: 131.

22. For example, by setting up a body independent of government – a Currency Commission – which would regulate the money supply within a legally enforceable framework. The trouble is, however, that Parliament can alter any such laws under the present constitution.

23. F. A. Hayek (1976) *Denationalisation of Money*, Hobart Paper 70, London: IEA, 2nd edn 1978; Hayek (1976) *Choice in Currency*, Occasional Paper 48, London: IEA.

24. Taking the period 1700 to 1914, with 1913=100, the lowest prices (78) were around 1735 and the highest around 1870 (130): Phyllis Deane and W. A. Cole (1962) *British Economic Growth, 1688-89*, Cambridge: Cambridge University Press.

25. See F. A. Hayek (1986) 'Market standards for money', *Economic Affairs*, April/May; Symposium on Hayek's 'Standard', *Economic Affairs*, June/July, 1986; Kevin Dowd (1988) *Private Money*, Hobart Paper 112, London: IEA.

CHAPTER NINE ECONOMIC GROWTH AND ITS COSTS

1. See E. J. Mishan (1984), reprinted in Mishan, 1986.
2. The creation of the National Economic Development Council in 1962 was one indication of how government assumed that it should be concerned with growth.
3. The social costs of road-widening and new road-building are not properly taken account of in Britain. Whenever congestion increases this is interpreted as a sign that 'demand' has increased; what it does signify is that the price of using that stretch of road is too low (usually, in practice, zero). This is typical of the inefficiency of the political process.
4. E. J. Mishan (1986) 'Fact, faith and myth', *Encounter*, November.
5. R. H. Coase (1960) 'The problem of social cost', *Journal of Law and Economics*, October.
6. See *The Economics of Politics*, IEA Readings no. 18, 1978; Gordon Tullock (1976) *The Vote Motive*, Hobart paperback 9, London: IEA. William C. Mitchell (1988) *Government as it is*, Hobart paper 109, London: IEA.
7. See Steven S. Cheung (1978) *The Myth of Social Cost*, London: IEA, for a full exposition of these ideas.
8. See Julian L. Simon and Herman Kahn (1984) *The Resourceful Earth*, Oxford: Blackwell; Charles Maurice and Charles W. Smithson (1983) *The Ultimate Resource*, London: Martin Robertson.
9. See E. J. Mishan (1972) 'Economic growth: the need for scepticism', *Lloyds Bank Review*, October, p. 3.
10. See S. C. Littlechild, 'The problem of social cost' in Spadaro (1978); it includes a useful bibliography.

CHAPTER TEN CONCLUDING NOTES

1. See Jeffrey H. Reiman (1981) 'The fallacy of libertarian capitalism', *Ethics*, October.
2. This is what Hegel would have called an absence of *Sittlichkeit*. See Raymond Plant (1985) 'Hirsch, Hayek and Habermas: dilemmas of distribution' in A. Ellis and K. Kumar (eds) *Dilemmas of Liberal Democracies*, London: Methuen, Chapter 3. The principle is similar in meaning to 'citizenship'.
3. Numerous knowledgeable commentators, however, have identified something called 'Thatcherism', for example, Kenneth Minogue and Michael Biddiss (eds) (1987) *Thatcherism*, London: Macmillan; Peter

Jenkins (1987) *Mrs Thatcher's Revolution*, London: Jonathan Cape; Anthony Hartley (1987) 'The remoulding of British politics', *Encounter*, Sept/Oct.

4. For example, F. A. Hayek (1949) 'The intellectuals and socialism', *University of Chicago Law Review*, 16, reprinted in Hayek, (1967); F. A. Hayek (ed.) (1954) *Capitalism and the Historians*, London: Routledge; G. J. Stigler (1963) *The Intellectual and the Market Place and Other Essays*, New York: Collier-Macmillan.

5. See David G. Green (1987) *The New Right*, Brighton: Wheatsheaf, pp. 153–209; Brittan, (1988): 245–301; Norman P. Barry (1987) *The New Right*, London: Croom Helm.

6. The Conservatives might have been better advised to call it 'liberation'.

7. This was seen in the postal workers' strike in September 1988.

8. John Burton (1985) *Why No Cuts?*, Hobart Paper 104, London: IEA.

9. See S. C. Littlechild (1986) *The Fallacy of the Mixed Economy*, 2nd edn, Hobart Paper 80, London: IEA.

10. David Sawers (1987) *Competition in the Air*, Research Monograph 41, London: IEA.

11. Arthur Seldon (ed.) (1988) *Financial Regulation – or Over-regulation?*, London: IEA.

12. David Henderson (1986) *Innocence and Design*, Oxford: Blackwell.

13. Samuel Brittan (1968) *Left or Right: The Bogus Dilemma*, London: Secker & Warburg.

BIBLIOGRAPHY

Allison, L. (1984) *Right Principles: A Conservative Philosophy of Politics*, Oxford: Blackwell.

The Autumn Statement (1987) London: HMSO

Barry, N. P. (1979) *Hayek's Social and Economic Philosophy*, London: Macmillan.

Bauer, P. T. (1982) *Equality, the Third World and Economic Delusion*, London: Methuen.

Beckerman, W. (1974) *In Defence of Economic Growth*, London: Jonathan Cape.

Berlin, I. (1969) *Four Essays on Liberty*, Oxford: Oxford University Press.

Blaug, M. (1980) *The Methodology of Economics*, Cambridge: Cambridge University Press.

Bosanquet, N. (1983) *After the New Right*, London: Heinemann.

Brittan, S. (1973) *Capitalism and the Permissive Society*, London: Macmillan.

Brittan, S. (1983) *The Role and Limits of Government*, Hounslow: Temple Smith.

Brittan, S. (1988) *A Restatement of Economic Liberalism*, Houndmills: Macmillan.

Brodbeck, M. (ed.) (1968) *Readings in the Philosophy of the Social Sciences*, New York: Macmillan.

Brownstein, B. P. (1980) 'Pareto optimality, external benefits and public goods: a subjectivist approach', *Journal of Libertarian Studies* IV, (1): 93–106.

Bruce, M. (1968) *The Coming of the Welfare State*, 4th edn, London: Batsford.

Buchanan, J. M. (1979) *What Should Economists Do?* Indianapolis: Liberty Press.

Buchanan, J. M. and Thirlby, G. F. (1973) *L. S. E. Essays on Cost*, London: Weidenfeld & Nicolson.

Burman, P. (1979) 'Variations on a dialectical theme', *Journal of the Philosophy of Social Science*, 9:357–75.

Butler, E. (1983) *Hayek: His Contribution to the Political and Economic*

Thought of our Time, Hounslow: Temple Smith.

Caldwell, B. (1982) *Beyond Positivism*, London: Allen & Unwin.

Coddington, A. (1983) *Keynesian Economics: the Search for First Principles*, London: Allen & Unwin.

Cornforth, M. (1968) *The Open Philosophy and the Open Society*, London: Lawrence & Wishart.

Crick, B. (1987) *Socialism*, Milton Keynes: Open University Press.

Cunningham, R. L. (ed.) (1979) *Liberty and the Rule of Law*, College Station, Texas: A and M University Press.

Dolan, E. G. (ed.) (1976) *The Foundations of Modern Austrian Economics*, Kansas City: Sheed & Ward.

Downie, R. S. (1976) 'Comment on Thomas Wilson, "Sympathy and Self-interest"', in T. Wilson and A. S. Skinner (eds) *The Market and the State*, repr. edn, Oxford: Oxford University Press, pp. 99–105.

Friedman, M. (1962) *Capitalism and Freedom*, Chicago: The University Press.

Friedman, M. and Friedman, R. (1980) *Free to Choose*, Harmondsworth: Penguin Books.

Friedman, M. and Friedman, R. (1985) *The Tyranny of the Status Quo*, Harmondsworth: Penguin Books.

Gamble, A. (1979) 'The free economy and the strong state: the rise of the social market economy', in R. Milliband and J. Saville (eds) *The Socialist Register*, London: Merlin Press, pp. 1–25.

Gellner, E. (1968) 'Holism versus individualism', in M. Brodbeck (ed.) Readings in the Philosophy of the Social Sciences, New York: Macmillan.

Gellner, E. (1985) *Relativism and the Social Sciences*, Cambridge: Cambridge University Press.

Grassl, W. and Smith, B. (eds) (1986) *Austrian Economics*: London: Croom Helm.

Gray, J. (1986) *Hayek on Liberty*, 2nd edn, Oxford: Blackwell, 1st edn, 1984.

Green, D. G. (1982) *The Welfare State: for Rich or for Poor?* Occasional paper 63, London: IEA.

Green, D. G. (1985) *Which Doctor?* Research Monograph 40, London: IEA, pp. 26–7.

Green, D. G. (1986) *Challenge to the NHS*, Hobart Paperback 23, London: IEA.

Green, D. G. (1988) *Everyone a Private Patient*, Hobart paperback 27, London: IEA.

Griffiths, B. (1983) *Morality and the Market Place*, London: Hodder & Stoughton.

Griffiths, B. (1984) *The Creation of Wealth*, London: Hodder & Stoughton.

Hahn, F. and Hollis, M. (1979) *Philosophy and Economic Theory*, Oxford: Oxford University Press.

Hanson, C. G. and Mather, G. (1988) *Striking out Strikes*, Hobart Paper 110, London: IEA.

Hare, R. M. (1963) *Freedom and Reason*, Oxford: Oxford University Press, repr. edn, 1978.

Harris, D. (1987) *Justifying the Welfare State*, Oxford: Blackwell.

Hart, H. L. A. (1983) *Essays in Jurisprudence and Philosophy*, Oxford: Clarendon Press.

Hattersley, R. (1987) *Choose Freedom: The Future for Democratic Socialism*, Harmondsworth: Penguin Books.

Hayek, F. A. (1944) *The Road to Serfdom*, London: Routledge & Kegan Paul, repr. edn, 1979.

Hayek, F. A. (1960) *The Constitution of Liberty*, London: Routledge & Kegan Paul, repr. edn, 1976.

Hayek, F. A. (1967) *Studies in Philosophy, Politics and Economics*, London: Routledge & Kegan Paul.

Hayek, F. A. (1976) *The Sensory Order*, London: Routledge & Kegan Paul.

Hayek, F. A. (1978) *New Studies in Philosophy, Politics and Economics*, London: Routledge & Kegan Paul.

Hayek, F. A. (1979) *The Counter-revolution of Science*, 2nd edn, Indianapolis: Liberty Press.

Hayek, F. A. (1980) *Individualism and Economic Order*, Chicago: University of Chicago Press, Midway reprint.

Hayek, F. A. (1982) *Law, Legislation and Liberty*, 3 vols, London: Routledge & Kegan Paul.

Hayek, F. A. (1983) *A Tiger by the Tail*, 2nd edn, Hobart paperback 4, London: IEA.

Hayek, F. A. (1984a) *Money, Capital and Fluctuations*, R. McCloughry (ed.), London: Routledge & Kegan Paul.

Hayek, F. A. (1984b) *Unemployment and the Unions*, 2nd edn, Hobart paper 87, London: IEA, p. 52.

Hayek, F. A. (1988) *The Fatal Conceit: The Errors of Socialism*, W. W. Bartley III (ed.), London: Routledge.

Hindess, B. (1987) *Freedom, Equality and the Market*, London: Tavistock.

Hirsch, F. (1977), *Social Limits to Growth*, London: Routledge & Kegan Paul.

Hobbes, T. (1984) *Leviathan*, Harmondsworth: Penguin Books.

Hutchison, T. W. (1977) *Knowledge and Ignorance in Economics*, Oxford: Blackwell.

Hutchison, T. W. (1981) *Politics and Philosophy of Economics*, Oxford: Blackwell.

Hutchison, T. W. (1986) 'Philosophical issues that divide liberals: omniscience or omni-nescience about the future', in I. Kirzner (ed.) *Subjectivism, Intelligibility and Economic Understanding*, London: Macmillan, Chapter 10.

Jordan, B. (1982) *Mass Unemployment*, Oxford: Blackwell.

Keynes, J. M. (1973) *The General Theory of Employment, Interest and Money*, London: Macmillan (first published, 1936).

Kirzner, I. (1986) *Subjectivism, Intelligibility and Economic Understanding*, London: Macmillan.

Kolakowski, L. (1981) *Main Currents of Marxism, vol, 3: The Breakdown*, Oxford: Oxford University Press.

Kristol, I. (1978) *Two Cheers for Capitalism*, New York: Basic Books.

Lachmann, L. M. (1977) *Capital, Expectations and Market Process*, Kansas City: Sheed, Andrews & McMeel.

Leube, K. R. and Zlabinger, A. H. (eds) (1984) *The Political Economy of Freedom*, Munich: Philosophia Verlag.

Lipsey, R. G. (1983) *An Introduction to Positive Economics*, 6th edn, London: Weidenfeld & Nicolson.

Lucas, J. R. (1979) 'Liberty, morality and social justice' in R. L. Cunningham (ed.) *Liberty and the Rule of Law*, College Station, Texas: A and M University Press, pp. 146–66.

Lucas, J. R. (1984) *The Principles of Politics*, Oxford: Oxford University Press.

Lukes, S. (1973) *Individualism*, Oxford: Blackwell.

MacCallum, G. C. (1967) 'Negative and positive freedom', *The Philosophical Review*, July.

Machen, T. (1979) 'Reason, morality and the free society' in R. L. Cunningham (ed.) *Liberty and the Rule of Law*, College Station, Texas: A and M University Press, pp. 268–93.

Machlup, F. (ed.) (1977) *Essays on Hayek*, London: Routledge & Kegan Paul.

Mackie, J. L. (1977) *Ethics: Inventing Right and Wrong*, Harmondsworth: Penguin Books.

Menger, C. (1950) *Principles of Economics* (trans. and ed. by J. Dingwall and B. F. Hoselitz) Glencoe, Ill. Free Press.

Mill, J. S. (1982) *On Liberty*, Harmondsworth: Penguin Books (first published, 1859).

Minford, P. (1985) *Unemployment: Cause and Cure*, 2nd edn, Oxford: Blackwell.

Minford, P. (ed.) (1987) *Monetarism and Macroeconomics*, IEA readings no. 26, London: IEA.

Minogue, K. (1963) *The Liberal Mind*, London: Methuen.

Minogue, K. (1985) *Alien Powers*, London: Weidenfeld & Nicolson.

Mises, L. von (1966) *Human Action*, 3rd revised edn, Chicago: Contemporary Books.

Mises, L. von (1978) *Ultimate Foundations of Economic Science*, Kansas City: Sheed, Andrews & McMeel.

Mises, L. von (1981) *Socialism*, Indianapolis: Liberty Fund.

Mishan, E. J. (1967) *The Costs of Economic Growth*, Harmondsworth: Penguin Books.

Mishan, E. J. (1984) 'GNP – measurement or mirage', *National Westminster Bank Review*, November.

Mishan, E. J. (1986) *Economic Myths and the Mythology of Economics*, Brighton: Wheatsheaf.

Musgrave, R. A. (1976) 'Adam Smith on public finance and distribution', in T. Wilson and A. S. Skinner (eds) *The Market and the State*, repr. edn, 1978 Oxford: Oxford University Press pp. 296–319.

Nagel, E. (1961) *The Structure of Science*, London: Routledge & Kegan Paul.

Norman, E. R. (1977) *The Denigration of Capitalism*, London: Standing

Conference of Employers of Graduates, 1st Annual Lecture.

Norman, R. (1987) *Free and Equal*, Oxford: Oxford University Press.

Nozick, R. (1974) *Anarchy, State and Utopia*, Oxford: Blackwell.

Nozick, R. (1977) 'On Austrian Methodology', *Synthese* 36: 353–92.

Oakeshott, M. (1962) *Rationalism in Politics and Other Essays*, London: Methuen.

Oppenheim, F. (1981) *Political Concepts*, Oxford: Blackwell.

Passmore, J. (1984) *A Hundred Years of Philosophy*, Harmondsworth: Penguin Books.

Paul, E. F. (ed.) (1983) 'Distributive Justice', *Social Philosophy and Policy*, vol 1, issue 1, Autumn.

Paul, E. F. (ed.) (1984) 'Liberty and Equality', *Social Philosophy and Policy*, vol 2, issue 1, Autumn.

Paul, E. F., Paul, J., and Miller, F. D. Jr. (eds) (1985) *Ethics and Economics*, Oxford: Blackwell.

Pelczynski, Z. and Gray, J, (eds) (1984) *Conceptions of Liberty*, London: Athlone Press.

Popper, K. R. (1960) *The Poverty of Historicism*, 2nd edn, London: Routledge & Kegan Paul.

Popper, K. R. (1966) *The Open Society and its Enemies*, 2 vols, 5th edn, London: Routledge & Kegan Paul.

Popper, K. R. (1979) *Objective Knowledge*, Oxford University Press.

Quinton, A. (ed.) (1967) *Political Philosophy*, Oxford: Oxford University Press.

Rawls, J. (1971) *A Theory of Justice*, Cambridge, Mass.: Harvard University Press.

Raz, J. (1987) *The Morality of Freedom*, Oxford: Clarendon Press.

Rothbard, M. N. (1957) 'In defence of extreme apriorism', *Southern Economic Journal* 23: 315–18, January.

Rothbard, M. N. (1970) *Man, Economy and State*, 2-vol. edn, Los Angeles: Nash Publishing.

Rothbard, M. N. (1977) *Power and Market*, 2nd edn, Kansas City: Sheed, Andrews & McMeel.

Rothbard, M. N. (1982) *Ethics of Liberty*, Menlo Park, Cal.: Institute for Humane Studies.

Rothbard, M. N. (ed.) (1987) *The Review of Austrian Economics*, vol. 1, Lexington, Mass.: D. C. Heath.

Ryan, A. (ed.) (1979) *The Idea of Freedom: Essays in Honour of Isaiah Berlin*, Oxford: Oxford University Press.

Ryan, A. (1984) *Property and Political Theory*, Oxford: Blackwell.

Schumpeter, J. A. (1954) *History of Economic Analysis*, Oxford: Oxford University Press; twelfth printing, London: Allen & Unwin, 1981.

Sen, A. (1987) *On Ethics and Economics*, Oxford: Blackwell.

Sennholz, M. (1956) *On Freedom and Enterprise: Essays in Honour of Ludwig von Mises*, Princeton, N.J.: D. van Nostrand.

Shackle, G. L. S. (1972) *Epistemics and Economics*, Cambridge: Cambridge University Press.

Shackle, G. L. S. (1973a) 'Keynes and today's establishment in economic theory: a view', *Journal of Economic Literature*, 11 June, pp. 516–19.

Shackle, G. L. S. (1973b) *An Economic Querist*, Cambridge: Cambridge University Press.

Shackle, G. L. S. (1979) *Imagination and the Nature of Choice*, Edinburgh: Edinburgh University Press.

Shand, A. H. (1984) *The Capitalist Alternative*, Brighton: Wheatsheaf Books.

Simon, J. L. (1983) *The Ultimate Resource*, Oxford: Martin Robertson.

Sinnett, M. W. (1987) '"Method versus methodology" a note on *The Ultimate Resource*', in M. N. Rothbard (ed.) *The Review of Austrian Economics*, vol 1, Lexington, Mass.: D. C. Heath.

Skidelsky, R. (1983) *John Maynard Keynes vol. 1: Hopes Betrayed*, London: Macmillan.

Spadaro, L. M. (ed.) (1978) *New Directions in Austrian Economics*, Kansas City: Sheed, Andrews & McMeel.

Tawney, R. H. (1964), *Equality*, London: Unwin (first published, 1931).

Watkins, J. W. N. (1968) 'Methodological individualism and social tendencies' in M. Brodbeck (ed.) *Readings in the Philosophy of the Social Sciences*, New York: Macmillan.

Watson, G. (1985) *The Idea of Liberalism*, London: Macmillan.

Wicksteed, P. H. (1933) *The Commonsense of Political Economy*, 2 vols, London: Routledge & Kegan Paul.

Wilson, T. and Skinner, A. S. (eds) (1976) *The Market and the State*, repr. edn, Oxford: Oxford University Press.

Yeager, L. (1987) 'Why subjectivism', in M. N. Rothbard (ed.) *The Review of Austrian Economics*, vol. 1, Lexington, Mass.: D. C. Heath, pp. 5–31.

INDEX

Acton, Lord 99
Allison, L. 111, 135, 211 n
altruism 66, 75, 78–81, 83, 95, 96, 150
analytic/synthetic distinction 10, 12, 211 n
Anderson, D. 209 n
a priori statements 9–12; Mises on 8–13
Aristotle 8, 32, 212 n
Aron, R. 205 n
Austrian school, on: conservation 189; equality 118–31; freedom 94–105; growth 187–90; macroeconomics 175; money 175–6; state welfare 152–5; trade unions 175–7
axioms 204–5 n

Balogh, Lord 206 n
Barry, N. P. 14
Bastiat, F. 69
Bauer, P. 133, 143
Beckerman, W. 184–7
Beenstock, M. 213 n
behaviourism 23; see Broad
Benn, S. I. 213
Benn, T. 174
Bentham, J. 62–6, 208 n
Berlin, I. 91, 109–10
Beveridge, W. 148, 213 n
Blaug, M. 7, 205 n
Bohr, N. 24, 43, 206 n
Bosanquet, N. 151
Brittan, S. 64, 76, 200, 214, 217 n
Broad, C. D. 23, 78
Buchanan, J. 27
Burke, E. 38, 67, 104
Burton, J. 217

Caldwell, B. 11
capitalism 49, 79, 95–6, 173–4, 192; destruction of 178; late 173; and liberalism 112–14
Cartesian rationalism 39, 99, 153
catallaxy 208 n
central planning 153
charity 122
Cheung, S. 217
Chicago school 1
Christianity 76–7, 80, 194
citizenship 139–42, 149–50, 158, 159, 160, 216 n
class struggle 152
Coase, R. H. 185, 217
Coddington, A. 27
coercion 99, 105, 110, 130, 192
collective bargaining 169
collectivism 31, 33
Comte, A. 17, 22, 38, 205 n
Congdon, T. 197
conservation 189–90
Conservative party 201
constructivism 38, 66–7, 101, 106, 153
Cornforth, M. 107
cost 22; subjectivity of 24–5, 189; social 189, 217 n
cost-benefit analysis 64
Crick, B. 94, 126, 137
Crosland, T. 93, 211 n
cultural standards 193, 194

Darwin, C. 38–9, 54
Darwinism 54, 78, 101
Day, J. P. 209 n
demand management 166–8
Descartes, R. 39, 43

224